Terrorism and the Pandemic

Weaponizing of COVID-19

Rohan Gunaratna and Katalin Pethő-Kiss

berghahn
NEW YORK • OXFORD
www.berghahnbooks.com

First published in 2023 by
Berghahn Books
www.berghahnbooks.com

First paperback edition published in 2025

Library of Congress Cataloging-in-Publication Data

A C.I.P. cataloging record is available from the Library of Congress
Library of Congress Cataloging in Publication Control Number:
2022045366

British Library Cataloguing in Publication Data

A catalogue record for this book is available from the British Library

ISBN 978-1-80073-801-0 hardback
ISBN 978-1-80539-747-2 paperback
ISBN 978-1-80073-773-0 web pdf
ISBN 978-1-80073-789-1 epub

https://doi.org/10.3167/9781800738010

An electronic version of this book is freely available thanks to the support of libraries working with Knowledge Unlatched. KU is a collaborative initiative designed to make high-quality books Open Access for the public good. More information about the inititative and links to the Open Access version can be found at knowledgeunlatched.org.

Contents

List of Illustrations

Figures

Tables

Introduction

The Threat

The global COVID-19 pandemic continues to attract the attention of threat groups. Although conventional means—the gun and the bomb—will remain terrorists' preferred mode of attack, threat groups have expressed an interest in exploiting the virus. Terrorist and extremist groups, cells, and personalities will not let up using what works for their stated purposes. Rather than using tested and proven traditional weapons, will contemporary and future threat groups use bioweapons? Some terrorist and extremist groups, especially the Islamic State and right-wing extremist groups, have shown intentions to weaponize the virus. Unlikely to disappear in the near future, the contagion worldwide reached six and a half million deaths in 2022 and is expected to further increase in 2023.

Modified organisms can certainly be weaponized, but the weaponized versions would not come from a backstreet lab. The infrastructure to produce a sophisticated weapon needs highly trained scientists. Such weaponization would most probably come from government-run programs. The analogy would be nuclear weapons, where terrorists cannot manufacture them but they can get hold of weapons created by governments and use them. Bioweapons are invisible, replicate, and self-perpetuate. Because of the widespread availability of SARS-CoV-2 causing COVID-19 disease, will there be a paradigm shift from traditional terrorism to bioterrorism?

The Context

Coronavirus, known officially as SARS-CoV-2 (COVID-19), is an evolving threat. Threat entities have explored and exploited the pandemic to advance their agenda. Although lockdowns inhibited virus attacks in government-controlled areas, terrorist attacks continued unabated in the conflict areas. While government entities and military forces abided by lockdown measures, postponing training and scaling down operations, insurgent and terrorist groups operated relatively freely and mounted attacks. Both on the battlefields and off the battlefields, threat groups have invested in digital acceleration, maintaining strength and ideological influence during COVID-19.

From disseminating propaganda to raising funds, these threat groups foment racial and religious tension and violence. By engaging in such support activity, terrorist and extremist groups fuel the recruiting momentum. They link up online with like-minded groups and build communities of supporters and sympathizers. Some Islamic violent fanatics argue that COVID-19 is a "Soldier of God," "a divine retribution," and they encourage waging "Corona jihad" to infect opponents. While Muslim fanatics have advocated infecting Muslim officials and non-Muslims, far right groups have urged direct action of deliberately spreading the virus to "non-whites"—mainly minorities and immigrants. Right-wing extremists have mounted cyberattacks on anti-pandemic and health institutions, seeking to accelerate the crisis (UN CTED 2020).

With COVID-19 having developed into a global pandemic, terrorist ideologies and extremist thinking influence the human terrain. Ideologies of violent groups also fuse with the thinking of political parties, bolstering each other. The far right influences a segment of the general population against migrants and immigration as well as people of color and minorities. Muslim threat entities politicize, radicalize and mobilize a tiny segment of communities to use the virus to their advantage and target their adversaries. Muslim threat groups and Islamist parties feed off each other, affirming the terrorism-political nexus.

SARS-CoV-2 (COVID-19) is easily accessible and relatively low-risk, and it can be rapidly transmitted and inconspicuously spread. Will threat groups as yet weaponize it? Considering that younger and less susceptible assailants can be used to infect older and vulnerable populations, will they deliberately spread coronavirus in target communities and countries? Considering recent developments, concerns of the security and intelligence community are real. Governments and community partners need to monitor evolving ideologies and operational capabilities of a spectrum of threat groups and personalities to mitigate the possibility of COVID-19 attacks.

Understanding the Threat

A small number of threat groups with access to resources have expressed an interest in developing and using biological and other weapons of mass destruction (WMD). Will the pandemic instigate or inspire

Islamic State and al-Qaeda, the two most powerful insurgent and terrorist groups in the world, to invest in WMD stealth programs?

Since the beginning of the contemporary wave of international terrorism in 1968, there has never been so much virus-related chatter. Terrorist groups worldwide have expressed interest in COVID-19. Rogue actors have already engaged in its malicious spread, particularly within law enforcement and medical research facilities. In the United Kingdom, infected assailants used spit as a weapon on police officers. The spokeswoman for the Police Federation said: "We have seen some vile and disgusting acts by a minority, weaponizing COVID-19 by spitting and coughing at officers. It is therefore absolutely right and proper that the home secretary is clear that those who do so should feel the full weight of the law. Those responsible for weaponizing the virus are the lowest of the low" (Weaver and Dodd 2020). Belly Mujinga, a 47-year-old British railway ticket office worker, died after a man deliberately coughed on her. Transport Salaried Staffs' Association said: "She is one of the far too many frontline workers who have lost their lives to corona virus" (DW, 12 May 2020). In Belgium, where several cases of spitting were reported, offenders could be fined up to €2,400 and could face prison terms of up to two years. If claiming to be infected to scare others, the offenders were subjected to the same penalties (Brussels Times, 31 March 2020). A Pennsylvania woman, Margaret Cirko, 35, coughed and spat on US$35,000 worth of produce and merchandise at a grocery store. Arrested and charged with two felony counts of terrorist threats, one count of threats to use a "biological agent" and one count of criminal mischief. She reportedly said: "I have the virus. Now everyone is going to get sick" (Halpin and Kalinowski 2020). Except for one-to-one infection, it is difficult to weaponize; still it has been a great security concern that an assailant could infect VIPs, security, or frontline officials.

New York-based Muslim Brotherhood activist Bahgat Saber—with 143,195 followers—called for Egyptians to intentionally infect government officials and state employees in a Facebook post on 1 March 2020. "If you are a soldier, you can go into the defense ministry, and shake hands with all the generals of the military and the police. The same is true with the justice system" (Naar 2020). In a Facebook Live session, Saber said, "If you have contracted corona virus, you should exact revenge! Avenge yourself, avenge the honor of your women, avenge the people who are in prison, and avenge the oppressed people. Go there. Why die alone? When you die, why die alone?" (ibid.). The US House Committee on Homeland Security drew the attention of the US Department of Homeland Security to concerns over white supremacist groups and radical Islamist groups who sought to use the pandemic "to leverage political deals and accelerate the collapse of society" (Counter Extremism Project 2020). The FBI also issued a report to local police agencies, pointing out that extremist groups "are encouraging one another to spread the virus, if contracted, through bodily fluids and personal interactions" (Middle East Transparent· 28 April 2020).

The COVID-19 pandemic has significantly transformed a plethora of circumstances in the threat environment. This changing threat landscape determines the thinking and actions of terrorist and extremist groups, networks, and cells. We have summarized our findings on these changes in accordance with two spectrums, namely conflict and in nonconflict zones.

Conflict Zones

Since 11 March 2020, lockdowns and partial lockdowns together with other pandemic restrictions have created a paradoxical effect on the battlefields. In the first four and a half months after the pandemic outbreak, the jihadist threat increased in conflict zones—more specifically in East and West Africa, Iraq, Syria—because of the following reasons:

1. The crisis situation forced governments to divert their resources to save lives and livelihoods. This reallocation has resulted in novel vulnerabilities terrorists have been keen to attack.
2. At the same time, to minimize the risk of infection, international troops were withdrawn from the most critical areas. This seriously paralyzed those enhanced technical capabilities local governments were provided with in their counterterrorism efforts.
3. The only major battlefield where the terrorist threat has not increased with the pandemic outbreak is Afghanistan. The diminished threat in the country at the beginning of 2020 was due to the Doha Declaration, in which the Afghan Taliban and the Afghan Government engaged in negotiations, with US assistance.

Nonconflict Zones

After the World Health Organization declared the spread of COVID-19 a pandemic on 11 March 2020, the number of terrorist attacks decreased off the battlefields. However, there was a surge in terrorism with developments in France. On 25 September 2020, a 25-year-old Pakistani man,

Zaher Hassan Mahmood, stabbed two French citizens and seriously wounded another one. The lone wolf attacker was influenced by the 2015 Charlie Hebdo terrorist act, which was perpetrated in revenge for the cartoons of Prophet Muhammad (BBC News, 26 September 2020). Some weeks later, on 16 October 2020, a French teacher, Samuel Paty, was beheaded by Abdoullakh Abouyedovich Anzorov, an 18-year-old Muslim Russian refugee of Chechen ethnicity, days after the controversial cartoons of the Prophet had been shown to his pupils. On 29 October 2020, a 21-year-old Tunisian man, Brahim Aouissaoui, stabbed three French people at a church in Nice. On the same day, French police foiled an alleged Nice-copycat attack near the Saint-Martin's Church in Sartrouville. Near Avignon, in Montfavet, a man was shot dead after threatening police with a handgun on 29 October 2020 (BBC News, 3 November 2020). Within hours of the Nice and Avignon incidents, a guard was attacked outside the French consulate in Jeddah in Saudi Arabia (NDTV, 29 October 2020). On the last evening prior to the lockdown in Austria, a gunman opened fire with assault rifles in six places in Vienna on 2 November 2020. The perpetrator was killed by police while wearing a fake suicide vest. The attacker was identified as Kujtim Fejzullai, an Islamic State supporter who had tried to travel to Syria (BBC News, 3 November 2020).

If not for these developments in France, the downturn trend in terrorist incidents would have continued. However, the attacks in France precipitated anger among Muslims and fury among extremists and terrorists, leading to a spike in the threat in Europe and beyond. It was the continuation of the Charlie Hebdo incident but more specifically linked to the trial, which had been scheduled for 6, 9, 10 and 11 November 2020 (France 24, 2 November 2020). French president Emmanuel Macron's support for the right to caricature Prophet Muhammad further heightened the anti-France sentiment across the fundamentalist Muslim world. The shooting in Austria illustrated the extremist networks' ability to respond to current events in a timely manner. Although the number of terrorist incidents increased in Europe in the second half of 2020, this trend was still well below the year prior to the pandemic outbreak.

In the United Kingdom and in the European Union, supporters and sympathizers of Liberation Tigers of Tamil Eelam (LTTE) have stepped up their recruitment and radicalization activities since the pandemic outbreak (Waduge 2020). The insurgent and terrorist group fighting for a mono-ethnic homeland in Northeastern Sri Lanka was defeated by the Sri Lanka security forces in May 2009. The militant separatist group was notorious for conducting the largest number of suicide attacks before the advent of the Islamic State (CISAC 2020). LTTE members currently residing in Western Europe are, however, of great security concern. The premier front in France, Tamil Coordinating Committee (TCC) held an event on 27 November 2020 to commemorate their leader Velupillai Prabhakaran's 66th birthday in the La Chapelle area. Organized annually by the LTTE international network, radical Tamils participate in the Mahaveer Day to mark their dead, including their suicide attackers. According to the Sri Lankan Embassy in France, French police had removed posters put up in La Chapelle on the days leading up to the event (Tamil Guardian, 28 November 2020). In parallel, pro-LTTE activists celebrated the martyrs day in the United Kingdom. Photos taken at the ornate and impressively prepared event show 10–30 LTTE sympathizers commemorating their dead at a warehouse in Balham, South London on 27 November 2020. Reportedly, the British police closely monitored the happenings (Nivunhella 2020).

Changes in Modus Operandi

The pandemic's impact on terrorism is highly complex and multifaceted. Its medium and long-term effects are yet to be seen. Nonetheless, the immediate operational changes it has induced can already be tracked. Restrictive epidemiological measures have introduced novel challenges in extremists' and terrorists' operational circumstances. Off-the-battlefield lockdowns have resulted in challenges to mounting an attack but also hindered well-established supply chains. Resorting to armed assault instead of deploying improvised explosive devices may suppose that the movement of goods was restricted and terrorists' access to operational resources was perhaps limited during lockdowns. These findings could be of great importance for counterterrorism agencies to map and better understand extremists' supply systems.

In conflict zones, the crisis offered radical Islamist fighters highly advantageous novelties. Without the support of international troops, local security forces have been struggling to counter terrorist operations. The heightened level of military presence, as well as the symbolic value of security forces during a crisis, have made military personnel and facilities their number one targets. Although, we need to mention here the exception of Mozambique. While Islamic State operatives previously ambushed government institutions and military compounds, supposedly taking advantage of the pandemic crisis situation since March 2020, radical Islamist groups have attacked cities, towns, and critical infrastructure (Meir Amit Intelligence 2020). In line with this, the Mozambique port Mocimboa da Praia was also captured by the Islamic State (Bowker 2020).

Propaganda Activities

COVID-19 has had a significant impact on terrorists' and violent extremists' online agitation acts. Intensified right-wing extremist activities have been striving to capitalize on the pandemic since the outbreak. Rigorous virus propaganda by both radical Islamists and right-wing groups have incited violent acts, and they have attempted to recruit in the digital realm. While the number of potential online audiences substantially increased because of the pandemic restrictions, these restrictions had serious operational consequences for the right wing offline. Consequently, demonstrations as traditional means for recruitment and building transnational connections with like-minded groups were eliminated. It is, again, yet to be seen how these threat groups can recover from the loss of these cross-border links.

At the time of the pandemic outbreak, extremists increased their propaganda activities in the digital world. They incorporated COVID-19 into their narratives and posted more frequently on their existing websites. Both radical Islamist and far right groups were determined to exploit the elevated online public presence. As the findings of our study show, to bolster their agenda, they circulated conspiracy theories, incited violence, and attempted to recruit new members. Interestingly, however, despite the initial intensity of extremists' and terrorists' actions in the cybersphere, the number of posts significantly decreased as the pandemic spread further.

Nonetheless, there are serious issues that remained great security concerns. First, the unsupervised Internet activity of the younger generation requires particular attention. Being exposed to radical online content in a highly unstable crisis situation may generate a super-susceptible audience for threat groups (Kruglanski et al. 2020). Second, the pandemic induced an enhanced level of politicization in many societies (Aatresh 2020). It was feared that this may accelerate polarization and ultimately engender more violence. Finally, another important consideration here is that, historically, crisis situations have generally made people turn to religion (Sherwood 2018). There is a risk that those who begin to engage in religious ideologies may fall victim to radicalization.

Policy Recommendations

The elevated level of digital presence inherently requires special attention from authorities. Building upon these novel operational circumstances, effective mechanisms and collaborations are to be developed. Detecting and moderating or removing radicalized online content is only one side of the problem. Governments and publicly trusted voices explicitly and publicly communicate that these posts are harmful for young people. At the same time, the younger generation should be taught to think critically when encountering potentially radicalized ideologies. Over-politicized online narratives as well as misinformation campaigns have significantly diminished the credibility of government communications. In order to restore the trust in governments, effective strategic campaigns should be implemented to diminish the power of extremist narratives.

The pandemic has introduced novel responsibilities for both law enforcement and military agencies. The enforcement of newly adopted epidemiological restrictions has resulted in a shift of security agencies' priorities. This reallocation of tasks has redirected scarce resources from counterterrorism efforts. COVID-19 has exacerbated state-level considerations, and this may undermine the success of global and transnational achievements. All in all, we cannot let the pandemic ruin already established international counterterrorism instruments and partnerships. Efforts should be fortified to maintain previous achievements in the field.

The pandemic drew attention to new types of security threats. Given the increased significance of medical facilities and grocery stores, their value as potential terrorist targets has also increased remarkably. In line with this, security arrangements of these types of facilities should be re-evaluated. It is also feared that the devastating consequences of COVID-19 may encourage individuals to seek innovative ways to carry out acts of bioterrorism. More specifically, there is a pressing need to develop capacities to counter deliberate attempts to infect others. One noteworthy example here may be an alert from the Federal Bureau of Investigation back in April 2020. The FBI issued the report to inform local police agencies about extremist groups' recommendations from their Telegram channels on how to spread coronavirus to law enforcement and minority communities (Middle East Transparent, 28 April 2020).

Outline of the Book

Following this introductory chapter, the book is organized into seven parts. Chapter 1, titled "The Evolution of the Threat," is a review of the past, the present, and the likely future of terrorist threats. This discussion maps the global threat landscape at the time the pandemic was declared and examines active violent extremists and terrorist entities both immediately before and after the outbreak of COVID-19. This section includes radical Islamist as well as right-wing agendas and incidents in conflict and nonconflict zones. Later in the chapter, a concise outline of prevalent academic standpoints and debates on COVID-19's impact on terrorism is put forward. This review aims to introduce the scholarship by mapping and exploring noted academics' contributions and the current status quo on the pandemic's impact on terrorism and violent extremism. In the final section, we identify and analyze potential political, social, economic, and psychological causes of terrorism in the context of COVID-19, and public health crises in general, to evaluate whether such emergencies create novel vulnerabilities terrorists can exploit.

Chapter 2, titled "How Have Radical Islamists Capitalized on the Pandemic?" endeavors to provide a better understanding of novel trends and dynamics in Islamist terrorism since the COVID-19 outbreak in China. Accordingly, radical Islamist narratives are first extensively elaborated. Secondly, changes in the volume and nature of radical Islamist threats are tracked. To do this, the threat landscape between 11 March and 31 July 2020 is contrasted with attacks that emerged in the same period in 2018. The comparison is based upon four perspectives: the number of attacks, their targets together with their modus operandi, and the active radical Islamist terrorist groups in the respective geographic regions. The discussion covers countries in both conflict zones (Syria, Iraq, Afghanistan, East and West Africa) and nonconflict zones (Southeast Asia, Europe, United States). In the concluding section, the role of Ramadan 2020 in radical Islamist activities is assessed.

COVID-19 has offered a unique opportunity for far right extremists to capitalize on the pandemic and thereby advance their malicious efforts. To gain a better understanding of how the associated threat has evolved since the outbreak, Chapter 3, titled "How Far Right Extremists Exploited the Coronavirus Crisis," has examined far right operations, incitements, and propaganda activities between 11 March and 31 July 2020 in both Europe and North America. By examining these groups' applied tactics and narratives, insights into far right extremist groups' operations can be investigated. The concluding section of this chapter has been devoted to Australia- and New Zealand-based right-wing extremist activities.

The pandemic has been used to bolster narratives across all extremist ideologies. Chapter 4, titled "Beyond the Radical Islamist and Right-Wing Threat," scrutinizes the activities of other extremist entities such as radical left-wing groups as well as ecoterrorists.

The discussion in Chapter 5, titled "Novel Terrorist Tactics and Targets," elaborates on the changes COVID-19 has introduced into violent extremists' operational circumstances. First, both the radical Islamist and the far right threat landscape are assessed. Building upon this analysis, observations on how the pandemic has changed extremists' operational tactics and targets are put forward.

Chapter 6, titled "Future Trajectories for Emerging Radical Islamist and Far Right Trends," has two purposes. First, the chapter takes account of future trajectories for both the emerging radical Islamist and far right trends. Second, the challenges associated with novel threats are examined.

With the attempt to establish an accurate picture of the terrorist threat landscape, this book's findings could serve as a basis for amendments to be made in counterterrorism strategies both in conflict and nonconflict zones. In the Conclusion, titled "Policy Recommendations," the implications on future counterpolicy actions are put forward.

Two datasets are annexed to the book. The first delineates the key radical Islamist and far right messages on the pandemic, and the second provides statistics on terrorists' and extremists' COVID-19-related activities.

The introduction has set the scene for the upcoming discussion in the book. The story starts in the early months of 2020. We guide the reader through the terrorist threat landscape at the time of the pandemic outbreak. To better understand the evolving security arrangements and ongoing insurgent dynamics in conflict and nonconflict areas, we strive to detect novelties in terrorist and extremist agendas and modus operandi. An extensive examination of emerging incidents after 11 March 2020 seeks to answer the questions this introductory chapter has raised. Drawing on these implications, we will highlight where we need to re-evaluate counterterrorism policies and constructs.

Conclusion

This introductory chapter has attempted to take account of changes in the terrorist threat landscape since the COVID-19 pandemic outbreak. Novelties in modus operandi, the most relevant terrorist attacks, and propaganda activities both in conflict and nonconflict zones have been examined. Building upon our assessments, implications for future counterpolicies have been presented.

References

Aatresh, Aishani. 2020. "Science, Society, and Security: Politicization in the Age of COVID-19." *Harvard Political Review*, May 30.

Bowker, Tom. 2020. "Battle Looms in Mozambique over Extremists' Control of Port." *AP News*, 25 August.

Halpin, James, and Bob Kalinowski. 2020. "Hanover Township Woman Charged in Gerrity's Supermarket Coughing Episode." *The Times-Tribune*, 26 March.

Kruglanski, Arie W., Rohan Gunaratna, Molly Ellenberg, and Anne Speckhard. 2020. "Terrorism in Time of the Pandemic: Exploiting Mayhem." *Global Security: Health, Science and Policy* 5(1): 121–32.

"Liberation Tigers of Tamil Elam." 2020. Stanford CISAC website. Retrieved May 2022 from https://cisac.fsi.stanford.edu/mappingmilitants/profiles/liberation-tigers-tamil-elam#: ~ :text = July percent208 percent2C percent202015-,The per cent20Liberation percent20Tigers percent20of percent20Tamil percent20Eelam percent20(LTTE) percent20were percent20a percent20militant,armed percent 20forces percent20in percent20May percent202009.

"Member States Concerned by the Growing and Increasing Transnational Threat of Extreme Right-Wing Terrorism." 2020. United Nations Security Council Counter-Terrorism Committee Executive Directorate, CTED Trends Alert. Retrieved May 2022 from https://www.un.org/securitycouncil/ctc/sites/www.un.org.se curitycouncil.ctc/files/files/documents/2021/Jan/cted_trends_alert_extreme_right-wing_terrorism.pdf.

Naar, Ismaeel. 2020. "Coronavirus: Muslim Brotherhood Activist Calls on Egyptians to Infect Officials." *Al Arabiya English*, 18 March.

Nivunhella, Sujeeva. 2020. "Pro-LTTE Activists Organize Grand 'Heroes Day' Commemoration in the UK." *The Island*, 29 November.

Sherwood, Harriet. 2018. "Non-Believers Turn to Prayer in a Crisis, Poll Finds." *The Guardian*, 14 January.

"Spotlight on Global Jihad April 7–22, 2020." 2020. The Meir Amit Intelligence and Terrorism Information Center website. Retrieved May 2022 from https://www .terrorism-info.org.il/en/spotlight-global-jihad-april-7-22-2020/.

"Tech and Terrorism: Online Extremists Exploit Coronavirus Pandemic to Incite Violence and Encourage Terrorism." 2020. Counter Extremism Project website. Retrieved May 2022 from https://www.counterextremism.com/press/tech-ter rorism-online-extremists-exploit-coronavirus-pandemic-incite-violence-en courage.

Waduge, Shenali. 2020. "LTTE Has Taken Murder, Extremism and Mayhem to the West." *Sinhala Net*, 8 October.

Weaver, Matthew, and Vikram Dodd. 2020. "Coronavirus Outbreak Police Examine CCTV Footage of Suspect Who Spat at UK Rail Worker Who Later Died." *The Guardian*, 13 May.

CHAPTER 1

The Evolution of the Threat

> If Muslims cannot defeat the kafir [unbelievers] in a different way, it is permissible to use weapons of mass destruction . . . . Even if it kills all of them and wipes them and their descendants off the face of the Earth.
> —Nasir al-Fahd, Saudi cleric's fatwa, *Foreign Policy*, 28 August 2014.

Introduction: The Pandemic

Today, the world faces an unprecedented global health crisis. Although coronavirus is not as deadly as the Spanish flu—February 1918–April 1920 (History.com 2020)—it has led to a dramatic loss of human lives and livelihoods. (The death toll of Spanish flu is estimated to have been between 20 and 50 million people.) Since the emergence of COVID-19 in China in December 2019, the world has witnessed heightened geopolitical rivalry, growing distrust in governments, and enhanced hostility between ethnic and religious communities. Away from the glare of international media, violent extremists and terrorists have adjusted to the novel circumstances and capitalized on the vulnerabilities the pandemic has created for their own benefit. Reactive measures to curb the spread of COVID-19 have inherently altered behavioral patterns and regiments in all aspects of life. Besides the social and economic consequences of the pandemic situation, fears have circulated that an economic downturn may add extraordinary impetus to the existing fragmentation of communities. It is also concerning whether coronavirus has exposed vulnerable segments to radical and violent online content and inspired new efforts at bioterrorism. But have terrorists and extremists changed their modus operandi and attempted to weaponize the virus? To what extent could they exploit the crisis in their propaganda?

To answer all these questions, we need to better understand the global threat landscape at the time of the pandemic outbreak. Therefore, this introductory section attempts to take account of the pre-existing conditions terrorists and extremists were contending with prior to

COVID-19. This starting scene includes radical Islamist and right-wing agendas, both in conflict and nonconflict zones.

The Radical Islamist Threat Landscape

Contemporary radical Islamists aim to establish an Islamic state governed exclusively by Islamic law. They legitimize the use of violence by citing classical Islamic doctrines on jihad (Europol 2020). Radical Islamist terrorism refers to "a violent ideology exploiting traditional Islamist concepts" (MD Staff 2020). It is a "violent sub-current of Salafism, a revivalist Sunni Muslim movement that rejects democracy and elected parliaments, arguing that human legislation is at variance with God's status as the sole lawgiver" (Europol 2020). Al-Qaeda and the Islamic State are the major representatives of radical Islamist groups.

Syria

In the Syrian Arab Republic, a relative improvement in the security situation was reported for the first quarter of 2020. Ankara and Moscow agreed to a temporary ceasefire in Idlib Province and began working toward a joint Turkish-Russian security corridor (International Crisis Group 2020). The biggest concerns in Syria remained around the security of detention facilities and camps (United Nations Security Council 2020) providing shelter for numerous youngsters with a heightened level of openness to radicalization As a territory-controlling armed entity, the Islamic State may have been defeated in early 2019—but as a comprehensive threat actor in the region, it was only seriously injured (Cordesman 2020b). In fact, several questions remained. How would IS fighters be demobilized, disarmed and reintegrated into society? (BTI Transformation Index 2020). And how would the coronavirus affect Islamic State's behavior? Would the coronavirus assist or hinder IS in its terrorist endeavors?

In early 2020, the estimated combined number of IS fighters in Iraq and Syria was more than 10,000, dispersed in small cells (United Nations Security Council 2020). Islamic State was reconstituting itself in these tiny safe havens that sheltered their operations in remote, isolated areas and therefore protected them from exposure to the virus. The pandemic generated humanitarian crises and high unemployment rates, and the Iraqi government's failures in ensuring basic services provided disillusioned civilians a reason to be recruited by the Islamic

State. Despite the fact that IS had lost many members in the chain of command, it was still a viable group in Syria and Iraq because of its self-financing capability as well as its continuous recruitment activities (US Department of State 2019).

Iraq

Iraq was in a particularly "fragile situation" (Cordesman 2020a) at the time of the outbreak, with conditions made even more fragile by the rapid spread of COVID-19. It had hardly recovered from the war against the Islamic State, so the political system remained unstable and dependent upon the support of both Iran and the United States. Despite the gradual changes in political leaders, still corruption and institutional incapacity paralyzed government efforts to provide stability (BTI Transformation Index 2020). Countrywide five-month-long protests called on longstanding demands for change, economic reform, and an end to corruption. Grave concerns existed in relation to authorities resorting to "excessive force" against demonstrators. Additionally, regional dynamics continued to affect Iraq. For example, there were deep tensions between ethnic Shi'ite and Sunni and Kurdish areas of the country. Operating in a "war of attrition," IS operatives aimed to exploit the coronavirus crisis by sustaining rural insurgency and carrying out sporadic operations in larger cities (United Nations Security Council 2020).

A strong state, organized on the monopoly of force, was required to effectively address Islamic State's ability to exploit the pandemic (UN CTED 2020). At the same time, programs were to be established concerning the repatriation of IS families. Moreover, advanced technology and military training were necessary for Iraqi security forces to more effectively fight against the Islamic State. Radical Islamists may have been defeated militarily, but the fundamental causes and factors that enabled the terrorist entity to develop still exist.

Afghanistan

The increasing threat of insurgents and weak political institutions constitute the major challenges for the Afghan state. Kabul's domestic political crisis deepened when Afghanistan's two rival leaders both declared themselves as leaders of the country (International Crisis Group 2020). As the state's monopoly on the use of force is limited, in recent years, the ever-growing power of the Taliban has jeopardized the stability of Afghan governance (BTI Transformation Index 2020). After an extensive period of negotiation between the United States and the Taliban, on 21 February 2020, the parties agreed upon a seven-day reduction in violence across Afghanistan. After the successful completion of this agreement, a formal US-Taliban peace agreement could have been signed. The document would have included a pledge from the US to cease targeting terrorist groups in the country, and at the same time, the number of US troops operating in Afghanistan would have been reduced from 13,000 to 8,600 (United Nations Security Council 2020). Following the Doha Agreement in February 2020, the Taliban would have resumed intense military pressure on Afghan security forces, especially in rural areas (International Crisis Group 2020).

Regardless of serious losses of its senior leaders in late 2019, the threat posed by the Islamic State remained persistent. The Islamic State's South Asian Province (IS Khorasan) was still ambitious and capable of implementing high-profile operations in Afghanistan. Some 2,100 IS fighters established the new Afghan core area in Kunar Province (United Nations Security Council 2020). It was also worrisome that existing accounts for Salafism in Kunar and Nangarhar provinces may push young residents toward IS as a response to the Afghan state's practices of repression (Mir 2020). The terrorist organization was also striving to attract Taliban operatives who are against the US-Taliban agreement, but several former Tehrik-e Taliban Pakistan (TTP) members also joined IS forces. Because of IS Khorasan's established informal contacts with other terrorist groups, including Jamaat-ul-Ahrar, TTP, and Lashkar-e-Islam, it was believed the associated security threat may address the neighboring countries of Afghanistan (United Nations Security Council 2020). Al-Qaeda—with an estimated 400–600 fighters—were still covertly active in the country (United Nations Security Council 2020).

Africa

Following a seven-month battle in 2016, the Libyan government forces cleared the last Islamic State North African territorial stronghold. Although IS was significantly weakened at that time, the terrorist organization continued to pose a serious security threat to Libya in the midst of the ongoing conflict in the country (BTI Transformation Index 2020). IS operated from its safe havens in the less-controlled southern parts of the country and still attacked military checkpoints and police stations. Also, there were two worrisome factors that required attention. Firstly, the influx of weapons into the Libyan conflict zone raised serious concerns that IS would exploit the opportunities provided by this new black market (United Nations Security Council 2020). Secondly, it was also feared whether there were members of designated terrorist groups among those 7,000–15,000 fighters who had arrived from Syria to participate in the Libyan conflict (United Nations Security Council 2020).

After Libya, the Islamic State built a significant capability in the Greater Sahara. In the region of Greater Sahara—Mali, Niger, and Burkina Faso—the influence of Islamic State was growing rapidly. The previous peaceful coexistence of Jama'at Nasr al-Islam wal Muslimin (JNIM) and the Islamic State in the Greater Sahara (ISGS) was at risk. Intensive ISGS propaganda activities had condemned JNIM for the "flexible implementation of sharia" (United Nations Security Council 2020) and its willingness to sit down with the government of Mali. The ISGS relied on the logistical supply chain with the Islamic State West Africa Province (ISWAP), and this further enhanced the threat group to operate independently. Regardless of focused counterterrorism operations in the area, ISGS still maintained strongholds in the tri-border area between Burkina Faso, Mali, and Niger (United Nations Security Council 2020). ISWAP and its almost 3,500 fighters intensively attacked Nigeria, southern Niger, and northwestern Cameroon.

The Islamic State in Somalia had suffered serious personnel losses in military counter operations in late 2019, but the group remained resilient and resumed covert operations. Al-Qaeda affiliate Harakat al-Shabaab al-Mujahidin (al-Shabaab) was expanding across Somalia. They were attacking high-profile (both civilian and military) as well as foreign targets. Al-Shabaab leadership was urging followers to carry out attacks beyond Somalia, in the neighboring countries. As a result, low-scale cross-border incursions were reported in Kenya. Meanwhile, the threat posed by the Islamic State Central Africa Province (ISCAP) was evolving, with local recruits and foreign fighters operating in their forces. Additionally, improved improvised explosive device capability and the application of asymmetric tactics were observed by authorities. There was a persistent endeavor to consolidate regional IS online propaganda with its affiliates in Eastern, Southern and Central Africa. In this vein, IS in Puntland aimed to function as a command center for Islamic State operatives in the Democratic Republic of Congo and Mozambique (United Nations Security Council 2020).

Europe

The threat of Internet-driven home-grown extremists remained of great concern in Europe. In 2019, nearly 60 percent of jihadi attackers had the citizenship of the country in which the attack or plot took place. Online platforms and encrypted Internet applications were used for recruitment and training purposes by both national citizens and resident foreigners. The risk of migrants being exposed to radical online inspirations was one of the greatest threats. The release of imprisoned foreign terrorist fighters in 2020 was another worrisome factor because of concerns over the effectiveness of rehabilitation programs. Reported incidents referred to the clandestine networks of women members of terrorist organizations facilitating the information exchange for radicalized prisoners. This drew attention to the threat posed by women terrorists and radicalized female inmates that should have been appropriately addressed (Europol 2020). Al-Hawl camp in the Syrian Arab Republic was of acute concern because of two factors. First, repatriating potentially radicalized women from the camp held serious security threats. And second, limited IS attempts to establish cells in Europe from Al-Hawl camp were detected. In North Europe and in the Western Balkans, the Islamic State or al-Qaeda sympathetic imams constitute new challenges for authorities. Their underground recruiting activities require constant attention. In parallel, IS-inspired Central Asian (Tajik, Uzbek, Kyrgyz) and Chechen terrorist networks have emerged with intentions to carry out attacks and recruit among migrants (United Nations Security Council 2020).

Southeast Asia

Regardless of consistent counterterrorism efforts, the contemporary threat posed by the Islamic State was still persistent (United Nations Security Council 2020) and concentrated in Sulu-Sulawesi Seas. Unsurprisingly, this tri-border area of Indonesia, Malaysia, and the Philippines had been historically struggling to govern the territorial disputes of maritime borders (Borelli 2017). Nevertheless, as a result of focused countermeasures and established channels for intelligence sharing, there was a better understanding of active local radical Islamist groups' operational circumstances. The inconsistent security of maritime borders enabled a vibrant route for operatives. Great concern remained in relation to foreign fighters arriving from Iraq and Syria, who may have further improved the operational capabilities of local threat groups. The role of women in the operational planning, financing, and execution of attacks in the region continued to be of particular attention. According to the latest estimations, approximately 1,500 Indonesians traveled to the conflict zone. Among them, roughly 700, including 400 minors, were believed to have been staying in Syrian detention centers. Both the public and the official policies were against the repatriation of these nationals (United Nations Security Council 2020).

Just prior to the pandemic outbreak, two terrorist threat predictions resonated. First, whether the defeat of IS by the West and the death of al-Baghdadi would result in an elevated level of intensity among foreign operatives. And second, whether the repatriated fighters from Syria could significantly upgrade the capacity of Southeast Asian-based—mainly low potency—terrorists. None of these predictions have materialized, as foreign fighters arriving from the battlefields were caught on arrival by authorities (Jones 2020).

Constant fights between radical Islamists and the Philippines military/security forces characterized the security landscape in the southern Philippines. Islamic State's four local affiliates (Abu Sayyaf Group, Bangsamoro Islamic Freedom Fighters, Maute Group, and Ansarul Khilafah Philippines) facilitated extraordinary opportunities for training and operational planning. Authorities had constant struggles combating radical Islamist online activities, including recruitment, radicalization, and fundraising via social media platforms. Local threat groups were reported to be self-sustaining; online campaigns, smuggling of arms or vehicles, and kidnap for ransom remained their preferred means for fundraising (United Nations Security Council 2020).

United States

The threat landscape was characterized by a highly decentralized network of organizations sharing a wide range of ideologies (Jones et al. 2020). Incidents were not isolated in specific geographic areas, suggesting that terrorism was a national and not a regional phenomenon (Jones et al. 2020). It was anticipated that the threat posed by foreign terrorist organizations would likely remain overseas because of constant US counterterrorism efforts. Nevertheless, considering that these entities maintain an interest in carrying out operations in the United States, this may result in the rise of so-called "inspired attacks" on the homeland (US Department of Homeland Security 2020).

Right-Wing Extremism and Terrorism

Right-wing extremism is generally defined as a specific ideology of "antidemocratic opposition towards equality" (Carter 2018). This is, though, not a uniform ideology but rather includes united sub-tenets along with the rejection of diversity and minority rights (Europol 2020). The concept is usually associated with antisemitism, racism, xenophobia, nationalism, authoritarianism, and conspiracy theories (Ravndal 2016).

The enemy articulated in these ideologies is thought to be the main threat to the survival of the nation or race (Jupskås and Segers 2020). Different concepts have been used for the term right-wing terrorism. As a unique form of political violence, it can be interpreted somewhere between a "hate crime" and "organized terrorism" (Koehler 2016). The extreme right-wing could be defined as activists who commit criminal activity motivated by a political or cultural opinion that may cover racism, extreme nationalism, fascism, and neo-Nazism (Greater Manchester Police Counter Terrorism Branch Prevent Team 2018).

There was a 320 percent rise in right-wing terrorism on a global scale in the five years up to 2020 (UN CTED 2020). Along with space security, climate security, and emerging technologies, right-wing extremism has become one of the most concerning global security threats. The highly complex nature of right-wing threat groups makes the combat against them challenging for governments and authorities. They are complex because of their wide range of grievances, including racism, misogyny, antisemitism, anti-LGBTQ sentiments, Islamophobia, and anti-governmental ideologies, which fuel radicalized individuals (UN News, 6 July 2020).

Extreme right-wing terrorism predominantly affects Europe, Australasia, and North America. The following discussions explain the right-wing threat landscape prior to the pandemic outbreak in these geographic areas.

Europe

Right-wing extremist attacks in 2019 drew attention to the relevance of online communication as a mean for strengthening international links among violent extremists. The perpetrators of the Christchurch, Poway, El Paso, Baerum and Halle right-wing attacks were members of like-minded transnational online communities and were inspired by one another (Europol 2020). The worrisome exponential influence of social media provided these threat groups with extraordinary opportunities for spreading hateful ideology and encouraging violence (Daines 2020). The pandemic as a "security issue" (Gjørv 2020) has fanned the flames of this increasingly loud chorus of destabilizing voices in society. Of particular concern is the impact of extremist disinformation campaigns with regard to the pandemic. Existing and emerging far right conspiracies and fake news can potentially accelerate polarization in Western societies (Macklin 2020) and/or inspire lone actors or autonomous cells to commit violent crimes (Ravndal et al. 2020). Another worrisome factor is the tight connectivity of far right entities. Besides communicating with each other in the digital subcultures, there are ever-growing concerns of their links to conflict zones and training camps (Ong and Pantucci 2020).

Australia

The Australian authorities thwarted far right-related violent acts in 2020. One far right extremist was seeking to travel to a conflict zone, while another was arrested for attempting to acquire firearms and manufacture an improvised explosive device. Later, in Melbourne, a man planning to attack left-wing targets was detained (Carroll 2020). The Australian 2020 terrorist threat assessment concluded that right-wing extremism is a top priority. Australian Security Intelligence Organization (ASIO) Director-General Mike Burgess said, "The numbers are small, but growing" (Daily Sabah, 18 September 2020). As the Australian Federal Police announced on 20 October 2020, "the most concerning phenomenon is the online radicalization of youngsters" (Coughlan 2020a). ASIO reported that far right extremism then accounted for up to 40 percent of its counterterrorism workload, up from 15 percent in 2016. The pandemic has further accelerated the complaining right-wing extremists' narratives and has made them more organized, sophisticated, and active (Daily Sabah, 18 September 2020). The threat landscape has included small right-wing cells in Australian suburbs using Nazi symbols and delivering weapon and combat training. Also, Australian far right activists reportedly had joined international white supremacist groups spreading extremist propaganda and inciting violent acts on their online forums, such as the one called Base. The associated threat was characterized by low capability (knife, gun, or a vehicle) (Whyte 2020).

New Zealand

The far right threat became evident when 28-year-old Brenton Tarrant killed 51 people in the Christchurch Mosque shootings in New Zealand in 2019. In the following year, 60–70 groups and 150–300 right-wing activists were estimated to be operating in the country (The Guardian, 10 March 2020). Notably, numerous countermeasures were launched to monitor these threat groups and individuals. Rapid action was taken to ban military-style semiautomatics and assault weapons, which were popular weapons with far right terrorist groups. New Zealand and France founded the so-called Christchurch Call, which outlines collective, voluntary commitments from fifty governments and ten online service providers to eliminate online terrorist and violent extremist content. Terrorists' use of technology has remained a threat, and even greater investments are necessary to enable law enforcement and intelligence agencies to intercept radical actors and their networks (Jones 2019).

In March 2020, a week prior to the first anniversary of the Christchurch attack, a member of the white supremacist group Action Zealandia was arrested in relation to a terror threat made against Al-Noor Mosque in Christchurch (Daalder 2020). Action Zealandia claims to be the "New Zealand European identity" (Counter Extremism Project 2020) and was formed in 2019. It is widely seen as a successor to the far right Dominion Movement, which described itself as "fraternity of young New Zealand nationalists" united by the belief that "Europeans are the defining people of this nation and that they were essential in its creation" (McCleery 2019).

United States

"Racially and ethnically motivated violent extremists—specifically white supremacist extremists—will remain the most persistent and lethal threat in the Homeland," concluded the US Department of Homeland Security in 2020 (US Department of Homeland Security 2020). An aggravated competition among far left and far right violent groups has been observed. This rivalry may push these entities into a spiraling situation in which actions of one group intended to heighten its security may lead the rival groups to take similar measures. This increased tension can result in an elevated level of weaponization and conflict. It is also notable that demonstrations have become the primary target for both antifascist and anarchist movements. The political polarization, the pandemic, concerns about a potential economic decline, existing racial injustice, and current social alienation may all induce increased domestic terrorism (Jones et al. 2020).

Scholarly Debates on COVID-19's Impact on Terrorism

The pandemic's impact on terrorism has already been subject to scholarly discourses. Important aspects of the phenomenon have been elaborated on by prominent academics. This section first encompasses a concise outline of the scholarly discourse on COVID-19 and terrorism. This review aims to introduce the relevant scholarship by mapping and exploring the academic contributions in the field. This book attempts to take a step forward and build upon these scholarly assertions by providing a comprehensive assessment of the current threat landscape. This assessment includes identifying opportunities and challenges the pandemic has provided hate groups.

Opportunities and Challenges during a Pandemic

Terrorism practitioners and scholars have assessed COVID-19's impact on terrorism in different ways. All their evaluations can be grouped under three approaches.

The first group of authors believes that COVID-19 has enabled terrorist activity. The novel circumstances since the pandemic outbreak have offered violent extremists across all ideological agendas new ways to encourage followers to mount attacks as well as to advance ideological objectives and recruit new members (Whiter 2020). COVID-19 continues to disrupt public health systems and has become the most dominant content in violent extremist online communications (Weimann and Masri 2020). The pandemic has been perceived by violent extremists as "an opportunity" (Daymon and Criezis 2020) to create "a more hospitable global environment for recruitment, growth and action than before" (Cruickshank and Rassler 2020). Since the emergence of SARS-CoV-2, hate groups have flooded their platforms with recruitment propaganda and calls for violence against minorities (Counter Extremism Project 2020). Al-Qaeda even called on non-Muslims to take the time spent in lockdown to study the Koran (Hanna 2020; Simons and Bianca 2020). Terrorist organizations' responses to COVID-19 have included labeling it as "an echo of traditional state structures" and accusations of blame regarding the origins of the disease (Taneja and Pantucci 2020). Extremist entities have named who to blame for the problems the situation has caused them. As a result of their conspiracy theories, anti-Chinese sentiments have broadly surfaced both in the West and in Asia (Pantucci 2020). Interestingly, while in March 2020 the Islamic State incited attacks on Chinese people and interests, no specific resources have been deployed for these efforts (Azman 2020).

The chaos caused by COVID-19 is a unique chance for these threat groups to aggravate resentment and destroy social cohesion (Voronkov 2020). Violent extremists across all ideologies have been promoting their conspiracy theories, tailor-made for the pandemic (Basit 2020). The International Crisis Group has been particularly concerned with places "where the global health challenge intersects with wars on political conditions that could give rise to new crises or exacerbate existing ones" (International Crisis Group 2020). A general tactic of the extreme right was to hijack anti-lockdown protests to induce social tension and to call for acts of violence (Ong 2020). Government failures in addressing the crisis together with social distancing practices that they put in place triggered a wave of "disenfranchisement" (Pantucci 2020), leading to a new impetus in political violence and another drive for "catalyst plots" (Brennan 2020). While extremists responded in various ways to the pandemic, all aimed to leverage it for their own radical purpose and exploit the antigovernment atmosphere. They adopted new global narratives to show their supremacy and better "governance capability" (Taneja and Pantucci 2020). Generally, extremists are keen to pose as superiors to the existing state, although, amidst the pandemic, some of them were struggling to operate as quasi-states and provide essential public services, including public healthcare, for their supporters (Taneja and Pantucci 2020). Simultaneously, the daunting economic consequences of the pandemic pushed many individuals into serious financial hardship, perhaps making them more disillusioned and prone to joining extremist movements (Green 2020).

The second group of authors believes that COVID-19 has hindered terrorist activity. The short-term opportunities of coronavirus such as the "captive [online] audience" and government failures in addressing the crisis facilitated the circulation of extremist narratives and conspiracy theories. At the same time, the pandemic generated various short-term risks for violent extremists (UN CTED 2020), as it changed the ways in which terrorist organizations operated. Obviously, epidemiological restrictive measures created serious challenges to terrorists' operational capacity. They resulted in far fewer crowded places, hindered terrorist groups' access to food, medicine, money, and weapons, and moreover distracted erstwhile media attention given to terrorist activities (ibid. 2020). Because of the reallocation of roles and funds of law enforcement agencies, terrorism together with national counterterrorism and policing strategies are going through a substantial reconceptualization (Whiter 2020). Travel bans and the temporary closure of borders may result in the rise of home-grown terrorism as a potential future trajectory for the evolving terrorist threat. This is because such restrictive measures make operational logistics particularly challenging for extremist groups, as their routes and means are more noticeable to the authorities (Simons and Bianca 2020).

Terrorist organizations themselves are also concerned with the physical threat of infection by COVID-19, leading hate groups to take a safety-first approach and highlight that "Islam is a hygiene-oriented religion" (Hanna 2020). In the meantime, instead of encouraging followers to mount attacks in the West, Islamic State asked them to "stay away from the land of the epidemic" (Hernandez-Morales 2020). There is an even heightened level of infection risk perceived when considering vulnerable radical Islamists in Indonesian prisons and Syrian refugee camps (UNODC 2021). Radical Islamists as potential carriers of coronavirus should also be pondered here. In this regard, they can be categorized into two perpetrator variables: non-IS and pro-IS militants. Non-IS radicals declared that regardless of social distancing rules they would congregate and pray and thus had the potential to spread the virus. A pro-IS group, since they resort to mounting attacks, claimed that they would not comply with any regulation imposed by Western governments and continued to live their normal life, thus they also potentially introduced the virus into their communities (Raj 2020). Lone actors are a great security concern as virus carriers. Extensively available extremist propaganda should be mentioned here, which may drive individuals to resort to lone wolf-like plots (Modern Security Consulting Group 2020).

The third group of authors is not yet sure whether the pandemic has enabled or hindered terrorist activities, but they all articulate the novelty COVID-19 has introduced into terrorist operational circumstances. A considerable share of scholarly publications by this group has dealt with the impact of COVID-19 on terrorism. Assessing the short- and long-term impacts of the pandemic, Andrew Silke (2020) asserted that coronavirus had already had a significant effect on terrorism in a variety of ways. Drawing on the fact that authorities were busy enforcing restrictive measures, their distracted attention may have been exploited by violent nonstate actors to incite mounting attacks. Recent threats against medical facilities have highlighted the need to enhance the security of certain critical infrastructure. At the same time, due to the prevalence of online extremist activities, there is a heightened risk of radicalization in the short to medium term. Despite the hurdles of biological terrorism, the pandemic may have also increased the interest in biological warfare. Another long-term consideration is the reallocation of counterterrorism funds, which will have made certain countries even more vulnerable and exposed to the threat of terrorism (Silke 2020). As the United Nations stated, the impact of the virus has varied between conflict and nonconflict zones, as the short-term terrorist threat has increased in conflict zones but has fallen in nonconflict areas (Deccanherald, 23 July 2020). To balance the hype of terrorism during the pandemic, all relevant factors should be considered in this regard, including the deep concerns around a successful bioterror attack by using an infected individual and the mitigating conditions the pandemic has created for the operational circumstances of violent extremists. It is critical to examine both the "exacerbating" and the "mitigating" factors to put forward a real assessment of the "evolving" terrorist threat.

Short-, medium- and long-term effects can be distinguished when considering COVID-19's impact on violent extremism. Drawing on a pandemic context, not only potential "governance vacuums" but also social restrictions can indulge both a "captive audience" and opportunistic attacks in the short term. In the longer run, government responses may generate tensions and deepen socio-economic impacts. Arguably, the COVID-19 pandemic has become a core topic for radical narratives and threat groups who have been seeking to exploit the crisis (Avis 2020).

It is also worth hoping that for any current or future pandemic the "widespread indiscriminate infection does not align with terrorist goals." Elevated biomedical research investments have resulted in a larger pool of scientists and knowledge, which are highly beneficial advancements for malicious violent nonstate actors, who can more effectively misuse these capabilities. Meanwhile, revisited health emergency preparedness remarkably mitigates the effect of a disease outbreak. Another important factor that suggests lower levels of terrorist capabilities for a successful bioterror attack is the fragmented organization of both radical Islamist and far right threat groups. For such an organizational structure, it is particularly challenging to develop a multidisciplinary bioweapon (Koblentz and Kiesel 2021).

Three potential novel terrorist targets can be identified when examining extremist narratives since the pandemic outbreak. Firstly, given the initial emergence of coronavirus in China, hatred toward Asian minorities has substantially increased (Dezler 2020). Secondly, as hospitals and medical facilities play a pivotal role in the fight against the virus, these critical infrastructures may be subject to future terrorist attacks. Thirdly, 5G-related conspiracies have argued that this emerging technology has facilitated the spread of the virus. Recent changes in remote work advocate and increase the significance of 5G, which adds a further perceived symbolic relevance to instances of people attacking 5G towers (Stern, Ware, and Harrington 2020).

Considering potential directions for the evolvement of future terrorism, the most significant effects of the pandemic on terrorism have been the following. Engaging in prosocial activities brings a certain "degree of legitimacy" together with enhanced opportunities for recruitment and funding for these threat groups; while this was denied, uncertainty since the outbreak may have increased the public's susceptibility to radicalization. Government responses to COVID-19 have often resulted in divisions within a society, exacerbating antigovernment attitudes. Future cataclysmal pandemic circumstances may provide inspiration for apocalyptic-millenarian extremists. Currently, an enhanced general digital presence has obviously increased extremists' online propaganda activities. Given the disruption COVID-19 has caused, a future dangerous virus may lead to the re-establishment of bioterrorism and encourage violent extremists to weaponize it. With the heightened symbolic relevance of medical facilities and the serious security concerns with regard to CBRNE storage and prisons, the reallocation of resources "introduce[s] frictions into the counterterrorism process," substantially undermining the success of these efforts (Ackerman and Peterson 2020).

There is a need for a "balanced assessment" of violent extremists' activities and narratives during a pandemic. Ongoing threats should be regularly and thoroughly reassessed. According to Sam Mullins (2020), the few incidents that constitute acts of terrorism and that happened during the COVID-19 pandemic had very weak links to it, thus the mobilizing potential of the pandemic with regard to terrorism was "relatively weak." The fact that we may have been more exposed to radical online content or the negative social and economic consequences of the pandemic may not inherently result in the mobilization of terrorism. The challenges terrorists faced because of the pandemic outbreak should also be noted here. Financial shorting together with the risk of infection posed significant challenges for terrorist organizations. Another concern that has circulated refers to the extent of terrorist intent to engage in biological terrorism. Extremist narratives, however, underpin that, for instance, far right activists would rather stay home and watch "the society destroy itself" (Mullins 2020). Incidents have justified the continued implementation of operational hurdles to prevent a bioterror attack, not to mention future epidemiological restrictions such as tight border controls and lockdowns, which during COVID-19 made the implementation of terrorist attacks even more challenging. The potential benefits violent nonstate actors may gain from a pandemic means that noteworthy challenges of the phenomenon cannot be disregarded when assessing the associated threat (Mullins 2020).

It is contested whether terrorist attacks in 2020 in Afghanistan, Iraq, Syria, Somalia, or Nigeria happened in accordance with the pandemic outbreak or whether they would have emerged anyway. The prediction that a spike in terrorist activities in the West was guaranteed was speculative. Likewise, there is little open-source evidence to substantiate any claim that there was an increase in the amount of extremist content online after the outbreak of the virus. It is not to say that as the pandemic continues violent actors' activities will not get worse and law enforcement/intelligence agencies should not devote sufficient attention and resources to counter malevolent extremist intentions. Arguably, there is still not enough solid evidence available to assess the full impact of COVID-19 on terrorism (Gurski 2020).

Some Implications for Developing Countries

Threats are of a different nature when considering the pandemic's consequences in developing countries, where terrorists can more easily advance their campaigns of violence and exploit general public dissatisfaction with the government. In the developing world, the coronavirus has deepened poor economic and social discrepancies, amplified existing food and financial shortages, and enabled conditions that are more optimal for "terrorist violence" (Bellinger and Kattelman 2020). While attempting to increase the legitimacy of their actions, terrorist entities become more state-like and adopt mandatory norms that they would usually seek to defy.

In the Sahel, limited resources, poor health conditions, and the lack of public health services and other societal vulnerabilities may drive the countries in the region further into destabilization. Jama'at Nasr al-Islam wal Muslimin (JNIM)—an al-Qaeda umbrella affiliate—and Islamic State in the Greater Sahara (ISGS)—a recognized Islamic State affiliate—could take advantage of these unstable conditions and exploit these vulnerabilities. Without appropriate foreign counterterrorism operations, the region's chances of eliminating the contributing factors to radicalization and violent extremism might further decrease (Coleman 2020). Reportedly, Iraqi forces face extraordinary challenges in fighting Islamic State's small guerrilla units. Such military operations urgently need high technical solutions, especially capabilities for reconnaissance, air support, and intelligence information, which have been provided by the United States (Magid 2020).

Theoretical Considerations on the Pandemic's Impact on Terrorism

In this section, we identify and analyze potential political, social, economic, and psychological causes of terrorism in the context of COVID-19, and public health crises in general, to evaluate whether such emergencies create novel vulnerabilities terrorists can exploit. For the purpose of this analysis, a broad interpretation of the causes of terrorism has been applied.

The State of Research

The impact of a pandemic is an important security concern. It has been argued that terrorism does not arise in a vacuum (Shughart 2006). An extreme event like a pandemic may induce changes in pre-existing circumstances. Through these mechanisms, such an emergency event can ultimately influence terrorism. It is plausible that turmoil in the aftermath of a pandemic outbreak creates or exacerbates vulnerabilities that terrorist groups might exploit. As the World Health Organization (WHO) stated in 2012, "infectious diseases have shaped societies, driven conflict, and spawned the marginalization of infected individuals and communities throughout history" (WHO 2012). In a similar vein, the Munich Security Conference report in 2016 affirmed that "in addition to the human toll, major outbreaks can also have significant impacts on economies and pose a political risk to governments, particularly those in fragile states that fail to control the disease. Because of their threat to human health, to economies, and to the stability of states as a whole, lapses in health security can become issues of international security" (Munich Security Conference 2016). Infectious diseases were identified as a national security threat in 1995 based upon the assessment of the US National Science and Technology Council. In a 2000 report, the US National Intelligence Council stated that "(re-)emerging infectious diseases threatened U.S. citizens and armed forces, exacerbated social and political instability in countries and regions of U.S. interest" (Patrick 2011). Outbreaks of infectious diseases do not only cause human losses but seriously affect political, social, and economic circumstances (Menzel 2020).

There are different forms of terrorism, and each has its own preconditions. However, certain direct or indirect factors may help us better understand why acts of terrorist violence occur (Newman 2006). The definition of terrorism and, accordingly, the causes of it are both highly contested concepts in the scholarly literature (Lia and Skjølberg 2004; Schmid 2005). Yet, to provide a rigorous theoretical framework for the analysis in this section, an outline of the prevailing causes of terrorism is needed. When analyzing the reasons for terrorism, "this plethora of different elements, their mutual relations and the conditions that influence them" (Lia and Skjølberg 2004) should be scrutinized. It is important to stress here that terrorists are "rational and intentional actors" (Bjørgo 2005), who take into consideration these precipitants during their operation. We also need to see that these factors operate in causal processes and interplay among societal, group, and individual factors (Marone 2021). The discussion on this complex phenomenon does not purport to be complete, nor could it be. The purpose of this review is to offer a wide-ranging discussion of the idiosyncratic processes that may have an impact on the future evolution of terrorism. In the interest of exhaustiveness, for the purpose of this research, four sets of the underlying causal factors were identified: political, social, economic, and psychological circumstances.

Political Factors

In the aftermath of a public health emergency, security and maintaining control can suffer significantly. Political tensions may also arise from the state's failure to provide essential facilities during the management of and the recovery from a natural disaster. Crisis management forces authorities to reconsider priorities and reallocate government resources. This can generate political, social, and economic instabilities (Price-Smith 2002). As a result, the disruption caused by such an extreme event can easily incentivize terrorist action (Berreni and Ostwald 2011). Failed or weak states without the capacity to provide basic needs to their citizens provide fertile ground for the emergence of terrorism. Terrorists are keen to exploit this power vacuum (Bjørgo 2005). This happened, for instance, in Pakistan, following the devastating floods in the country in 2010. Taliban together with other terrorist groups capitalized on weakened state control and intensified their operation (Hasan 2010).

Political instability and terrorism are not unrelated (Hall 1994). A political crisis can ultimately be responsible for a surge in global terrorism (Schumacher and Schraeder 2019). State instability could generate conditions for "creating" terrorists as well as opportunities for terrorists to flourish (Piazza 2007). Infectious disease outbreaks can result in a lower level of political stability, considering that public services together with state capacity can be seriously eroded (Patrick 2011). A crisis situation like a pandemic can induce social tension and increase citizens' lack of faith in government (Rohwerder 2014). Such extreme events may have a serious impact on a country's social as well as political stability (Studies IfS 2014).

A surge in conspiracy theories may also generate public distrust in governments. Misleading or manipulated information was circulated during both the Spanish flu (Jackson 2018) and COVID-19 pandemic. After years of war propaganda, there was a general distrust of public information and governments during the 1918 flu pandemic. Conspiracy theorists blamed COVID-19 on the development of 5G networks, while allegedly radio waves were thought to be the reason for the 1918 flu (Woodward 2020). Trust in public health communication and transparent information, however, has turned out to be crucial. Misleading statements and fake news shared on social media platforms can hamper efforts to curb the consequences of a pandemic (Cotter 2020). Disinformation campaigns together with conspiratorial thinking during a public health emergency event pose significant security concerns (Davies, Wu, and Frank 2021).

Social Factors

There are numerous social factors to consider during a pandemic that may lead to terrorism. First, experiencing discrimination based on ethnic or religious origin can give rise to political violence, which may manifest itself in ethnonationalist terrorism (Bjørgo 2005). Scapegoats and victims of conspiracy theories may feel total alienation from society. Like the use of "Spanish flu," "Chinese virus" during the COVID-19 pandemic quickly spread as a discriminatory term. This, combined with the intense fear of the pandemic, intolerance, propaganda narratives, racism, and stereotypes provided a breeding ground for hateful narratives and acts (Cotter 2020). Blaming foreigners for disease outbreaks is a catalyst for a rise in extremist narratives and activities, as seen with right-wing extremist voting during the Spanish flu. Historians and epidemiologists estimate that about a third of the world's population was infected, and 2.5 to 5 percent of the world's population died in the three waves of the 1918–1919 influenza pandemic (Africa Center for Strategic Studies 2020).

Similarly, a sense of social injustice can also be a strong motivating factor for terrorism (Bjørgo 2005). High social inequality may induce aggression, which may lead to violent acts of terrorism (Ola 2018). A disaster can arguably exacerbate pre-existing social divisions, leading to social-revolutionary terrorism. Research suggests that marginalized groups are disproportionately affected by the consequences of a disaster (Albala-Bertrand 1993; Bolin 2007; Cohen and Werker 2008). This together with the inequalities in the distribution of aid may also be an important determinant of terrorism (Azam and Delacroix 2006; Azam and Thelen 2008; Bandyopadhyay, Sandler, and Younas 2011; Basuchoudhary and Shughart 2010).

Alienation from a political system may lead to frustration. For these excluded individuals, terrorism may be a tempting option to exercise power (Bjørgo 2005). Lockdowns during COVID-19 provided extremists with the "ideal time to exploit youth grievances about their lack of agency, their families' economic distress, and their intense sense of disorientation, confusion, fear and anxiety" (Derish 2020). With digital schooling, the impact of lockdowns on the younger generation may deserve special attention. This captive young audience in the digital sphere is for terrorists an important pool for new recruits (Beach, Clay, and Saavedra 2020). The increase in general online presence also accelerated the spread of misinformation (Davies 2021).

The long-term consequences of a pandemic on the growth of a population are felt in areas that suffer the highest number of fatalities. Heavily affected towns in Germany during the Spanish flu had on average spent less per capita on their inhabitants in the decade following the outbreak. This generated notable problems within society, including an elevated level of violence, intolerance, and racism, meaning German urban centers were more likely to vote for extremist parties in the federal elections (Frankopan 2020).

One of the major differences between the Spanish flu and COVID-19 is the age groups affected. While the 1918 influenza targeted the youth, COVID-19 was extremely fatal to seniors (Derish 2020). Major losses in the older generation have inherently affected future societies (Blickle 2020). The effect of a pandemic on birth rate also has an impact on future societies. In 1921, in the aftermath of the Spanish flu, an increase in stillbirths and infant mortality was reported in Brazil. Girls were more likely to survive in the womb than boys, which scientists have argued was largely "because female fetuses are less vulnerable than male fetuses to diseases in general" (Frankopan 2020).

A pandemic may delay making decisions to have children because of the economic and public health instability. According to Beach et al., it has been implied by some studies that in the post-COVID era there has been a decline in births and an increase in miscarriages (Beach, Clay, and Saavedra 2020).

Economic Factors

Pandemics pose a severe threat to the security and stability of an economy (Sarkodie and Owusu 2020), creating a gloomy economic forecast (Kanupriya 2020). The COVID-19 pandemic contributed heavily to declining economic growth, unemployment, and stagnation in the affected countries (Eisawy 2020). The OECD projected that global GDP would drop between 6 and 7.6 percent and unemployment would increase by 3.8 to 4.6 percent in 2020 (OECD 2020). The International Monetary Fund's April 2021 World Economic Outlook predicted:

> a stronger recovery for the global economy in 2021 and 2022 compared to the forecast in the previous October, with growth projected to be 6 percent in 2021 and 4.4 percent in 2022. Nonetheless, the outlook presents daunting challenges related to divergences in the speed of recovery both across and within countries and the potential for persistent economic damage from the crisis. Cumulative per capita income losses over 2020–22, compared to pre-pandemic projections, are equivalent to 20 percent of 2019 per capita GDP in emerging markets and developing economies (excluding China), while in advanced economies the losses are expected to be relatively smaller, at 11 percent. (International Monetary Fund 2021)

Compared to the economic consequences of the Spanish flu on the labor market, COVID-19 will likely not generate a negative labor supply shock of the same volume (Beach, Clay, and Saavedra 2020). This is because of the age of the most affected population. While the 1918 influenza outbreak was lethal to the working age, COVID-19 has been fatal to the oldest. It is also noteworthy that approximately 2 percent of the population died in the 1918 influenza pandemic. This suggests that "the pandemic resulted in a 6 percent decline in real GDP per capita and an 8 percent decline in real consumption per capita on average. These values are remarkably close to the OECD projections for the real GDP decline in 2020" (Barro, Ursua, and Weng 2020). Production decline due to labor shortage was recorded both during the Spanish flu and COVID-19 (Bodenhorn 2020). At the same time, the negative labor supply shock resulted in increased wages (Jedwab, Johnson, and Koyama 2020).

Outbreaks of infectious diseases also have severe economic consequences, diminishing living standards, affecting productivity, reducing fiscal resources and government revenue, affecting trade, and exacerbating real or perceived income inequalities (Price-Smith 2002). Extremists have been capitalizing on novel vulnerabilities including economic hardship and global uncertainty. Their ideologies strive to advance divisiveness and hatred by inciting acts of violence (Burchill 2020).

We now provide an overview of theoretical discussions involved in the economic considerations of a pandemic. First, economic grievances due to the novel circumstances are taken into account (Gassebner 2011). The debate on the role of economic conditions when investigating the root causes of terrorism has remained unresolved (Burgoon 2006). It has been a highly contested issue whether poverty and adverse economic conditions play an important role in explaining terrorism. Scholarly standpoints arguing that poor economic circumstances increase the probability of civil conflict[1] have been challenged by empirical studies (Krueger and Laitin 2004; Piazza 2006). In a similar vein, Abadie could not identify a significant association between terrorism and economic variables (Abadie 2006). Furthermore, Feldmann and Perälä (2004) found no association between "economic performance or structural economic conditions and the incidence of nongovernmental terrorism." Other studies still could not confidently support the hypothesis that terrorism is rooted in economic grievances (Berman and Laitin 2008; Blomberg and Hess 2008; Blomberg and Rosendorff 2009; Krueger and Maleckova 2003; Tavares 2004).

Krueger and Laitin (2008) concluded that poverty is not an economic condition for terrorism. And Piazza (2006) has contested the so-called rooted-in-poverty thesis. His analysis revealed that neither the GDP growth, inflation, stable prices or unemployment "are significant predictors of either terrorist incidents or casualties," but he asserted that "low levels of economic and social development increase the appeal of political extremism and encourage political violence and instability" (ibid.). This is similar to Enders and Hoover's position (2012). They argued that there is a "non-linear relationship between income and terrorism" but asserted that middle income is more conducive to terrorism. Blomberg et al., however, argue that economic contractions do lead to an increased likelihood of terrorist activities (Blomberg, Hess, and Weerapana 2004). And Goldstein's study (2005) revealed that the overall terrorist risk is affected by unemployment rate.

When relating poverty and inequality with political violence, relative deprivation is considered "a link between economic disparity and the propensity of individuals to resort to violent action." Gurr (1970), Chen (2003), Paxson (2002), and Li and Schaub (2004) argued that economic conditions influence deprivation and the feeling of injustice and therefore can ultimately induce political tension. Pandemics can disproportionately affect certain groups in society (Gross et al. 2020). During the COVID-19 lockdowns, inequality emerged where some occupations could be done remotely while other businesses had to shut down (Montenovo et al. 2020). Remote working, thanks to accelerated digital modernization, went some way in reducing the economic impact of the COVID-19 pandemic, with the technology for this obviously lacking during the 1918 influenza (Nicola et al. 2020). Ultimately, social redistributive measures and policies at the national level (Burgoon 2006) and foreign aid (Azam and Delacroix 2006) are important instruments to alleviate citizen grievances and thereby reduce the occurrence of terrorism.

Psychological Factors

In the scholarly literature, modifiable social and psychological factors have been identified that contribute to the genesis of the terrorist mind-set. Victoroff (2005) argued that terrorist behavior is probably always determined by a combination of innate, biological, early developmental, and cognitive factors, temperament, environmental influences, and group dynamics. Certain novel social, economic, and psychological circumstances emerging with a pandemic seem to influence vulnerable individuals. In an apocalyptic experience, it may cause paranoia if all certainties in our lives are shaken (Guilhot 2020). Labeling some ethnic minorities and blaming them for spreading a virus can induce social tensions and conflict, leading to hatred and racism. Not only individuals but their families and the whole community may be affected by the accompanying psychological distress (Madhav et al. 2017).

Lockdowns, home offices and digital schooling quickly changed the regular ways of interacting during the COVID-19 pandemic. Social distancing established an irregular, more isolated lifestyle among average citizens (Russell Sage 2020), which has been strongly associated with anxiety, depression, and suicidal ideation (Doyle et al. 2020). With the feeling that the state is incapable of proving adequate protection in a public health emergency incident, public mistrust can seriously get around. This psychological stress among the population can incite an elevated level of antigovernment activities (Price-Smith 2002).

Conclusion

As the analysis has revealed, infectious disease outbreaks have serious political, social, economic, and psychological impacts. First, crisis management requires extraordinary resources and renders the possibility of political, social, and economic instability, which may be further exacerbated by manipulated disinformation campaigns. Violent nonstate actors may capitalize on the low level of stability in such challenging times. Second, political tension may arise from discrimination experienced as a scapegoat or victim of conspiracy theories during a pandemic. Frustration from these grievances makes isolated members of a society more likely to engage in political influence and violence. Third, a pandemic can have a serious effect on the global economy. Decline during COVID-19 was recorded globally both in real GDP and real consumption. Perceived economic hardship and uncertainty provide fertile ground for political extremist narratives. Fourth, the psychological impact of a pandemic, with social isolation to blame for increases in psychological stress, may lead to anxiety and depression, making people more vulnerable to hateful influences.

This chapter attempted to first introduce the security threat landscape at the time of the COVID-19 outbreak. Second, academic discourses on COVID-19's immediate impact on terrorism have been detailed. In line with this, we have explored emerging terrorist opportunities and challenges. In the final section, potential political, social, economic, and psychological causes of terrorism were examined in the context of COVID-19, and public health crises in general, to evaluate whether such emergencies create novel vulnerabilities terrorists can exploit.

Note

1. For instance, Joseph Kahn and Tim Weiner, "World Leaders Rethinking Strategy on Aid to Poor," *The New York Times*, 18 March 2002; Alberto Alesina, Sule Ozler, Nouriel Roubini and Phillip Swagel, "Political Instability and Economic Growth," *Journal of Economic Growth*, 1996, 1(2): 189–211; Paul Collier and Anke Hoeffler, "Greed and Grievance in Civil War," *Oxford Economic Papers*, 2004, 56(4): 563–95; Edward Miguel, Shanker Satyanath and Ernst Sergenti, "Economic Shocks and Civil Conflict: An Instrumental Variables Approach," *Journal of Political Economy*, 2004, 112(4): 725–53; and Todd Sandler, "The Analytical Study of Terrorism: Taking Stock," *Journal of Peace Research*, 2014, 51(2): 257–71.

References

Abadie, Alberto. 2006. "Poverty, Political Freedom, and the Roots of Terrorism." *American Economic Review* 96(2): 50–56.

Ackerman, Gary, and Hayley Peterson. 2020. "COVID-19 and Terrorism." *Perspectives on Terrorism* 14(3).

"Adjustment and Resilience Preventing Violent Extremism in Indonesia during COVID-19 and Beyond." 2021. UNODC website. Retrieved September 2022 from https://www.unodc.org/documents/southeastasiaandpacific/Publications/2021/indonesia/Main_COVID_CT_Indonesia_PRINT_EN.pdf.

"Afghanistan Country Report. 2020." 2020. BTI Transformation Index website. Retrieved May 2022 from https://www.bti-project.org/en/reports/country-report-AFG.html.

Albala-Bertrand, J. M. 1993. *The Political Economy of Large Natural Disasters: With Special Reference to Developing Countries*. New York: Oxford University Press.

Alesina, Alberto, Sule Ozler, Nouriel Roubini, and Phillip Swagel. 1996. "Political Instability and Economic Growth." *Journal of Economic Growth* 1(2): 189–211.

Avis, William. 2020. "The COVID-19 Pandemic and Response on Violent Extremist Recruitment and Radicalisation." K4D Helpdesk Report. Retrieved May 2022 from https://gsdrc.org/publications/the-covid-19-pandemic-and-response-on-violent-extremist-recruitment-and-radicalisation/.

Azam, Jean Paul, and Alexandra Delacroix. 2006. "Aid and the Delegated Fight against Terrorism." *Review of Development Economics* 10(2): 330–34.

Azam, Jean Paul, and Véronique Thelen. 2008. "The Roles of Foreign Aid and Education in the War on Terror." *Public Choice* 135(3–4): 375–97.

Azman, Nur Aziemah. 2020. "Divine Retribution: The Islamic State's COVID-19 Propaganda." *The Diplomat*, 3 March.

Bandyopadhyay, Subhayu, Todd Sandler, and Javed Younas. 2011. "Foreign Aid as Counterterrorism Policy." *Oxford Economic Papers* 63(3): 423–47.

Barro, Robert J., José F. Ursua, and Joanna Weng. 2020. "The Coronavirus and the Great Influenza Pandemic: Lessons from the "Spanish Flu" for the Coronavirus's Potential Effects on Mortality and Economic Activity." National Bureau of Economic Research.

Basit, Abdul. 2020. "The COVID-19 Pandemic: An Opportunity for Terrorist Groups?" *Counter Terrorist Trends and Analyses* 12(3): 7–12.

Basuchoudhary, Atin, and William Shughart. 2010. "On Ethnic Conflict and the Origins of Transnational Terrorism." *Defence and Peace Economics* 21(1): 65–87.

Beach, Brian, Karen Clay, and Martin H. Saavedra. 2020. "The 1918 Influenza Pandemic and its Lessons for COVID-19." NBER Working Paper Series. Retrieved May 2022 from https://www.nber.org/system/files/working_papers/w27673/w27673.pdf.

Bellinger, Nisha, and Kyle T. Kattelman. 2020. "How the Coronavirus Increases Terrorism Threats in the Developing World." *The Conversation*, 26 May.

Berman, Eli, and David D. Laitin. 2008. "Religion, Terrorism and Public Goods: Testing the Club Model." *Journal of Public Economics* 92(10–11): 1942–67.

Berreni, Claude, and Jordan Ostwald. 2011. "Earthquakes, Hurricanes and Terrorism, Do Natural Disasters Incite Terrorism?" *RAND Report*. Retrieved May 2022 from https://www.rand.org/pubs/working_papers/WR876.html.

Bjørgo, Tore. 2005. *Root Causes of Terrorism: Myths, Reality and Ways Forward*. Routledge.

Blickle, Kristian. 2020. "Pandemics Change Cities: Municipal Spending and Voter Extremism in Germany, 1918–1933." FRB of New York Staff Report No. 921. Retrieved May 2022 from https://www.newyorkfed.org/medialibrary/media/research/staff_reports/sr921.pdf.

Blomberg, S. B., and G. D. Hess. 2008. "The Lexus and the Olive Branch: Globalization, Democratization and Terrorism." In *Terrorism, Economic Development, and Political Openness*, ed. Philip Keefer and Norman Loayza, 116–47. Cambridge: Cambridge University Press.

Blomberg, S. B., and Peter B. Rosendorff. 2009. "A Gravity Model of Globalization, Democracy and Transnational Terrorism." In *Guns and Butter*, ed. Gregory D. Hess, 25–156. Cambridge: MIT Press.

Blomberg, S., Gregory. D. Hess, and Akila Weerapana. 2004. "Economic Conditions and Terrorism." *European Journal of Political Economy* 20(2): 463–78.

Bodenhorn, Howard. 2020. "Business in a Time of Spanish Influenza." National Bureau of Economic Research.

Bolin, Bob. 2007. "Race, Class, Ethnicity, and Disaster Vulnerability." In *Handbook of Disaster Research*, ed. Havidan Rodríguez, Enrico L. Quarantelli and Russell Dynes, 113–29. New York: Springer.

Borelli, Marguerite. 2017. "ASEAN Counter-terrorism Weaknesses." *Counter Terrorist Trends and Analyses* 9(9): 16.

Brennan, David. 2020. "How Neo-Nazis Are Exploiting Coronavirus to Push Their Radical Agenda." *Newsweek*, 31 March.

Burchill, Richard. 2020. "Extremism in the Time of COVID-19: Excerpt from a Bussola Institute Study." *Small Wars Journal*, 10 June.

Burgoon, Brian. 2006. "On Welfare and Terror: Social Welfare Policies and Political-Economic Roots of Terrorism." *Journal of Conflict Resolution* 50(2): 176–203.

Carroll, Jacinta. 2020. "The Christchurch Terrorist Attack – One Year On." *The Strategist*, 18 March.

Carter, Elisabeth. 2018. "Right-Wing Extremism/Radicalism: Reconstructing the Concept." *Journal of Political Ideologies* 23(2): 157–82.

Chen, Daniel. 2003. "Economic Distress and Religious Intensity: Evidence from Islamic Resurgence during the Indonesian Financial Crisis." *PRPES Working Paper* No. 39.

Cohen, Charles, and Eric Werker. 2008. "The Political Economy of Natural Disasters." *Journal of Conflict Resolution* 52(6): 795–819.

Coleman, Julie. 2020. "The Impact of Coronavirus on Terrorism in the Sahel." ICCT Publications, 16 April. Retrieved May 2022 from https://icct.nl/publication/the-impact-of-coronavirus-on-terrorism-in-the-sahel/.

Collier, Paul, and Anke Hoeffler. 2004. "Greed and Grievance in Civil War." *Oxford Economic Papers* 56(4): 563–95.

Cordesman, Anthony H. 2020a. "The Greater Middle East: From the 'Arab Spring' to the 'Axis of Failed States'." Center for Strategic and International Studies. Retrieved May 2022 from https://www.csis.org/analysis/greater-middle-east-arab-spring-axis-failed-states.

———. 2020b. "The Real World Capabilities of ISIS: The Threat Continues." Center for Strategic and International Studies website. Retrieved May 2022 from https://www.csis.org/analysis/real-world-capabilities-isis-threat-continues.

Cotter, Cédric. 2020. "From the 'Spanish Flu' to COVID-19: Lessons from the 1918 Pandemic and First World War." *Humanitarian Law and Policy*, 23 April.

Coughlan, Matt. 2020a. "Right-Wing Extremism on the Rise: Police." *Young Witness*, 20 October.

———. 2020b. "Tech and Terrorism: Extremist Groups Leverage Coronavirus Pandemic Online." Counter Extremism Project website. Retrieved May 2022 from https://www.counterextremism.com/press/tech-terrorism-extremist-groups-leverage-coronavirus-pandemic-online.

———. 2020c. "New Zealand: Extremism and Counter-Extremism." Counter Extremism Project website. Retrieved May 2022 from https://www.counterextremism.com/countries/new-zealand.

"COVID-19 and Conflict: Seven Trends to Watch." 2020. International Crisis Group website. Retrieved May 2022 from https://www.crisisgroup.org/global/sb4-covid-19-and-conflict-seven-trends-watch.

Crenshaw, Martha. 2011. *Explaining Terrorism, Causes, Processes and Consequences*. Routledge.

Cruickshank, Paul, and Don Rassler. 2020. "A View from the CT Foxhole: A Virtual Roundtable on COVID-19 and Counterterrorism with Audrey Kurth Cronin,

Lieutenant General (Ret) Michael Nagata, Magnus Ranstorp, Ali Soufan, and Juan Zarate." *CTC Sentinel* 13(6).

Daalder, Marc. 2020. "Action Zealandia Member Arrested for Threat." *Newsroom*, 5 March.

Daines, Nick. 2020. "The Evolving VRWE Challenge in Spotlight – Violent Right-Wing Extremism in Focus." *Spotlight*, May.

Davies, Garth. 2021. "Radicalisation and Violent Extremism in the Era of COVID-19." *Journal of Intelligence, Conflict and Warfare*, 31 May.

Davies, Garth, Edith Wu, and Richard Frank. 2021. "A Witch's Brew of Grievances: The Potential Effects of COVID-19 on Radicalisation to Violent Extremism." *Studies in Conflict and Terrorism*.

Daymon, Chelsea, and Meili Criezis. 2020. "Pandemic Narratives: Pro-Islamic State Media and the Coronavirus." *CTC Sentinel* 13(6).

Derish, Igor. 2020. "The 1918 Pandemic Was Linked to a Rise in Nazi Support: Will This Pandemic Be Similar?" *Salon*. Retrieved May 2022 from https://www.salon.com/2020/05/10/the-1918-pandemic-was-linked-to-a-rise-in-nazi-support-will-this-pandemic-be-similar/.

Dezler, Matt. 2020. "I Am Not a Virus – Anti-Chinese Racism and Coronavirus." TUC website. Retrieved May 2022 from https://www.tuc.org.uk/blogs/i-am-not-virus-anti-chinese-racism-and-coronavirus.

Doornbos, Harald, and Jenan Moussa. 2014. "Found: The Islamic State's Terror Laptop of Doom." *Foreign Policy*, 28 August.

Doyle, Alexis A., Mollie S. H. Friedlander, Grace D. Li, William Marble, Courtney J. Smith, Nitisha Baronia, Christopher R. Calkins, Trillium Chang, Mallory Harris, Seth Kolker, Abd Al-Rahman Traboulsi, Amanda D. Zerbe, and Malathi Srinivasan. 2020. "The Evidence and Tradeoffs for a 'Stay-at-Home' Pandemic Response: A Multidisciplinary Review Examining the Medical, Psychological, Economic and Political Impact of 'Stay-at-Home' Implementation in America." Working Paper. Retrieved May 2022 from https://papers.ssrn.com/sol3/papers.cfm?abstract_id=3578841.

"Ebola a Blow for Fragile States on the Road to Recovery." 2014. Studies IfS. Retrieved May 2022 from https://issafrica.org/iss-today/ebola-a-blow-for-fragile-states-on-the-road-to-recovery.

Eisawy, Ashraf Al. 2020. "Repurposing Covid-19: Pandemic as an Opportunity for Extremist Groups." Trendsresearch website. Retrieved May 2022 from https://trendsresearch.org/insight/repurposing-covid-19-dimensions-and-repercussions-of-extremist-groups-using-the-pandemic/.

Enders, Walter, and Gary A. Hoover. 2012. "The Nonlinear Relationship between Terrorism and Poverty." *American Economic Review* 102(3): 267–72.

"European Union Terrorism and Situation Trend Report." 2020. Europol website. Retrieved May 2022 from https://www.europol.europa.eu/activities-services/main-reports/european-union-terrorism-situation-and-trend-report-te-sat-2020.

"Extreme Right Wing Symbols, Numbers and Acronyms." 2018. Greater Manchester Police Counter Terrorism Branch Prevent Team website. Retrieved May 2022 from https://www.wrothamschool.com/wp-content/uploads/2021/06/Preventing-Right-wing-extremism.pdf.

Feldmann, A. E., and M. Perälä. 2004. "Reassessing the Causes of Nongovernmental Terrorism in Latin America." *Latin American Politics and Society* 46(2): 101–32.
Frankopan, Peter. 2020. "Past Pandemics Exacerbated Disadvantages – What We Can Learn from Them about the Coronavirus Recovery." PreventionWeb website. Retrieved May 2022 from https://www.preventionweb.net/news/view/72495.
Gassebner, Martin. 2011. "Lock, Stock and Barrel: A Comprehensive Assessment of the Determinants of Terror." *Public Choice*, August.
Gjørv, Gunhild Hoogensen. 2020. "Coronavirus, Invisible Threats and Preparing for Resilience." *NATO Review*, 20 May.
"Global Report for Research on Infectious Diseases of Poverty." 2012. Geneva: World Health Organization. Retrieved May 2022 from https://apps.who.int/iris/handle/10665/44850.
Goldstein, Kevin. 2005. "Unemployment, Inequality and Terrorism: Another Look at the Relationship between Economics and Terrorism." *Undergraduate Economic Review* 1(1).
Green, Adam. 2020. "Exclusive: Criminality, Terrorism and COVID-19." *International Security Journal*, 9 June.
Gross, Cary P. R., Essien Utibe, Pasha Saamir, Jacob R. Gross, Shi-yi Wang, and Marcella Nunez-Smith. 2020. "Racial and Ethnic Disparities in Population Level Covid-19 Mortality." *MedRxiv*.
Guilhot, Nicolas. 2020. "Why Pandemics Are the Perfect Environment for Conspiracy Theories to Flourish." *The Conversation*, 6 April.
Gurr, Ted Robert. 1970. *Why Men Rebel*. Princeton, NJ: Princeton University Press.
Gurski, Phil. 2020. "Where Is the COVID-19 Terrorism Spike?" Borealis. Retrieved May 2022 from https://borealisthreatandrisk.com/where-is-the-covid-19-terrorism-spike/.
Hall, C. M. 1994. *Tourism and Politics: Policy, Power and Place*. New York: Wiley.
Hanna, Andrew. 2020. "What Islamists Are Doing and Saying on COVID-19 Crisis." Wilson Center website. Retrieved May 2022 from https://www.wilsoncenter.org/article/what-islamists-are-doing-and-saying-COVID-19-crisis.
Hasan, S. S. 2010. "Pakistan Suicide Bomb on Police, Children among Dead." *BBC*, 6 September.
Hernandez-Morales, Aitor. 2020. "ISIS Tells Terrorists to Steer Clear of Coronavirus-Stricken Europe." *Politico*, 15 March.
"Homeland Threat Assessment October 2020." 2020. US Department of Homeland Security website. Retrieved May 2022 from https://www.dhs.gov/sites/default/files/publications/2020_10_06_homeland-threat-assessment.pdf.
"Iraq Country Report 2020." 2020. BTI Transformation Index website. Retrieved May 2022 https://bti-project.org/en/reports/country-report/IRQ.
Jackson, Norman A. 2018. "The 1918 Flu Pandemic and Its Aftermath." *Evolution: Education and Outreach*, 5.
Jedwab, Remi, Noel D. Johnson, and Mark Koyama. 2020. "The Economic Impact of the Black Death." Unpublished Manuscript.
"Jihadist Terrorism in the EU Since 2015." 2020. MD Staff website. Retrieved May 2022 from https://moderndiplomacy.eu/2020/11/06/jihadist-terrorism-in-the-eu-since-2015/.

Jones, Seth G. 2019. "The New Zealand Attack and the Global Challenge of Far Right Extremism." Center for Strategic and International Studies website. Retrieved May 2022 from https://www.csis.org/analysis/new-zealand-attack-and-global-challenge-far-right-extremism.

Jones, Seth G., Catrina Doxsee, Nicholas Harrington, Grace Hwang, and James Suber. 2020. "The War Comes Home the Evolution of Domestic Terrorism in the United States." Center for Strategic and International Studies website. Retrieved May 2022 from https://csis-website-prod.s3.amazonaws.com/s3fs-public/publication/201021_Jones_War_Comes_Home_v2.pdf.

Jones, Sidney. 2020. "COVID-19 and Extremism in Southeast Asia." *The Asia Pacific Journal* 18(15).

Joscelyn, Thomas. 2020. "How Jihadists Are Reacting to the Coronavirus Pandemic." Foundation for Defence of Democracies website. Retrieved May 2022 from https://www.fdd.org/analysis/2020/04/06/how-jihadists-are-reacting-to-the-coronavirus-pandemic/.

Kahn, Joseph, and Tim Weiner. 2002. "World Leaders Rethinking Strategy on Aid to Poor." *The New York Times*, 18 March.

Kanupriya. 2020. "COVID-19: A Socio-economic Perspective." *FIIB Business Review*, 12 May.

Koblentz, Gregory D., and Stevie Kiesel. 2021. "The COVID-19 Pandemic: Catalyst or Compilation for Bioterrorism?" *Studies in Conflict and Terrorism*, 14 July.

Koehler, Daniel. 2016. "Right-Wing Extremism and Terrorism in Europe Current Developments and Issues for the Future." *PRISM Journal* 6.

Krueger, Alan B., and David D. Laitin. 2004. "Faulty Terror Report Card." *The Washington Post*, 17 May.

———. 2008. "Kto Kogo? A Cross-Country Study of the Origins and Targets of Terrorism." In *Terrorism, Economic Development, and Political Openness*, ed. Philip Keefer and Norman Loayza, 148–73. Cambridge: Cambridge University Press.

Krueger, Alan B., and Jitka Maleckova. 2003. "Education, Poverty and Terrorism: Is There a Causal Connection?" *Journal of Economic Perspectives* 17(4): 119–44.

Lea, J. P. 1996. "Tourism, Realpolitik and Development in the South Pacific." In *Tourism, Crime and International Security Issues*, ed. A. Pizam and Y. Mansfeld, 123–42. Chichester: Wiley.

"Lessons from the 1918–1919 Spanish Flu Pandemic in Africa." 2020. Africa Center for Strategic Studies website. Retrieved May 2022 from https://africacenter.org/spotlight/lessons-1918-1919-spanish-flu-africa/.

"Letter Dated 16 July 2020 from the Chair of the Security Council Committee Pursuant to Resolutions 1267 (1999), 1989 (2011) and 2253 (2015) Concerning Islamic State in Iraq and the Levant, Al-Qaida and Associated Individuals, Groups, Undertakings and Entities Addresses to the President of the Security Council." 2020. United Nations Security Council website. Retrieved May 2022 from https://digitallibrary.un.org/record/3848705.

Li, Quan, and Drew Schaub. 2004. "Economic Globalization and Transnational Terrorist Incidents: A Pooled Time-Series Cross-Sectional Analysis." *Journal of Conflict Resolution* 48(2): 230–58.

Lia, Brynjar, and Katja Skjølberg. 2004. "Causes of Terrorism: An Expanded and Updated Review of the Literature?" Norwegian Defence Research Establishment. Retrieved May 2022 from https://www.researchgate.net/publication/

281274883_CAUSES_OF_TERRORISM_An_Expanded_and_Updated_Review_of_the_Literature.

"Libya Country Report 2020." 2020. BTI Transformation Index website. Retrieved May 2022 https://bti-project.org/en/reports/country-dashboard/LBY.

Macklin, Graham. 2020. "Coronavirus and the Far Right: Seizing the Moment?" *ISPI*, 15 May.

Madhav, Nita, Ben Oppenheim, Mark Gallivan, Prime Mulembakani, Edward Rubin, and Nathan Wolfe. 2017. "Pandemics: Risks, Impacts, and Mitigation." Retrieved May 2022 from https://www.ncbi.nlm.nih.gov/books/NBK525302/.

Magid, Pesha. 2020. "Islamic State Aims for Comeback Amid Virus-Expedited US Withdrawal." *Foreign Policy*, 6 April.

Marone, Francesco. 2021. "Hate in the Time of Coronavirus: Exploring the Impact of the COVID-19 Pandemic on Violent Extremism and Terrorism in the West." *Security Journal*, 7 January.

McCleery, Adam. 2019. "Secretive Right-Wing Group Dominion Movement which Described Immigrants as 'Unworthy Imports' Goes Underground Following Christchurch Terror Attack." *Daily Mail*, 26 March.

"Member States Concerned by the Growing and Increasingly Transnational Threat of Extreme Right-Wing Terrorism." 2020. UN CTED website. Retrieved May 2022 from https://www.un.org/sites/www.un.org.securitycouncil.ctc/files/files/documents/2021/Jan/cted_trends_alert_extreme_right-wing_terrorism.pdf.

Mendelsohn, Barak. 2017. "Power, Legitimacy, and the Self-Limiting Logic of Terrorism." *Georgetown Journal of International Affairs*, 1 March.

Menzel, Celina. 2020. "The Impact of Outbreaks of Infectious Diseases on Political Stability: Examining the Examples of Ebola, Tuberculosis and Influenza." Konrad Adenauer Stiftung website. Retrieved May 2022 from https://www.kas.de/documents/252038/253252/7_dokument_dok_pdf_52294_1.pdf/95dc732e-2eda-2698-b01f-7ac77d060499?version = 1.0&t = 1539647543906.

Miguel, Edward, Shanker Satyanath, and Ernst Sergenti. 2004. "Economic Shocks and Civil Conflict: An Instrumental Variables Approach." *Journal of Political Economy* 112(4): 725–53.

Mir, Asfandyar. 2020. "Afghanistan's Terrorism Challenge the Political Trajectories of al-Qaeda, the Afghan Taliban, and the Islamic State." Middle East Institute website. Retrieved May 2022 from https://www.mei.edu/publications/afghanistans-terrorism-challenge-political-trajectories-al-qaeda-afghan-taliban-and.

Montenovo, Laura, Xuan Jiang, Felipe Lozano Rojas, Ian M. Schmutte, Kosali I. Simon, Bruce A. Weinberg, and Coady Wing. 2020. "Determinants of Disparities in Covid-19 Job Losses." National Bureau of Economic Research website. Retrieved May 2022 from https://www.nber.org/papers/w27132.

Mudde, Cas. 2007. *Populist Radical Right Parties in Europe*. Cambridge: Cambridge University Press.

Mullins, Sam. 2020. "Terrorism and COVID-19: Are We Over-Estimating the Threat?" *Small Wars Journal*, 25 June.

"Munich Security Report 2016: Boundless Crises, Reckless Spoilers, Helpless Guardians." 2016. Retrieved May 2022 from https://espas.secure.europarl.europa.eu/orbis/document/munich-security-report-2016-boundless-crises-reckless-spoilers-helpless-guardians.

Newman, Edward. 2006. "Exploring the 'Root Causes' of Terrorism." *Studies in Conflict and Terrorism* 29(8): 749–72.

Nicola, M., Z. Alsafi, C. A. Sohrabi, Al-Jabir A. Kerwan, C. Iosifidis, M. Agha, and R. Agha. 2020. "The Socio-economic Implications of the Coronavirus Pandemic (COVID-19): A Review." *International Journal of Surgery* 78: 185–93.

"OECD Economic Outlook Volume 2020 Issue 1." 2020. OECD website. Retrieved May 2022 from https://read.oecd-ilibrary.org/economics/oecd-economic-outlook/volume-2020/issue-1_0d1d1e2e-en.

Ola, Temitope. 2018. "Re-Thinking Poverty, Inequality and Their Relationship to Terrorism." *Journal of Sciences: Basic and Applied Research* 21(2): 264–92.

Ong, Kyler. 2020. "Ideological Convergence in the Extreme Right." *Counter Terrorist Trends and Analyses* 12(4): 1–7.

Ong, Kyler, and Raffaello Pantucci. 2020. "From Fringe to Mainstream: The Extreme Rightwing in Europe." *Atlantic Files*, 1 July.

Pantucci, Raffaello. 2020. "After the Coronavirus, Terrorism Won't Be the Same." *Foreign Policy*, 23 April.

Patrick, Stewart. 2011. *Weak Links: Fragile States, Global Threats and International Security*. Oxford: Oxford University Press.

Paxson, Christina. 2002. "Comment on Alan Krueger and Jitka Maleckova, 'Education, Poverty, and Terrorism: Is There a Causal Connection?'" *Mimeo*, Princeton University.

Piazza, James A. 2006. "Rooted in Poverty? Terrorism, Poor Economic Development and Social Cleavages." *Terrorism and Political Violence* 18(1): 159–77.

———. 2007. "Draining the Swamp: Democracy Promotion, State Failure, and Terrorism in 19 Middle Eastern Countries." *Studies in Conflict and Terrorism* 30(6): 521–39.

Price-Smith, Andrew. 2002. *The Health of Nations: Infectious Disease, Environmental Change, and Their Effects on National Security and Development*. Cambridge, MA: Massachusetts Institute of Technology.

"Quarterly Report to Congress on Operation Inherent Resolve." 2020. Excerpted from Lead Inspector General. 12 April–30 June 2020. Retrieved May 2022 from https://www.stateoig.gov/system/files/lead_inspector_general_for_operation_inherent_resolve_april_1_2020_-_june_30_2020.pdf, p. 21.

Raj, Andrin. 2020. "Assessing the Terrorist Threat during the COVID-19 Pandemic." Religion and Security website. Retrieved May 2022 from https://religionandsecurity.org/2020/05/09/assessing-terrorism-during-the-COVID-19-pandemic/.

Ravik Jupskås, Anders, and Iris Beau Segers. 2020. "What Is Right-Wing Extremism?" Center for Research on Extremism, University of Oslo website. Retrieved May 2022 from https://www.sv.uio.no/c-rex/english/groups/compendium/what-is-right-wing-extremism.html.

Ravndal, Jacob Aasland. 2016. "Right-Wing Terrorism and Violence in Western Europe: Introducing the RTV Dataset." *Perspectives on Terrorism* 10(3): 2–15.

Ravndal, Jacob Aasland, Sofia Lygren, Anders Ravik Jupskås, and Tore Bjørgo. 2020. "Right-Wing Terrorism and Violence in Western Europe, 1990–2019." Center for Research on Extremism, University of Oslo website. Retrieved May 2022 from https://www.sv.uio.no/c-rex/english/groups/rtv-dataset/rtv_trend_report_2020.pdf.

Rohwerder, Brigitte. 2014. "Impact and Implications of the Ebola Crisis." Helpdesk Research Report. Retrieved May 2022 from http://www.gsdrc.org/docs/open/HDQ1177.pdf.

Russell Sage. 2020. "Social, Political, Economic, and Psychological Consequences of the COVID-19 Pandemic." Retrieved May 2022 from https://www.russellsage.org/research/funding/covid-19-pandemic.

Sandler, Todd. 2014. "The Analytical Study of Terrorism: Taking Stock." *Journal of Peace Research* 51(2): 257–71.

Sarkodie, Samuel Asumadu, and Phebe Asantewaa Owusu. 2020. "Global Assessment of Environment, Health and Economic Impact of the Novel Coronavirus (COVID-19)." *Environment, Development and Sustainability* 23: 5005–15.

Schmid, Alex P. 2005. "Root Causes of Terrorism: Some Conceptual Notes, a Set of Indicators, and a Model." *Democracy and Security* 1: 127–36.

Schumacher Michael J., and Peter J. Schraeder. 2019. "Does Domestic Political Instability Foster Terrorism? Global Evidence from the Arab Spring Era (2011–14)." *Studies in Conflict and Terrorism* 44(3): 198–222.

Shakir, A. 2010. "UN Halts Aid Distribution after Female Suicide Bomber Kills 46 in Pakistan." *Bloomberg*, 25 December.

Shughart, W. F. 2006. "An Analytical History of Terrorism, 1945–2000." *Public Choice* 128(1): 7–39.

Silke, Andrew. 2020. "COVID-19 and Terrorism: Assessing the Short and Long-Term Impacts." Pool Re and Cranfield University's Professor of Terrorism, Risk and Resilience Commentary.

Simons, Greg, and Cristina Bianca. 2020. "The Specter of Terrorism during the Coronavirus Pandemic." *E-International Relations*, 8 May.

"Spanish Flu." 2020. History.com website. Retrieved May 2022 from https://www.history.com/topics/world-war-i/1918-flu-pandemic#: ~ :text = Thepercent20Spanish percent20flu percent20pandemic percent20of,victims percent2C percent20includingpercent20somepercent20675percent2C000percent20Americans.

Spreeuwenberg, Peter, Madelon Kroneman, and John Paget. 2018. "Reassessing the Global Mortality Burden of the 1918 Influenza Pandemic." *Am J Epidemiol* 187(12): 2561–67.

Stern, Samantha, Jacob Ware, and Nicholas Harrington. 2020. "Terrorist Targeting in the Age of Coronavirus." International Institute for Counter-Terrorism. Retrieved May 2022 from https://ict.org.il/terrorist-targeting-in-the-age-of-coronavirus/.

"Syria Country Report 2020." 2020. BTI Transformation Index website. Retrieved May 2022 from https://bti-project.org/en/reports/country-report/SYR.

Taneja, Kabir, and Raffaello Pantucci. 2020. "Beware of Terrorists Offering COVID19 Aid." Observer Research Foundation website. Retrieved May 2022 from https://www.orfonline.org/expert-speak/beware-of-terrorists-offering-COVID19-aid-64731/.

Tavares, José. 2004. "The Open Society Assesses Its Enemies: Shocks, Disasters and Terrorist Attacks." *Journal of Monetary Economics* 51(5): 1039–70.

"Tenth Report of the Secretary-General on the Threat Posed by ISISL (Da'esh) to International Peace and Security and the Range of United Nations Efforts in Support of Member States in Countering the Threat." 2020. United Nations Security Council website. Retrieved May 2022 from https://digitallibrary.un.org/record/3849754?ln = ru.

"Terrorism and COVID-19: Validation and Opportunity." 2020. Modern Security Consulting Group website. Retrieved May 2022 from https://www.mosecon.com/terrorism-and-COVID-19-vindication-and-opportunity/.

"Terrorism in the EU: Geographically Widespread and Multifaceted." 2020. Europol Press Release, Europol website. Retrieved May 2022 from https://www.europol.europa.eu/newsroom/news/terrorism-in-eu-geographically-widespread-and-multifaceted.

"The Impact of the COVID-19 Pandemic on Terrorism, Counter-Terrorism and Countering Violent Extremism." 2020. United Nations Security Council Counter-Terrorism Committee Executive Directorate website. Retrieved May 2022 from https://www.un.org/securitycouncil/ctc/news/impact-covid-19-pandemic-terrorism-counter-terrorism-and-countering-violent-extremism-update.

"United Nations, Security Council 8739th Meeting." 2020. United Nations Security Council website. Retrieved May 2022 from https://www.securitycouncilreport.org/atf/cf/%7B65BFCF9B-6D27-4E9C-8CD3-CF6E4FF96FF9%7D/s_pv_8739.pdf.

US Department of State. 2019. "2019 Country Reports on Human Rights Practices: Syria." Retrieved May 2022 from https://www.state.gov/reports/2019-country-reports-on-human-rights-practices/syria/.

Victoroff, J. 2005. "The Mind of the Terrorist: A Review and Critique of Psychological Approaches." *Journal of Conflict Resolution* 49(3): 3–42.

Voronkov, Vladimir. 2020. "Countering Terrorism during the COVID-19 Pandemic." *The Jakarta Post*, 9 July.

Waraich, O. 2010. "Religious Minorities Suffering Worst in Pakistan Floods." *Time*, 3 September.

Weimann, Gabriel, and Natalie Masri. 2020. "The Virus of Hate: Far Right Terrorism in Cyber-Space." International Centre for Counter Terrorism website. Retrieved May 2022 from https://www.ict.org.il/Article/2528/The_Virus_of_Hate#gsc.tab = 0.

Whiter, James K. 2020. "The COVID-19 Pandemic: A Preliminary Assessment of the Impact on Terrorism in Western States." George C. Marshall European Center for Security Studies website. Retrieved May 2022 from https://www.marshallcenter.org/en/publications/occasional-papers/COVID-19-pandemic-preliminary-assessment.

Whyte, Sally. 2020. "'We'll Hunt You': ASIO Warns Right-Wing Extremists and Foreign Spies." *The Canberra Times*, 24 February.

Wieviorka, M. 1994. *The Making of Terrorism*. Chicago: University of Chicago Press.

Wojciechowski, Sebastian. 2017. "Reasons of Contemporary Terrorism an Analysis of Main Determinants." In *Radicalism and Terrorism in the 21st Century Implications for Security*, ed. Anna Sroka, Fanny Castro-Rial Garrone, and Rubén Darío Torres Kumbrián. Peter Lang: Frankfurt am Main.

Woodward, Calvin. 2020. "Virus-Afflicted 2020 Looks Like 1918 Despite Science's March." *AP News*, 5 May.

"World Economic Outlook." 2021. International Monetary Fund website. Retrieved May 2022 from https://www.imf.org/en/Publications/WEO/Issues/2021/03/23/world-economic-outlook-april-2021.

CHAPTER 2

How Have Radical Islamists Capitalized on the Pandemic?

Narratives Circulated on COVID-19 in the Radical Islamist Propaganda

As COVID-19 was moving from the phase of an epidemic to a pandemic, there were early signs that the global threat of terrorism was beginning to decline. With the global economy and social life coming to a standstill, most threat groups embarked on a phase of reflection and strategic rebuilding. However, Islamic State (IS) and al-Qaeda (AQ) urged their affiliates to exploit the COVID-19 situation and called for and mounted attacks—mostly in conflict zones. Although these threats were to be carried out worldwide, they were focused on specific parts of Asia, such as Indonesia, the Philippines, and the Maldives (SITE Intelligence Group 2020).

Radical Islamist propaganda encouraged followers to use the COVID-19 crisis as an opportunity for violence. A 19 March 2020 editorial in the Al-Naba newsletter drew the attention of jihadists to one of the obligations of Muslims today, namely "to inflict damage on [the enemy]" (SITE Intelligence Group 2020). This was echoed by an Indonesian-language Telegram post on 26 March, claiming "if COVID-19 could talk, maybe it would say: 'We have surrounded the Vatican, what are you waiting for, attack them' . . . COVID-19 has opened the path for us, let's join together in attacking them" (SITE Intelligence Group 2020). Parallel to this, IS Maldivians called on supporters to take advantage of the coronavirus pandemic and mount attacks. The Muslim Brotherhood urged people to use COVID-19 in attacks in Egypt. Another English-language post on an IS-aligned Telegram channel on 18 March 2020 highlighted that the panic caused by the pandemic was distracting governments, which supporters should exploit for carrying out operations: "So . . . take advantage of how they are now misdirected and forced to let loose the strong grip they had against us and to exhaust their finances and their resources upon this newly risen matter" (SITE Intelligence Group 2020). An Indonesian Islamic State-aligned

Facebook account also urged its followers to prepare for and commit acts of terrorism amidst the chaos. In the editorial of Al-Naba 226 published on 19 March 2020, the Islamic State incited lone wolf jihadists to capitalize on the paralysis and fear overtaking "Crusader" countries during the pandemic. "It would be their worst nightmare" if "fighters launched operations" while people are facing a "bleak economic future and overcrowded hospitals." They also reported "fear of this contagion has affected them more than the contagion itself" (International Crisis Group 2020). The author reminded readers that the "enemy did not show mercy on Muslims in Baghouz, Mosul or Sirte, and bombed houses of young and old, and women and children alike in multiple countries" (SITE Intelligence Group 2020).

Among the threat groups that embarked on a phase of reflection and rebuilding their capabilities during the pandemic was the Afghan Taliban. The Taliban signed an agreement with the United States, aimed at peace, and took advantage of the pandemic to proselytize Afghans by stating that COVID-19 should make them realize their weakness, mortality, and subservience to Allah. Describing the pandemic as "God's might," the Taliban called on people to turn to God (Jackson 2020).

COVID-19, a global threat of seismic proportions, piqued the interest of Islamic State and al-Qaeda. Their narratives ranged from COVID-19 being a "Soldier of God" (Meek 2020) to rhetoric about fighting unbelievers—a "Shia Iran" and the "anti-Islamic" West (ibid.). The very first coronavirus-related post by a terrorist group was by the supporters of the Islamic State monitoring the developments in Xinjiang, China (Johnson 2020).

With hundreds of Uighur fighters in Syria and Afghanistan, Islamic State and their supporters regularly expressed their views with regard to the developments in Xinjiang. On 27 January 2020, a poster designed and distributed by Quraysh Media depicted a person in a gas mask at the forefront and a city in the background. The English text read: "China Corona virus . . . a promise is a debt that we must not forget" (Azani, Barak, and Atiyas-Lvovsky 2020). Although the pro-Islamic State media did not identify the "promise", supporters exposed to Islamic State propaganda saw it as revenge for China's persecution of Uighur Muslims.

In the northwest Xinjiang province, the Chinese response to terrorism was to integrate the indigenous Uighurs with Han settlers, re-educate them (mainstream through rehabilitation), and enforce strict measures to restore local and traditional Islam by regulating the Islamic space (Millward and Peterson 2020). The narrative of Wuhan coronavirus and its outbreak in China as a punishment for the country was repeated as it evolved from an endemic to an epidemic and spread to other countries.

When the virus afflicted Iran, the Islamic State supporters said Iranian Shia are being punished for their "idolatry." When the virus spread to Europe and the US, IS supporters said Europeans and Americans are being punished for being "polytheist nations" (Hanna 2020). Stating that the virus mostly attacked unbelievers, these threat groups highlighted that China suffered because of its mistreatment of Uighurs, Iran because of the role of its Shia, and the West (Italy and the United States) because of their interventions, especially in Iraq and Syria. Islamic State supporters said COVID-19 is divine revenge for Muslim lives lost in Baghouz, the last territorial stronghold of the Islamic State in Syria, which was bombed by coalition airstrikes: "It is the prayer of the people of Baghouz whom you burnt alive. It has killed you. So reap the results of your actions" (SITE Intelligence Group 2020). They also described COVID-19 as an act of divine retribution for Western nations' support for Kurdish forces, who helped dismantle its caliphate.

The Islamist thinking that pandemics are God's dictate will continue. In the eyes of the Muslim threat groups, the virus did not infect believers. Portraying the coronavirus as divine retribution, Al-Azm Media Foundation published on 18 May 2020 the 15-minute 38-second video titled "And None Can Know the Hosts of Your Lord but He" (SITE Intelligence Group 2020). In its production, Al-Azm features clips from past IS videos that show fighters in Baghouz, Syria, bombs falling on IS-held territories, an English-speaking fighter celebrating the disasters from Hurricanes Irma and Harvey in the United States, and footage from news media concerning people who died from COVID-19, all to argue that the virus was sent by God to punish Western states and their allies and other foes for what befell Muslims. It then displays infographics on infections and deaths in the United States, Spain, Russia, Britain, Italy, France, Germany, Iran, China, Belgium, and Israel. Islamic State, al-Qaeda, and supporting groups compared the impact of COVID-19 on its enemies. Stating that America is not all-powerful and invincible, the Islamic State pointed out that in one week more Americans died of COVID-19 infection than the nearly 3,000 killed on 9/11 (Meek 2020). "It is a falsehood to worship America and to fear it instead of Allah the Almighty" (ibid.). Al-Qaeda propaganda arm As-Sahab said: "Allah, the Creator, has revealed the brittleness and vulnerability of your material strength. It is now clear for all to see that it was but a deception that could not stand the test of the smallest soldier of God on the face of the earth" (Meek 2020).

In Asia, an Indonesian-language Telegram post highlighted that "the virus has transferred the fear which was experienced by Muslims [in IS-controlled territories under Western bombardment] so that it is also felt by the infidel nations oppressing them" (SITE Intelligence Group 2020). Islamic State propaganda expressed joy on the spread of the virus and shared detailed charts of the growing number of deaths in the West. One post claimed that "Corona virus is doing the works of the mujahideen [, and] Muslims should enjoy how Allah is punishing kuffar for their support against Muslims" (SITE Intelligence Group 2020). On Friday 20 March 2020, a day before two coronavirus infections were confirmed in the Gaza strip, Imam Jamil Al-Mutawa declared in a sermon at the White Mosque in Gaza that COVID-19 is a "soldier of Allah" (Memri 2020). He referred to the empty streets of the United States, Italy, China, and Iran and contrasted it with the crowd in that mosque. He claimed that it is "the greatness of Allah" (ibid.) that "protected them and harmed" the others.

Users on a pro-IS messaging platform discussed the pandemic and its impact on those they deem the enemy. In English posts, on 12 March 2020, one jihadist wrote, "Corona virus is healing the hearts of the believers. Alhamdulillah [Praise be to Allah] Corona is divine punishment. Look who has been hit the worst, China (Arrogant atheists), Iran (Arrogant shia), and Italy (Arrogant Christians)" (SITE Intelligence Group 2020). On 9 March another user had posted photos of West Africa Province fighters as they executed Christians and stated: "This will be your streets Europe and the US. When the Corona virus weakens your infrastructure and economy. May you fall from virus or from jihad . . . Notice how Corona virus only affects the kufar, rafdah, and murtadeen" (SITE Intelligence Group 2020). Additionally, an IS supporter behind the online group called "Greenbirds" posted an image of coronavirus with the label "a soldier of Allah" and Qur'anic verse: "And none knows the soldiers of your Lord except Him" (SITE Intelligence Group 2020). The Islamic State-aligned Bunat Alamjad distributed a poster on 2 March with Chinese President Xi Jinping and North Korean Supreme Leader Kim Jong-un on it. The text referred to the coronavirus as a "nightmare for disbelieving countries" (SITE Intelligence Group 2020). The author questioned whether "those despotic and oppressive countries that deny the existence of Allah" (SITE Intelligence Group 2020) could "benefit from their scientific, medical and technological advancements when confronting with a virus, the size of which does not exceed an atom" (SITE Intelligence Group 2020). The message stated that Allah sent them the virus to "vex their lives and destroy their conditions and situations" (SITE Intelligence Group 2020).

The pro-al-Qaeda Thabaat News Agency on 19 March 2020 published Khalid al-Saba'i's paper, in which he regarded COVID-19 as a "soldier [unleashed by Allah on the] sects of disbelief" (SITE Intelligence Group 2020). The author incited Sunnis to "prepare to capitalize on the perceived devastation to hammer the final nail in the coffin of falsehood" (SITE Intelligence Group 2020) and to maintain assaults through jihad to establish Shariah-based governance. In contrast to the Islamic State narratives on COVID-19, al-Qaeda proclaimed that "The Way out of the Belly of the Whale [lies in] Commandments and Disclosures about Corona virus pandemic" (Joscelyn 2020).

There are, however, other confusing statements in the radical Islamist propaganda. Islamist terrorists themselves feared the spread of the virus. Their narratives highlighted that the pandemic was a physical threat to radical Islamists when considering the heightened level of infection risk for extremists in Indonesian prisons and Syrian refugee camps. It is also noteworthy that while previously the Islamic State was urging its followers to attack major European cities, terrorists were asked to stay clear from these areas because of the pandemic. In the case of radical Islamists already staying in Europe, they are told not to return to their homeland but aim to sicken infidels in accordance with a Shariah directive printed in an Al-Naba newsletter. Describing the virus as "Army of Allah" and "the smallest army of Allah" (SITE Intelligence Group 2020), "Balik I.," a radical convert in the Philippines, posted a Facebook message on 19 May 2020 and another one on 21 May 2020, claiming that Muslims in Mindanao are not doing anything to stop the abuses of the "kuffar" (infidels) and mocked them for not taking action (SITE Intelligence Group 2020).

Islamic State newsletter Al-Naba presented an infographic on Shariah directives on dealing with the coronavirus pandemic. In accordance with this, everything that happens is decreed by God, even infection by disease (SITE Intelligence Group 2020). The infographic counseled supporters on safety measures they should take at this time. Interestingly, all of Al-Naba's information cited Hadiths of the Prophet Muhammad[1] from the seventh century. Suggestions included covering one's mouth when sneezing, washing hands before placing them in a communal pot, and for healthy individuals not to enter areas affected by an epidemic, and those afflicted not to leave those areas. As the Islamic State declared:

> Islam is a hygiene-oriented Religion. It lays great stress on principles of prevention so as to protect one from all forms of the disease. This is implemented through a system of personal hygiene that takes the form of a regular routine that is repeated several times throughout the day. The laws on preventative measures include the necessity of using only the right hand for eating, drinking and all decent activities, and the left hand for cleaning the body. Our Prophet (pbuh) ordered the Muslims to abide by certain

> norms and etiquettes such as covering one's face with a cloth or any protective cover when sneezing or coughing. The Prophet (pbuh) taught us that he would recognize his sincere followers on the Day of Judgement by marks on their bodies that indicate repeated daily practice of cleaning and purification of one's body and soul. (SITE Intelligence Group 2020)

> The importance of hygiene and cleanliness for preventing disease and warding off viruses manifests itself in several facets of Islam. A simple illustration of this is that for fourteen centuries, Muslims have unanimously included chapters on laws regarding cleanliness and hygiene in the first section of their books on Fiqh or Islamic law. Laws of Fiqh regulate all aspects of Muslim life, from the personal to matters of economy, society, and the state, and it is instructive that the introduction to these books begins with rules on hygiene. Western societies must study how Islam, more than fourteen centuries back, came with a preventive cure to tackle the spread of viral diseases. The Prophet (peace be upon him) issued strict orders that anyone who finds himself in an area infected by a viral disease must not leave that area or travel to any other region, town, or village lest the infection spreads to new localities. The Prophet (pbuh) taught us that the one who patiently remains in his locality when a viral disease spreads, his reward equals that of a martyr because of his choice to preserve and protect human life and prosperity in other localities. (SITE Intelligence Group 2020)

As a follow-up to the infographic published by IS in Al-Naba 225 on Shariah directives for dealing with epidemics, the prominent IS-aligned Al-Battar Media Foundation created a video presentation of the information (SITE Intelligence Group 2020). The video, published on 15 March 2020, used the original Arabic infographic that came in the digital newspaper on 12 March 2020.

Most terrorist groups and their followers defied quarantine restrictions, mosque closures, and lockdown measures and incited attacks during the COVID-19 pandemic, neglecting the safety precautions required to prevent infection. A post from Balik I.'s account asserted that, unlike shopping malls, mosques are being kept closed because no one is fighting for them. Balik I. then urged followers to engage in violence, stating: "Being patient in the abuses of the kuffar? Brother and sisters, that is not the right kind of patience for you. Instead, be patient with the orders of Allah, that is, fight to protect Islam" (SITE Intelligence Group 2020).

In a related vein, the COVID-19 pandemic provided radical Islamists with opportunities to consolidate their internal support. Radical Islamists liked to mount public criticism of the government, stirring up supporters and thus contributing to the risk of potential upheaval. Some radical Islamists believed that the crisis could trigger major political instability and that it offered them the opportunity to overthrow secular rulers. An al-Qaeda-linked Indonesian website highlighted that "secular leaders, who have ruled from a strong position with the support of the infidel superpowers, are being tested. Can they control this situation amidst the pandemic outbreak without the strong support they usually receive from their foreign bosses?" (SITE Intelligence Group 2020). Regardless of the significant differences and competition between violent extremists, IS, al-Qaeda, and nonviolent Islamists all highlighted the government's failings, together constituting an increasingly loud chorus of destabilizing voices in society.

Similar to the radical Islamist statements, the Afghan Taliban used the pandemic to make Muslims and non-Muslims alike recognize their weaknesses, mortality, and subservience to God. An English article published on the Taliban website asserted that COVID-19 "as a microscopic organism . . . has instilled fear in mankind and brought the global economy and social life to a standstill. [It is] an instance of [God's] might that forced the staunchest atheist to take refuge in religion as a last resort. [This makes people realize] that humanity is not everlasting and not all-powerful, but God is. . . . Humans distant from Islam must consider this tribulation as a time of reflection and change while the Muslims, in general, must also return back to Allah . . . by seeking forgiveness for their sins and renewing their commitment to religious principles" (Kruglanski et al. 2020).

Presently, grave concerns exist with regard to the potential threat of the next wave of the virus coming from Islamic State fighters in Syrian displaced person camps (Alexander 2020). Syrian Democratic Forces (SDF) are holding around 10,000 Islamic State fighters in prisons across northeast Syria. At least 11,000 of these prisoners are IS women and children at Al-Hawl camp and other nearby displaced person camps (International Crisis Group 2020). These facilities are of great epidemiological concern because they are so densely populated and practice poor hygiene. Because of these fears, very few people are allowed to visit the camp. Information on the spread of the virus is circulated among the detainees by social media apps, texts, and phone calls. Authorities say that among the thousands of Islamic State families being held there some women are defying the orders, saying the virus is part of God's threat against infidels (Kruglanski et al. 2020).

Discussion

This chapter continues with an introductory section that aims to briefly set the radical Islamist threat landscape between 11 March and 31 July

2020. This is then contrasted with attacks that happened in the same period during 2018, for which information from the Global Terrorism Database (University of Maryland) has been used. For the 2020 discussion, incident reports from the SITE Intelligence Group and The Meir Amit Intelligence and Terrorism Information Center provided the information. The comparison is based on four perspectives: the number of attacks, their targets together with their modus operandi, and the active radical Islamist terrorist groups in the respective geographic regions. By quantitatively assessing a number of terrorist incidents, this section endeavors to provide a better understanding of novel trends and dynamics in Islamist terrorism since the virus outbreak in both conflict and nonconflict zones. To ensure a consistent analysis, the same geographic regions are examined for both periods. Accordingly, incidents occurring in nonconflict zones such as Europe, Southeast Asia, and the United States as well as attacks in conflict zones such as Syria, Iraq, Afghanistan, and Africa provide the basis for this analysis. In this case, a terrorist attack is defined as "physical violence or threat thereof employed by terrorist actors involving single-phase acts of lethal violence (such as bombings and armed assaults), dual-phased life-threatening incidents (like kidnapping, hijacking and other forms of hostage-taking for coercive bargaining) as well as multi-phased sequences of actions (such as in disappearances involving kidnapping, secret detention, torture, and murder)" (Schmid 2012). The date 11 March is when the World Health Organization declared the coronavirus a pandemic.

Conflict Zones

Syria

In the middle of March 2020, Islamic State operatives attacked Syrian Democratic Forces (SDF) and their vehicles in nine simultaneous operations (Meir Amit Intelligence 2020). Between 13 and 18 March, IEDs were activated against SDF vehicles and personnel twenty-six times. On 22 March 2020, SDF fighters were targeted by machine gun fire. Between 25 and 29 March, IS operatives abducted SDF militants in three operations (European Asylum Support Office 2020).

In April 2020, Islamic State continued its highly intensive activities against SDF positions in the region. Improvised explosive devices were planted in eight plots, and targeted killings were carried out in another eight incidents (Meir Amit Intelligence 2020). On 7 April, the secretary of the Ba'ath Party was killed by machine gun fire in the city of Nawa (ibid.). Later in the month, Syrian soldiers and two commanders of the Syrian army were shot in three attacks (Meir Amit Intelligence 2020). In the last days of the month, eight IS attacks occurred: there were ambushes, IED activations, and targeted killings against SDF forces (Al-Khateb 2020).

Between 28 April and 3 May 2020, Islamic State operatives struck Syrian soldiers and SDF personnel in nine operations (Meir Amit Intelligence 2020). On 10 May 2020, the al-Qaeda-affiliated "Awaken the Believers" attacked positions of the forces supporting the Syrian army in the northern Al-Ghab Plain. In May, a further five IS attacks targeted SDF fighters. IEDs against SDF vehicles and targeted killings characterized fifteen IS activities in the region between 20–23 May. In the last week of May, the intensity of IS activities decreased, with SDF fighters and vehicles struck nine times (Meir Amit Intelligence 2020).

On 9 June 2020, an IED was activated against a tanker carrying oil for the Syrian regime, and in four other incidents SDF vehicles and a checkpoint were targeted (Meir Amit Intelligence 2020). In the middle of June, SDF vehicles were struck in four IS operations, and Syrian soldiers in three (Knights and Almeida 2020). In the following week, nine attacks were committed against SDF vehicles, oil tankers, and Syrian soldiers. In the last days of June, SDF checkpoints, their intelligence operatives, and oil tankers were targeted in eleven IS operations (Meir Amit Intelligence 2020).

In the first week of July 2020, Syrian soldiers, SDF militants, and their vehicles were struck by IEDs and machine gun fire in ten operations. In the middle of July, SDF fighters and Syrian soldiers were attacked in four operations. In the same period, SDF fighters and their vehicles were the targets of five more IS attacks. On 17 July 2020, an "agent" of the Turkish-sponsored rebel organization was targeted by gunfire. On 18 July, IS operatives ambushed a convoy of Iranian-affiliated militias and operatives of the Lebanese Hezbollah. Between 23 and 28 July, SDF militants and their vehicles together with Syrian soldiers were struck in thirteen IS operations in Syria. Additionally, IS claimed responsibility for a suicide attack among Syrian Military Security soldiers on 21 July (Meir Amit Intelligence 2020).

How Has the Radical Islamist Threat Evolved in Syria?

The significant difference in the number of Islamic State-claimed incidents between the two periods is obvious from the graph below, with an almost tenfold increase from 2018 to 2020.

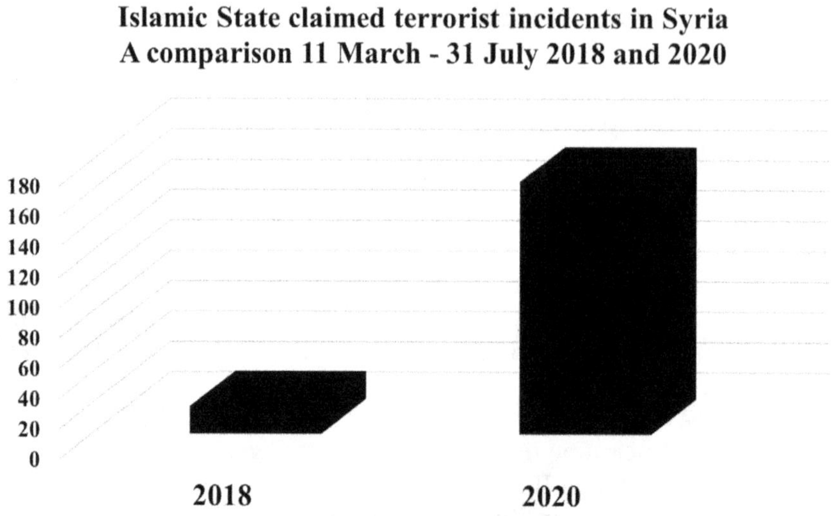

Figure 2.1. Islamic State-claimed terrorist incidents in Syria.
© Katalin Pethő-Kiss.

Military compounds and personnel remained the main IS targets, but apparently at an elevated scale. It is also significant that private citizens/property, businesses, and journalists were not attacked in 2020, although a new type of target emerged when the secretary of the Ba'ath Party was killed by machine gun fire in April 2020.

There is also a substantial change in Islamic State's modus operandi. In 2018, bombings were their most frequent means of attack, but in 2020 armed assault was at an extremely heightened scale and featured more frequently in their attacks. As Figure 2.2. shows, hostage-taking occurred roughly the same number of times in both 2018 and 2020.

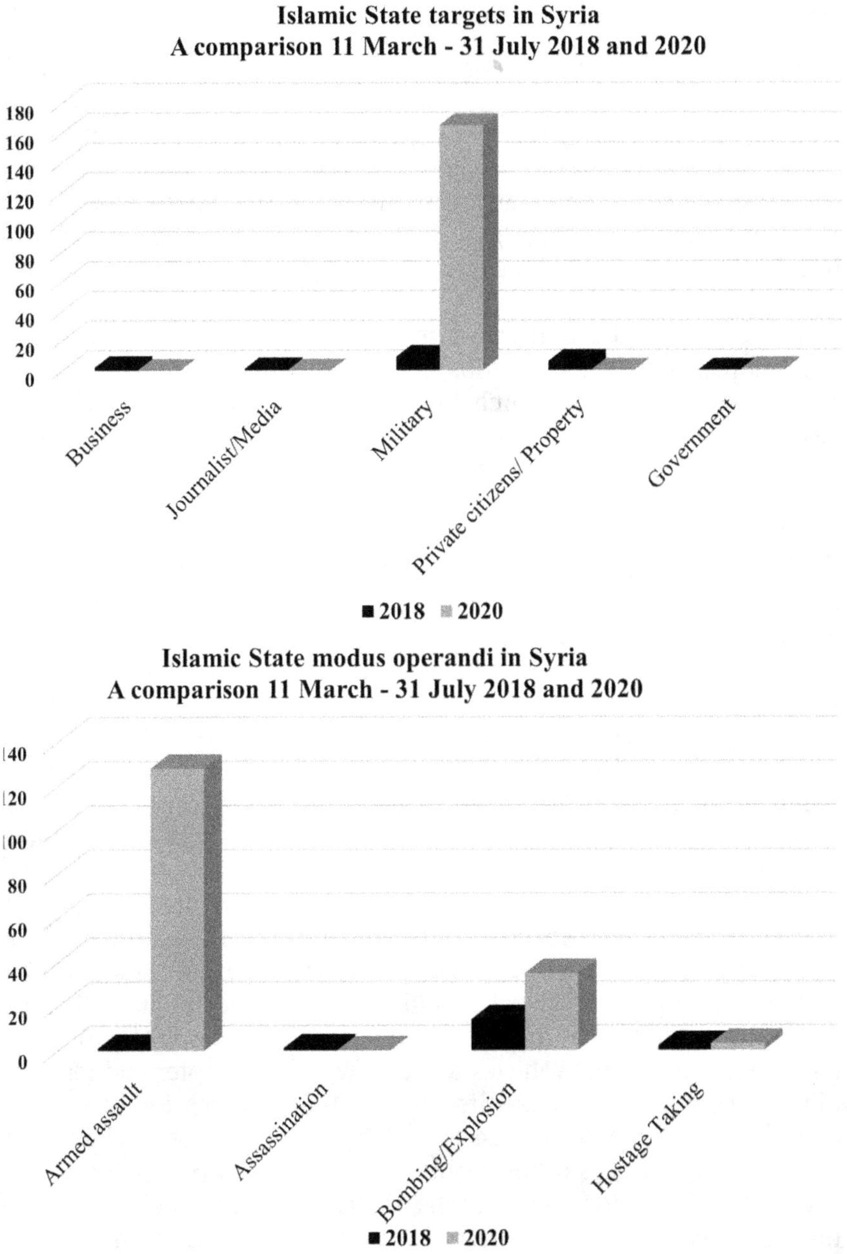

Figure 2.2. Islamic State targets and modus operandi in Syria. © Katalin Pethő-Kiss.

Iraq

Iraq remained the main arena of IS global activity. A significant increase can be observed in Islamic State's attack intensity in the region in 2020. Not only did the Islamic State expand its areas of operation, but it also diversified its activities. The trend is obviously linked with IS intentions to capitalize on the pandemic crisis situation (Cruickshank 2020).

In the middle of March 2020, IEDs and sniper fire were targeted at Iraqi soldiers, their army camps, and Tribal Mobilization forces in twenty-two operations. Between 17 and 22 March 2020, Iraqi army forces and their military vehicles were struck in thirteen missions. Iraqi armed and police forces, together with Tribal Mobilization fighters, were targeted by IS between 23 and 29 March 2020 in eighteen operations. During the last days of the month, IS attacked Iraqi military camps and the Tribal Mobilization's compound in seventeen operations (Meir Amit Intelligence 2020).

Between 7 and 22 April 2020, IS mounted thirty attacks targeting Iraqi military forces and Tribal Mobilization fighters. On 22 April 2020, a suicide bomber blew himself up at the entrance of the Intelligence and Counterterrorism Directorate of Kirkuk. Later in the month, Iraqi police forces and a SWAT team were struck in twenty operations. Iraqi soldiers and army camps were the targets of twenty-four IS attacks between 30 April and 4 May 2020 (Meir Amit Intelligence 2020).

Between 4 and 11 May 2020, IS militants raided Tribal Mobilization fighters and Iraqi government forces in a further eleven operations (Barak 2020). In its first documented attack in the Iraqi capital since November 2019, IS claimed thirty-six casualties among Shi'ites in five bombings in Baghdad on 11 May 2020. The next day the Islamic State claimed responsibility for a suicide bombing at a funeral of a police commander in IS Khorasan Province (SITE Intelligence Group 2020). In the middle of May, Tribal Mobilization and Iraqi military fighters and compounds were targeted in thirty-seven missions (Meir Amit Intelligence 2020). Army vehicles together with a helicopter and military officers were shot in sniper fires and IED detonations in eighteen IS operations between 20 and 24 May 2020 (Rubin, Jakes, and Schmitt 2020). In the last days of the month, the intensity of IS activity in Iraq decreased; IEDs detonations, mortar shells, sniper fire, and arson were the most common modus operandi in eleven strikes (Meir Amit Intelligence 2020).

At the beginning of June 2020, IS militants attacked Iraqi army compounds and Tribal Mobilization operatives six times (ibid.). On 13 June 2020, civilians of the Kaka'i sect were targeted by sniper fire. In the following days, Popular Mobilization militants and Iraqi compounds were struck in eleven IS operations (Al-Hashimi 2020). In the middle of June, Iraqi army vehicles and Popular Mobilization fighters were targeted in eleven IS missions. In the last days of June 2020, Iraqi soldiers and policemen were the targets of ten Islamic State operations (Meir Amit Intelligence 2020).

In the first week of July 2020, IS claimed responsibility for ten attacks targeting the Iraqi army and Popular Mobilization fighters. The most common form of attack between 7 and 13 July 2020 was the detonation of IEDs against the Shi'ite militias and the Iraqi security forces, in seventeen operations. Iraqi soldiers and Popular Mobilization fighters were again killed in twelve IS attacks between 14 and 20 July 2020. The most noteworthy attack that week was the killing of an Iraqi army brigade commander in an IS ambush about 30 km north of Baghdad. On 26 July 2020, an IED was activated against a vehicle of the Iraqi Interior Ministry's Commando Unit about 60 km north of Baqubah. Between 21 and 27 July 2020, Popular Mobilization vehicles and Iraqi armed forces were targeted in eleven IS operations (Meir Amit Intelligence 2020).

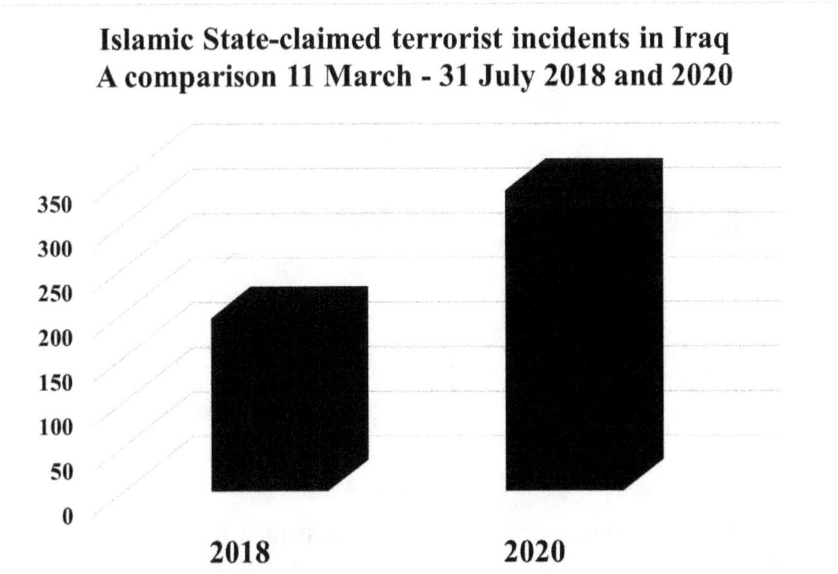

Figure 2.3. Islamic State-claimed terrorist incidents in Iraq. © Katalin Pethő-Kiss.

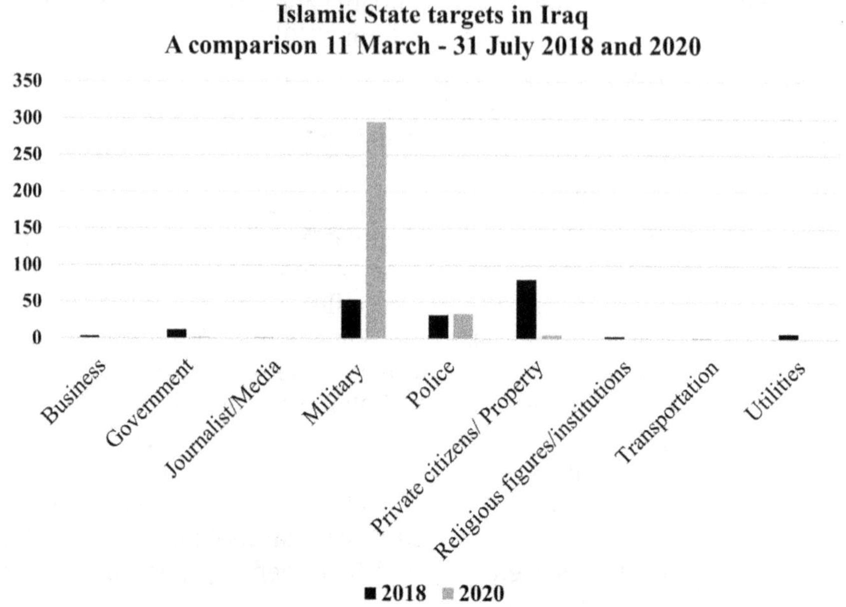

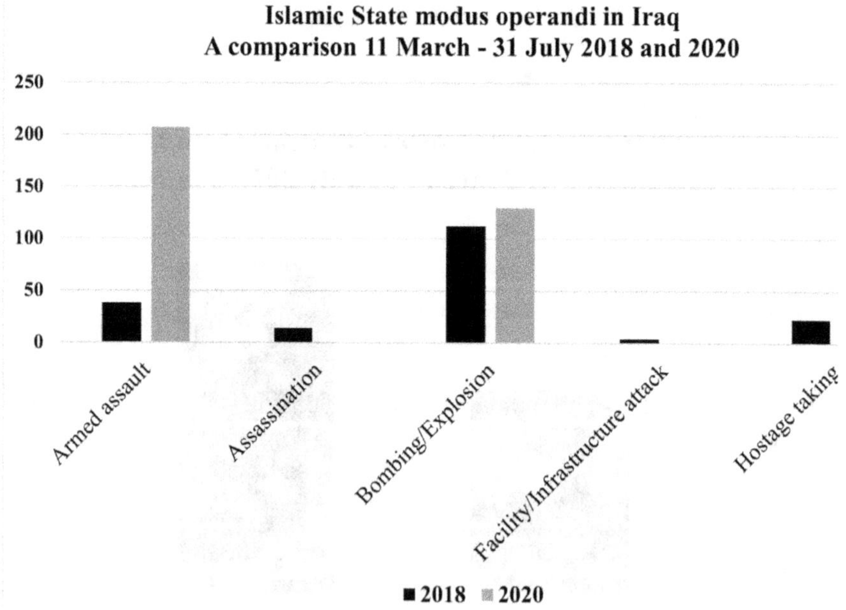

Figure 2.4. Islamic State targets and modus operandi in Iraq.
© Katalin Pethő-Kiss.

Euphrates Valley

Between 19 and 25 March 2020, SDF fighters, vehicles, and intelligence headquarters were targeted in five IS operations. In the last days of March, IS militants struck SDF forces again in five missions. In early April, IS activated IEDs and attacked SDF vehicles and personnel in eight attacks (Meir Amit Intelligence 2020).

How Has the Radical Islamist Threat Evolved in Iraq?

There is an almost 150 percent increase in the number of attacks for which the Islamic State claimed responsibility between 11 March and 31 July 2020. Obviously, it cannot be unequivocally confirmed that the evolving trend is due to the pandemic, but it is absolutely realistic that Islamic State took advantage of the crisis situation in Iraq and intensified its activities in the country.

It is beyond dispute that the military had a prominent symbolic role during the COVID-19 pandemic. Members of the armed forces were given extraordinary responsibilities in this crisis situation. Their enhanced presence and proximity during lockdown measures increased their exposure as targets, reducing their ability to respond to crises. Lockdown measures made traditional soft targets, such as private citizens and religious sites, almost impossible to attack, thereby substantially decreasing the psychological impact an act of terrorism strives to induce. Therefore, striking other targets of opportunity such as military and police headquarters made sense (Kruglanski et al. 2020).

Changes in Islamic State's modus operandi suggest that the pandemic has altered the circumstances in which the terrorist organization operates. Armed assault of low sophistication was more feasible and practicable in times of difficulties due to restrictive measures. IS fighters could not obtain the materials to make sophisticated weapons so they resorted to less complicated means of operation. The timing of attacks was of paramount importance as they knew the chaos due to the pandemic might not last long or offer exceptional opportunities to revive the radical Islamist relevance.

Afghanistan

The Taliban hosted al-Qaeda but have had a political office in Doha since 2013. The Qatari capital was the venue for signing the deal between the US and the Taliban. Governments worldwide are critical of the Taliban presence in Qatar, as it is tantamount to political recognition of the Taliban. With the Doha Declaration, the talks between the

Afghanistan government and Taliban started, the fighting stopped, and violence decreased. Until then Afghanistan had seen the largest number of terrorist attacks in any single country. "Afghanistan experienced 21 percent of all terrorist attacks worldwide in 2019, and 41 percent of all people killed in terrorist attacks (including assailants) in 2019" (Mashal and Rahim 2020). Just as the number of terrorist attacks had declined globally for six consecutive years since 2014, plots in Afghanistan also diminished following the US-led peace negotiations between the Taliban and the government in Kabul. Still, multiple terrorist plots were reported from the region. In a noteworthy incident on 13 July 2020, for instance, the Taliban mounted a devastating attack on an Afghan intelligence complex, killing at least eleven people and wounding more than sixty others. While the number of attacks committed by the Afghan Taliban decreased dramatically, in parallel the Islamic State became more active in Afghanistan in 2020 (Mashal and Rahim 2020).

Islamic State Khorasan Province resumed its continuous operation in the region. Because of the withdrawal of US troops from the country, COVID-19 provided an advantageous opportunity for the recovery of the threat group. Supposedly with the intention to disrupt the agreement between the US and the Taliban, on 20 March 2020, Islamic State operatives fired ten rockets at Bagram Airbase, where US army troops were stationed. An operative of IS Khorasan Province carried out a suicide bombing attack at a Sikh temple in Kabul on 25 March 2020. The next day, an IED was detonated against a gathering place of Sikhs and Hindus in the Afghan capital. In another recorded incident, an Afghan Special Forces commander was targeted with gunfire in the Nangarhar Province on 31 March 2020 (Meir Amit Intelligence 2020).

The Afghan Special Forces arrested the Emir and nineteen senior commanders of IS Khorasan Province on 4 April 2020 (ibid.). On 9 April 2020, Islamic State operatives fired rockets at Bagram US Airbase (United Nations Security Council 2020). At the beginning of May, IS fighters in Kabul took Sufi imam Abdel Hadi al-Naqshbandi hostage, and he was later executed. An IED was activated against two Taliban fighters on 6 May 2020. A Taliban fighter was targeted with gunfire on 11 May 2020. Later the same day, an IED was activated against a senior officer at the Afghan National Directorate of Security (Meir Amit Intelligence 2020). Another improvised explosive device struck the vehicle of a commander of the forces supporting the Afghan army on 16 May 2020. The next day, another IED attack targeted Afghan police in Kabul. On 24 May 2020, Islamic State militants fired rockets at Bagram US Airbase. Later in the month, hand grenades were thrown at an Afghanistan police checkpoint in Jalalabad. In another incident, an IED was activated on a

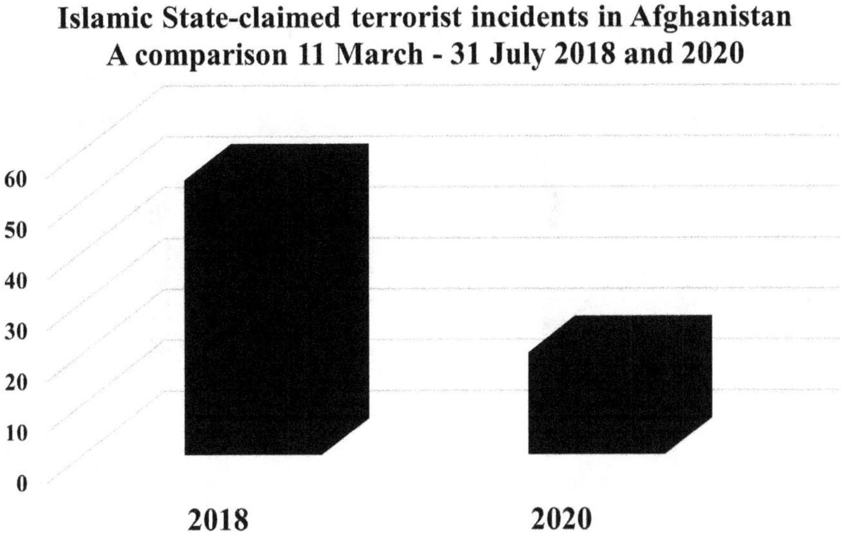

Figure 2.5. Islamic State-claimed terrorist incidents in Afghanistan. © Katalin Pethő-Kiss.

bus carrying employees of the Afghan government-affiliated Khurshid TV station in the capital Kabul on 30 May 2020. The next day, an IED was targeted at Afghan police forces in Kabul (Meir Amit Intelligence 2020).

On 25 July 2020, an investigator of the Afghan National Directorate of Security (NDS) was struck by gunfire in Jalalabad. The next day, a sticky bomb was activated against the vehicle of an Afghan NDS militant in the eastern Nangarhar Province. An IED was targeted at an Afghan police vehicle in Jalalabad on 28 July 2020. On 29 July, a limpet charge detonated on a bus carrying Shi'ites in the city of Herat (Meir Amit Intelligence 2020).

How Has the Radical Islamist Threat Evolved in Afghanistan?

As statistics demonstrate, the number of incidents IS Khorasan Province claimed responsibility for more than halved in the middle of 2020. First, losing its main territorial stronghold in Nangarhar and second the losses in its chain of command (Pikulicka-Wilczewska 2020) may explain this decrease.

As Figure 2.6. shows, the pandemic changed the main targets of Islamic State operations. Strikes against military, police, and private citizens were frequent but carried out at a lower level of intensity. No

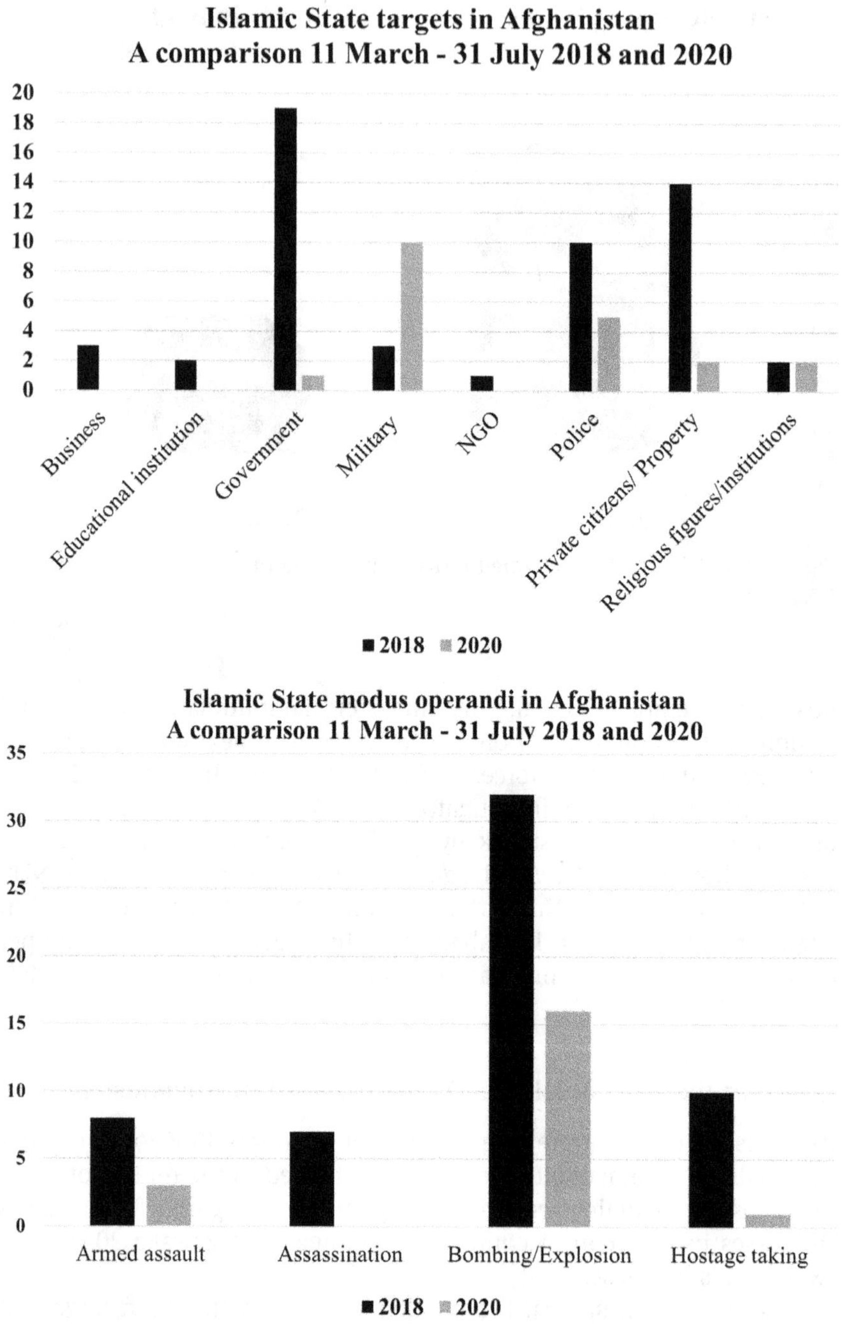

Figure 2.6. Islamic State targets and modus operandi in Afghanistan. © Katalin Pethő-Kiss.

assassinations occurred, and only one hostage-taking event happened, but the prevalence of bombing over armed assault remained.

Africa

Egypt

In the Sinai Peninsula, between 11 and 14 March 2020, Islamic State Sinai Province ambushed Egyptian military vehicles in three attacks. An IED was activated against an Egyptian military patrol on 19 March 2020. In the last days of March, IS militants attacked Egyptian military vehicles, personnel, and camps in five operations. Ambushes continued in April with nine IED detonations against Egyptian army vehicles and patrols (Meir Amit Intelligence 2020). The group claimed six operations between 22 April and 3 May 2020; all were IED detonations targeted at Egyptian soldiers. The group fired at Egyptian forces and activated three IEDs in North Sinai in the middle of May. IS Sinai Province attacked a checkpoint east of Sheikh Zuweid, killing four Egyptian soldiers on 20 May 2020 (SITE Intelligence Group 2020). An IED was activated against an armored Egyptian military vehicle on 30 May (Rubio 2020). As Islamic States's first attack in South Sinai since August 2019, it claimed a roadside IED detonation on a military vehicle in Wadi Maghara (SITE Intelligence Group 2020). Early June 2020, IS Sinai Province killed three Egyptian soldiers in an armed assault (United Nations Security Council 2020). On 21 June 2020, the group assaulted a gathering in Wadi Maghara. During the last days of the month, IS attacked Egyptian security forces in seven operations in the vicinity of Bir al-Abed (SITE Intelligence Group 2020). In one of its most active weeks, at the beginning of July 2020 IS Sinai Province claimed eight attacks on Egyptian forces. On 24 July 2020, the group carried out a dual VBIED suicide operation, targeting positions in Bir al-Abed (SITE Intelligence Group 2020). In the last days of July, two IEDs were detonated at Egyptian army tanks, soldiers were targeted by sniper fire, and two Egyptian officers were abducted and then executed (Meir Amit Intelligence 2020). There is a recognizable change throughout the period in the group's modus operandi, as instead of the previous trend in IED detonations on military vehicles, in-person armed assaults became more frequent (SITE Intelligence Group 2020).

Libya

Islamic State Libya Province detonated a roadside IED at the entrance of a battalion post in Taraghin town, south of Sabha, on 25 May 2020 (Reuters, 25 May 2020). Libya Province's Fezzan division claimed the

IED activated against a police station on 28 May 2020. Some days later, the group struck projectiles at the LNA-operated Tamanhant airbase (SITE Intelligence Group 2020).

Mozambique

Islamic State operatives attacked five Mozambican army and Mozambican police centers on 23 and 25 March 2020. In early April, IS militants ambushed a Mozambican military camp and seized control of two villages in the region (Meir Amit Intelligence 2020). IS Central Africa Province claimed an armed assault on Mozambican soldiers on 5 May 2020. Later in the month, the group executed two Mozambican soldiers and targeted Mozambican militia as well as homes of Christians via armed assault in the Muidumbe district of Cabo Delgado (SITE Intelligence Group 2020). Islamic State operatives attacked two compounds in Cabo Delgado on 27 June 2020 (BBC, 27 June 2020).

Niger, Nigeria, and Chad

IS West Africa Province militants struck four army camps in Niger between 10 and 16 March 2020. In the last days of March, IS operatives hit various Nigerian military compounds, ambushed their vehicles (Meir Amit Intelligence 2020), and later targeted a military post in Diffa, on the border with Nigeria (SITE Intelligence Group 2020). Several soldiers were killed in 11, 16, and 29 May 2020 Islamic State attacks (Meir Amit Intelligence 2020). IS West Africa Province claimed an armed assault on Nigerian soldiers, as well as a series of arson attacks on government buildings, all in the city of Diffa on 24 and 26 July (Campbell 2020).

Islamic State West Africa Province attacked Nigerian military headquarters on 14 and 17 April 2020 in Chad (Meir Amit Intelligence 2020). The group targeted Chadian soldiers in Kega and captured two aligned intelligence members in Krajakia in late May (SITE Intelligence Group 2020). IS West Africa Province claimed responsibility for an attack against a Nigerian military base on 3 May 2020. Islamic State operatives struck a Nigerian military camp on 18 May 2020. Two days later, the group captured Chadian military officers, who were then executed. Chadian soldiers and an army camp were ambushed on 8, 10, and 14 July (Meir Amit Intelligence 2020).

Nigeria remained Islamic State's most consistent bastion outside of Syria and Iraq. IS ambushed Nigerian security forces and struck their camp in Borno state in five operations between 10 and 15 March 2020 (ibid.). Islamic State operations against Nigerian military bases continued, with two army sites attacked on 21 and 24 March (Umar and Olukoya 2020). IS West Africa Province claimed a series of attacks carried out in the Lake Chad area on Nigerian security forces on 6 April 2020 (Meir Amit Intelligence 2020). In the middle of April, IS West Africa carried out six operations, targeting Nigerian forces (SITE Intelligence Group 2020). On the Eastern part of Yobe state, IEDs were activated against Nigerian military vehicles and personnel on 2 May 2020 (Meir Amit Intelligence 2020). A series of roadside IEDs killed seventeen Nigerian soldiers as a result of an IS operation in Nigeria on 3 May (SITE Intelligence Group 2020). Islamic State news outlet Amaq reported arson attacks on two Christian churches in Geldi town on 7 May. There were three armed assault incidents between 7 and 12 May on Nigerian forces. In Yobe State, a Nigerian military base was struck (Zenn 2020). IS West Africa Province attacked Nigerian army camps and convoys together with Nigerian police forces in seven incidents between 18 and 22 May (Meir Amit Intelligence 2020). In the following days, IS West Africa Province claimed three armed assaults and ten projectile strikes targeting Nigerian soldiers in various villages of its foothold Borno. In late May, Islamic State carried out five operations, consisting of four armed assaults and an IED detonation targeting Nigerian forces in Borno. In early June, the group issued claims for three attacks—all armed assaults—targeting Nigerian soldiers in Borno (SITE Intelligence Group 2020). More than eighty civilians died in an 8 June 2020 plot, when IS West Africa Province raided a village in Borno state (Meir Amit Intelligence 2020). As a result of three armed assaults, the Islamic State killed more than eleven Nigerian soldiers between 17 and 20 June 2020 (SITE Intelligence Group 2020). The group claimed responsibility for five attacks on Nigerian military camps and vehicles between 24 and 28 June (Meir Amit Intelligence 2020). In the first weeks of July 2020, IS West Africa Province claimed an armed assault targeting Civilian Joint Task Force (CJTF) personnel in Gombe and eleven additional armed assaults targeting Nigerian forces. Thirteen operations targeted Nigerian forces, Cameroonian forces, Nigeria-government-aligned militiamen, and a Christian community between 23 and 31 July 2020 (SITE Intelligence Group 2020).

Cameroon and DRC

In Cameroon, at the end of May, Islamic State claimed its first cross-border attack since June 2019 in the country from the Nigerian side of Lake Chad. Early June 2020, IS West Africa Province hit on an army position in Sagmé and ambushed a Cameroonian army compound (SITE Intelligence Group 2020). Thirty-four soldiers were killed on 20 June when an Islamic State suicide bomber activated a car bomb among a group of Cameroonian soldiers near Lake Chad (Meir Amit Intelligence 2020). On 27 July, the group carried out its third attack in the country in 2020 in targeting a military post in Sagmé town, Fotoko (SITE Intelligence Group 2020).

In the Democratic Republic of Congo, there were two clashes between IS Central Africa Province and the Congolese army in the middle of April 2020 (Meir Amit Intelligence 2020). Between 16 and 20 May, Islamic State claimed three attacks—two targeting Congolese soldiers and one targeting Christians—across various villages of Beni (Africa News, 15 May 2020). Thirteen Christians were killed in a 23 May IS operation targeting Christian civilians in northeastern Congo. On 24 May, a soldier and two Congolese military intelligence officers were executed by Islamic State. The group claimed to have killed thirteen Christians as the result of an armed assault in Kumbwa Kobo village near Eringeti on 25 May. Twenty soldiers were killed at a military compound on 26 May when IS attacked the base. Twenty other Congolese soldiers lost their lives in an armed assault on two military positions in Beni on 28 May. Later in June 2020, IS Central Africa Province killed eleven Christians in an armed assault, still in Beni. Two days later, the group claimed two more attacks on Christians and Congolese soldiers in the region. IS Central Africa Province claimed three armed assaults between 1 and 3 July. On 14 June, Islamic State operatives killed an officer at a Congolese military compound (SITE Intelligence Group 2020). The group targeted Congolese soldiers in two armed assaults in Beni on 20 and 22 June. The next day, the group attacked a new kind of target when killing five UN peacekeepers (Perkins 2020). As part of its "Battle of Attrition" campaign, IS Central Africa Province claimed three operations targeting Congolese forces between 29 and 30 July 2020 (SITE Intelligence Group 2020).

Mali, Somalia, Kenya

On 11 March 2020, Islamic State operatives activated an IED against a French and Malian military convoy (Meir Amit Intelligence 2020). In Mali, under the "Invasions in the Holy Month" military campaign, JNIM claimed four operations against security forces in early May (SITE Intelligence Group 2020). Thabaat News Agency issued messages claiming JNIM attacked a Malian army position in an unidentified location within Mopti province on 27 July 2020 (Al-Lami 2020).

In late April 2020, al-Shabaab carried out standard operations across six regions in Somalia, targeting Somali police officers as well as Ugandan and Burundian troops. Their tactics remained the same, namely armed assaults, assassinations, IED detonations, projectile strikes, and capture/execution (SITE Intelligence Group 2020). In the suburbs of the capital Mogadishu, two Somali policemen were targeted by machine gun fire on 9 May 2020 (Meir Amit Intelligence 2020). Mid-May Islamic State Somalia Province killed a Somali police officer in the Elasha area of Lower Shabelle (Weiss 2020). Marking its third attack in the country in June, the group claimed killing a Somali police officer when deploying a grenade at Wedo intersection. In late May, Islamic State killed a Somali law enforcement agent in a projectile strike on the outskirts of Mogadishu. On 4 June 2020, the group claimed its first operation in Afgoye—a past hotspot (2017–2019)—since late January with a grenade strike at a police headquarters (SITE Intelligence Group 2020). IS Somalia Province targeted Somali police patrols in Mogadishu on 8 June. A policeman was killed in a 22 June attack when a hand grenade was thrown at him (Meir Amit Intelligence 2020). Seven policemen were killed when an IED was activated in Mogadishu on 25 June 2020 (Rolbieczki, Van Ostaeyen, and Winter 2020). In the first days of July, IS Somalia Province wounded three police officers in a grenade attack in Mogadishu. As part of the "Battle of Attrition," the group attacked a joint US/Puntland security convoy on 22 July 2020. The next day they claimed to have killed four Somali police officers with a hand grenade at a Bakara intersection in Mogadishu. Between 16 and 22 July, al-Shabaab claimed twenty operations across six provinces in Somalia and one in Kenya, with standard operations. Al-Shabaab carried out eighteen operations across five provinces in Somalia and one in Kenya between 23 and 29 July 2020, targeting Ugandan troops and Somali

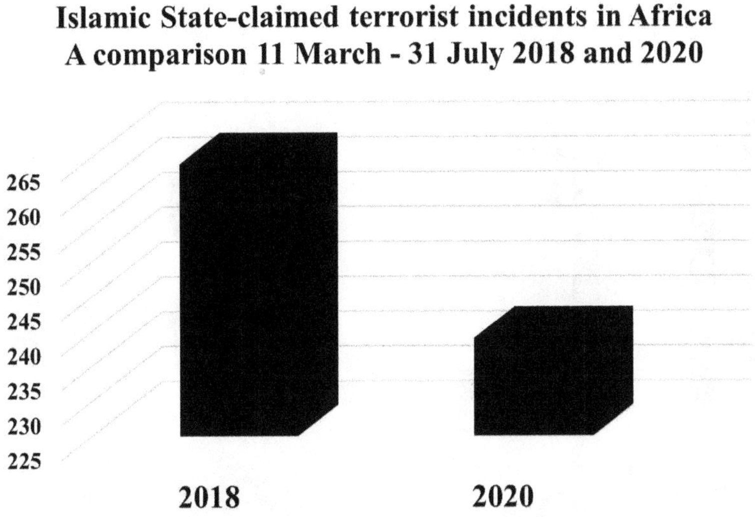

Figure 2.7. Islamic State-related terrorist incidents in Africa.
© Katalin Pethő-Kiss.

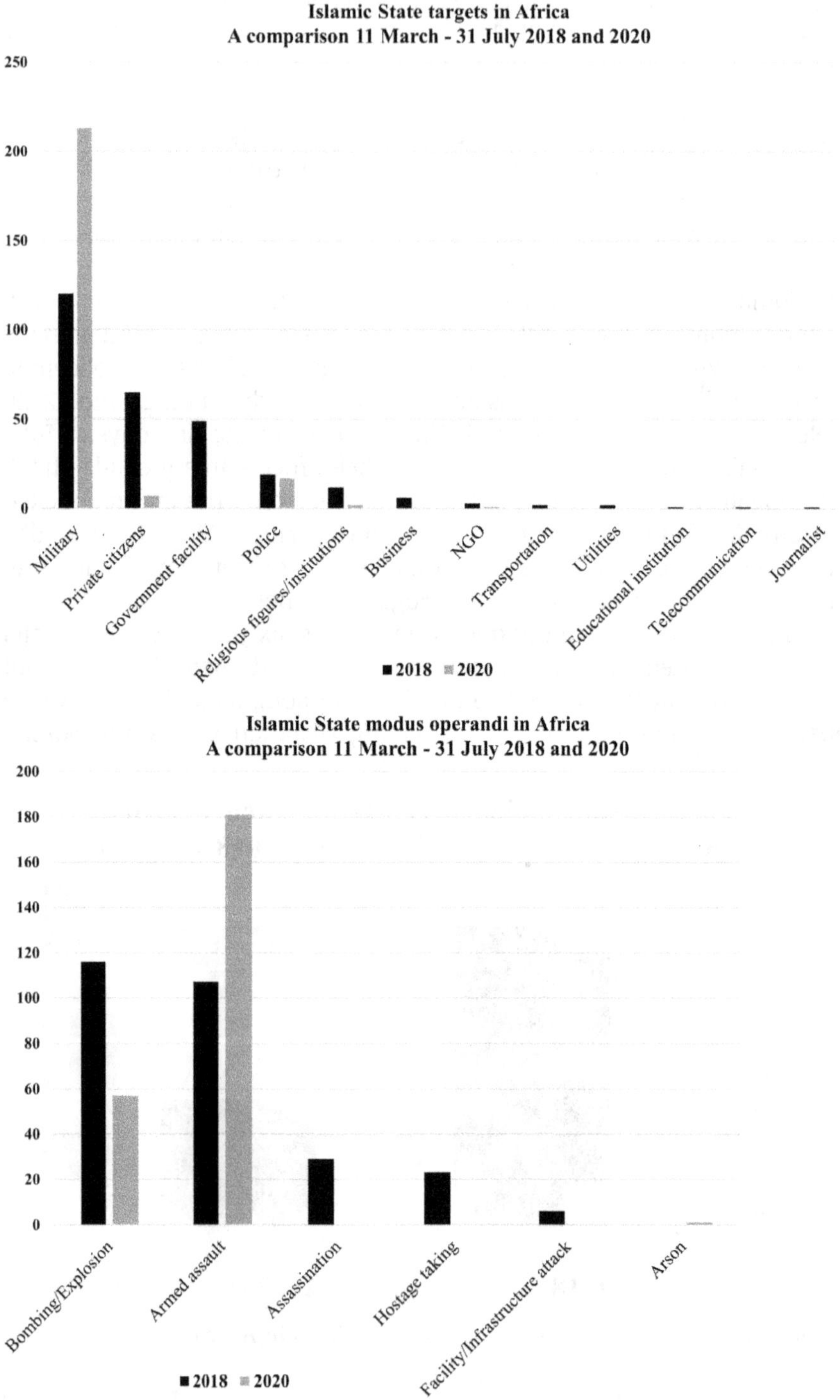

Figure 2.8. Islamic State targets and modus operandi in Africa.
© Katalin Pethő-Kiss.

special forces. At the end of July IS Somalia Province attacked a police checkpoint in Mogadishu (SITE Intelligence Group 2020).

How Has the Radical Islamist Threat Evolved in Africa?

A slightly fewer number of IS-linked incidents were reported in 2020. However, more obvious are the changes both in radical Islamist targets and modus operandi. The number of military targeted attacks nearly doubled, while strikes on private citizens, religious institutions, and businesses drastically decreased. Interestingly, police stations and personnel were attacked roughly the same number of times. This trend might reflect the consequences of restrictions having been put in place. As traditional gatherings were canceled, the more visible military forces became the primary jihadist targets.

There is, however, another observable change in Islamic State's operational tactics in Mozambique. Prior to COVID-19, the group ambushed government institutions and military camps, but after the outbreak they attacked cities, towns, and critical infrastructure to capitalize on the crisis situation (Meir Amit Intelligence 2020).

Islamic State's modus operandi also went through an elementary change, as IED attacks were replaced by armed assaults. Obviously, epidemiological restrictions resulted in disruptions in jihadist supply chains, and this is most likely the reason for this trend.

Nonconflict Zones

Europe

The 2020 European Union Terrorism Situation and Trend Report asserted that radical Islamist terrorism, more specifically foreign terrorist fighters, were a real security concern in the EU (Europol 2019). There were some significant terrorism-related plots in Europe between 11 March and 31 July 2020.

French police launched a terrorism investigation after two people were killed and five wounded in a knife attack in Romans-sur-Isère, near Grenoble on 4 April 2020. The Sudanese offender, an Islamic State-sympathizer, attacked more people at various shops before being arrested (BBC, 5 April 2020).

Four Tajik nationals were arrested as suspected members of an Islamic State cell on 15 April 2020. They were supposed to have joined IS in January 2019 and had continuously received orders from high-ranking IS members in Syria and Afghanistan inciting them to carry out attacks in Germany, in particular on US military bases and personnel (Gartenstein-Ross, Chace-Donahue, and Clarke 2020). A French man rammed his car into two police motorcyclists in a Paris suburb on 28 April 2020. The offender pledged allegiance with Islamic State after the incident (Reuters, 28 April 2020).

In the United Kingdom, the official terrorism threat level was reduced from "severe" to "substantial" in November 2019. Since then, three major incidents have occurred in the country, including the stabbing attack in a Reading park. On 20 June 2020, Khairi Saadallah was held on suspicion of killing three people at the scene. The Libyan national perpetrator was known to MI5; in 2019 he caught the attention of security services when information about his aspirations to travel abroad for terrorism purposes emerged. However, at that time no immediate security risk was identified (BBC, 22 June 2020).

Two Algerian citizens were arrested in a Spanish antiterror operation on 2 July 2020. According to the Catalan police, the two citizens were part of a cell that was planning an attack with explosives in Barcelona (Al Jazeera, 14 July 2020). As a result of a joint investigation with Moroccan security forces, earlier in May 2020 Spanish police arrested a suspected Islamic State terrorist. The radicalized Moroccan man broke the pandemic restrictions and was allegedly planning a militant attack in Barcelona (The Telegraph, 8 May 2020).

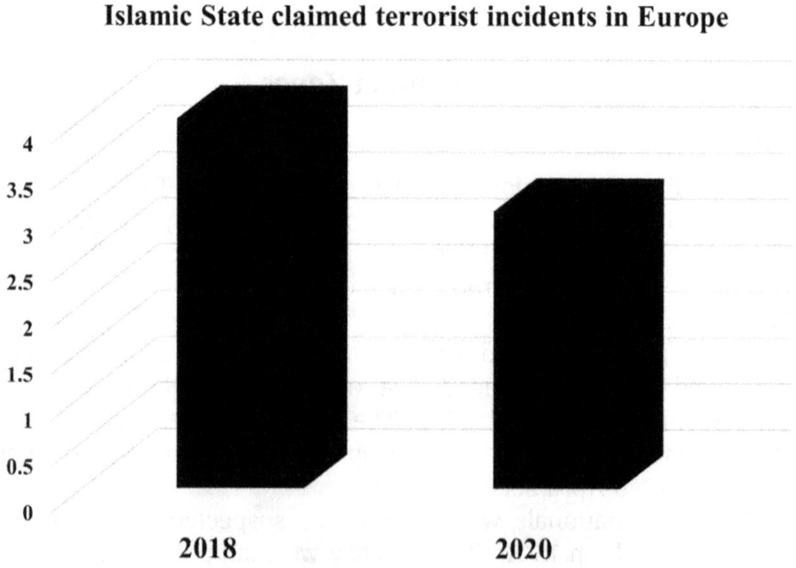

Figure 2.9. Radical Islamist terrorist incidents in Europe.
© Katalin Pethő-Kiss.

How Has the Radical Islamist Threat Evolved in Europe?

All the seven completed European plots in 2018 were of radical Islamist nature and were committed by lone individual actors (Europol 2019). As Figure 2.9. indicates, fewer completed terrorist attacks occurred be-

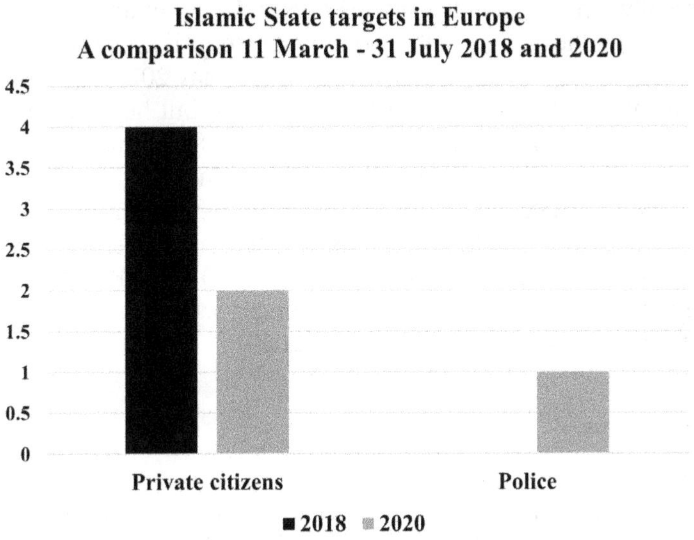

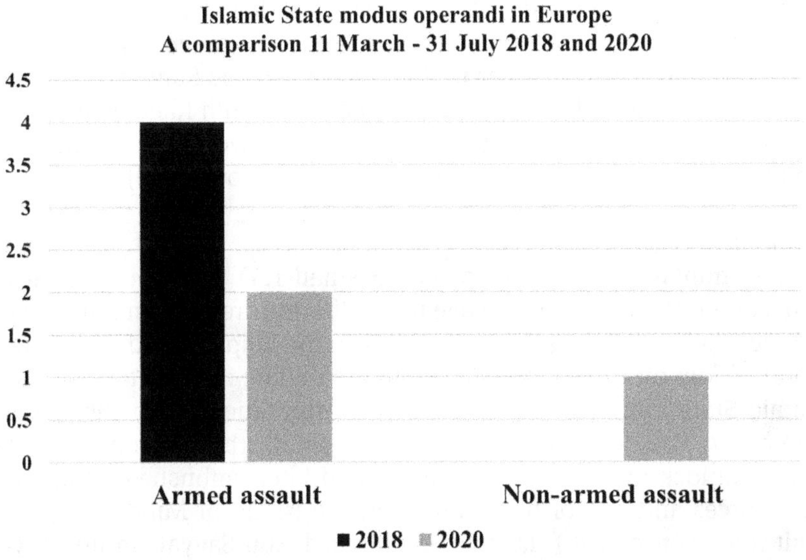

Figure 2.10. Radical Islamist targets and modus operandi in Europe.
© Katalin Pethő-Kiss.

tween 11 March and 31 July 2020, but there has not been a significant decrease in their numbers.

With regard to terrorist targets, no COVID-related changes can be observed. Notably, private citizens were the targets of radical Islamist attacks both in 2018 and 2020. Besides civilians, however, two police officers were stabbed and shot in the Liège attack (BBC News, 30 May 2018).

Typically, unsophisticated modus operandi (a gun and a knife) characterized the attacks, although in one instance in the heat of the attack a passer-by was taken hostage (BBC News, 30 May 2018). Regarding the Colombes attack, the perpetrator was unarmed, but he rammed his car into two stationary police patrols on motorcycles (Reuters, 28 April 2020). As mentioned above, radical Islamist-inspired individuals were responsible for the plots occurring in Europe within the examined time period. With regard to the Reading stabbing attack, there was no immediate evidence for allegiance to Islamic State or al-Qaeda. Khairi Saadallah was, though, under investigation as a person who might travel abroad "for extremist reasons" (Grierson et al. 2020).

Southeast Asia

Indonesia

Mujahidin Indonesia Timur claimed responsibility for plots allegedly taking advantage of the pandemic crisis situation in the middle of April 2020. Police killed two suspected MIT operatives after they attacked police officers in Poso city on 15 April. Some days later, the Islamic militant group kidnapped and killed a farmer in Kilo village. Islamic State militants set fire to a police car and attacked police officers in South Kalimantan province on 1 June 2020. IS operatives allegedly shot two Muslim farmers in the Poso regency on June 2 (International Crisis Group 2020).

Philippines

Islamist militants continued to mount small IED and suicide attacks against security forces and engage in small-arms firefights in Mindanao. Islamic State operatives exchanged fire with Filipino soldiers on the island of Jolo on 14 March 2020. From the middle of April till late July, Islamic State militants had numerous confrontations with the Philippine army. They exchanged fire on Jolo Island, threw hand grenades at a roadblock of the Philippine army and later ambushed Philippine army forces and one of their camps on the island of Mindanao (Meir Amit Intelligence 2020). Islamic State-linked Abu Sayyaf Group (ASG) clashed with the military in two operations in April. ASG took hostage of five Indonesians on 28 April 2020 (International Crisis Group 2020).

In its first documented attack during Ramadan, Islamic State East Asia Province claimed the deaths of two Philippine soldiers in a center located in Datu Hoffer, Maguindanao on 3 May 2020. An "exclusive" in Al-Naba 232 revealed a previously unclaimed attack in Sulu by fighters in East Asia Province, which resulted in the wounding of eight Philippine soldiers. According to the article, the casualties occurred on 23 April 2020, the first day of Ramadan, during an encounter in Latih village, Patikul town (SITE Intelligence Group 2020). In two other May operations, IS East Province militants attacked again Philippine army forces on the island of Mindanao (Meir Amit Intelligence 2020). Islamic State East Asia Province claimed to have killed and wounded an unspecified number of Philippine soldiers as the result of an armed assault on an army barracks in Maguindanao on 20 May 2020 (SITE Intelligence Group 2020) and some days later declared the responsibility for killing fifteen Philippine soldiers in a large-scale armed assault in Patikul municipality, Jolo, Sulu (Broches 2020). Confrontations between soldiers and Abu Sayyaf Group militants continued in two May operations. Operatives of Bangsamoro Islamic Freedom Fighters attacked military personnel on 3 May and on 18 and 19 May 2020 in Maguindanao province (International Crisis Group 2020).

Islamic State East Asia Province ambushed Philippine soldiers on Jolo Island on the first day of June 2020. Abu Sayyaf Group operatives attacked military personnel in three operations between 5 and 13 June. In Maguindanao province, members of Bangsamoro Islamic Freedom Fighters killed a soldier on 9 June 2020 in Sultan Kudarat town. IS militants fired machine guns at Filipino soldiers in the northern part of Jolo Island on 22 June 2020. The leader of Abu Sayyaf was reported dead after a clash with the Philippine armed forces in July 2020. Operatives of IS East Province ambushed Philippine army forces in two operations between 24 and 25 July (Meir Amit Intelligence 2020). In early July, IS East Asia Province targeted a checkpoint of Philippine soldiers on the Island of Maguindanao (SITE Intelligence Group 2020). Bangsamoro Islamic Freedom Fighters clashed with police and military in three operations in July. Abu Sayyaf Group attacked government forces in Patikul municipality on 6 July (AP News, 30 July 2020).

Borneo Island

In the southern part of Borneo Island, a police officer was killed when Islamic State mounted an attack on a police station on 1 June 2020 (Meir Amit Intelligence 2020). On the same day, a single Islamic State fighter struck a police station in South Daha district, South Hulu Sungai Regency (SITE Intelligence Group 2020).

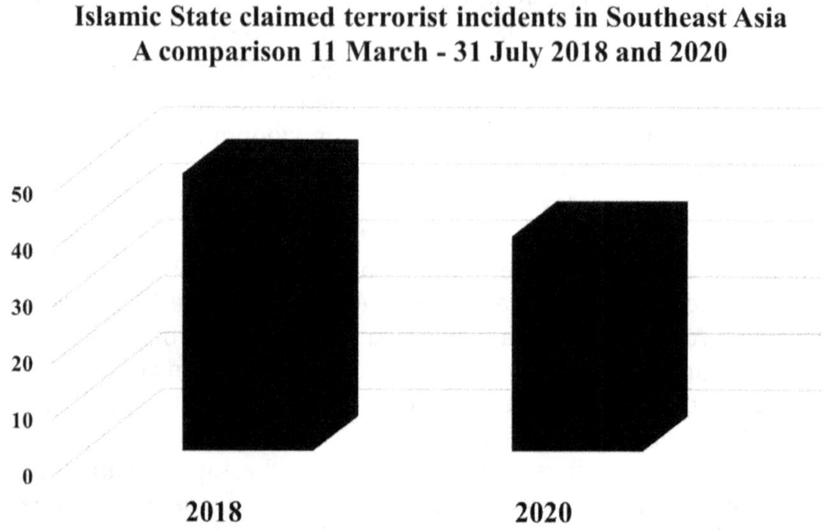

Figure 2.11. Radical Islamist terrorist incidents in Southeast Asia.
© Katalin Pethő-Kiss.

How Has the Radical Islamist Threat Evolved in Southeast Asia?

As the information in Figure 2.11 represents, there was a 23 percent decrease in the number of Islamic terrorist incidents from 2018 to 2020. In Indonesia, the decrease in the number of terrorist attacks and plots can be attributed to the following factors. First, radical Islamist movements became restricted because of the pandemic. Second, counterterrorism operations resulted in successful arrests and weapon hauls. Third, Indonesia-based networks were suffering from an apparent absence of financial assistance from foreign fighters based in Syria (Rahmah 2021).

The change in radical Islamist terrorists' targets is even more apparent. While Islamist fighters previously attacked national armies, private citizens, and police roughly the same amount, in 2020 the vast majority of radical Islamist terrorist incidents targeted military personnel and compounds. There were very few 2020 plots in which police and private citizens were struck. As Figure 2.12 shows, businesses, government facilities, educational institutions, religious figures/institutions, journalists, and means of transportation were no longer targets by prominent terrorist entities in 2020.

There is also a noteworthy change in the way radical Islamist terrorists plotted their attacks. While in 2018 46 percent of Islamist terrorist incidents occurred by activating an improvised explosive device or a

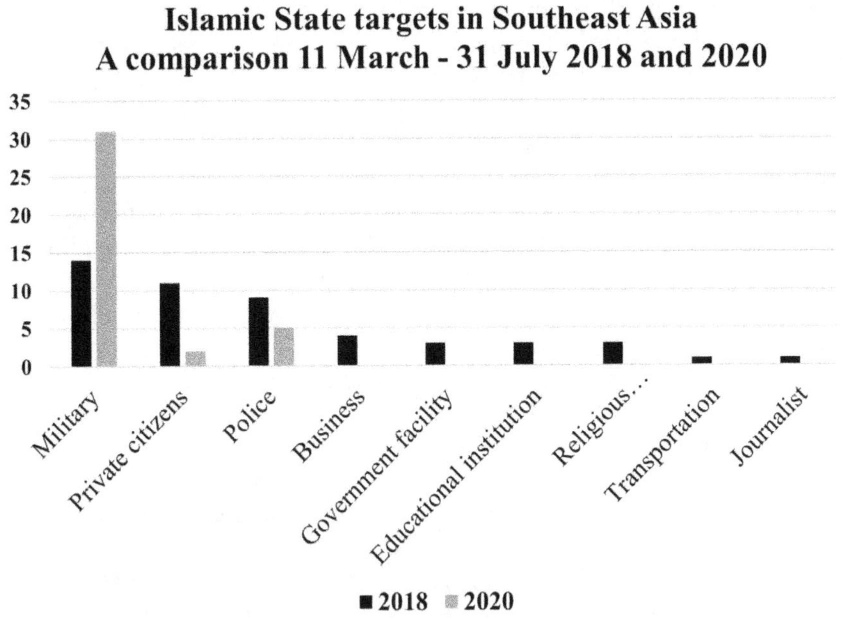

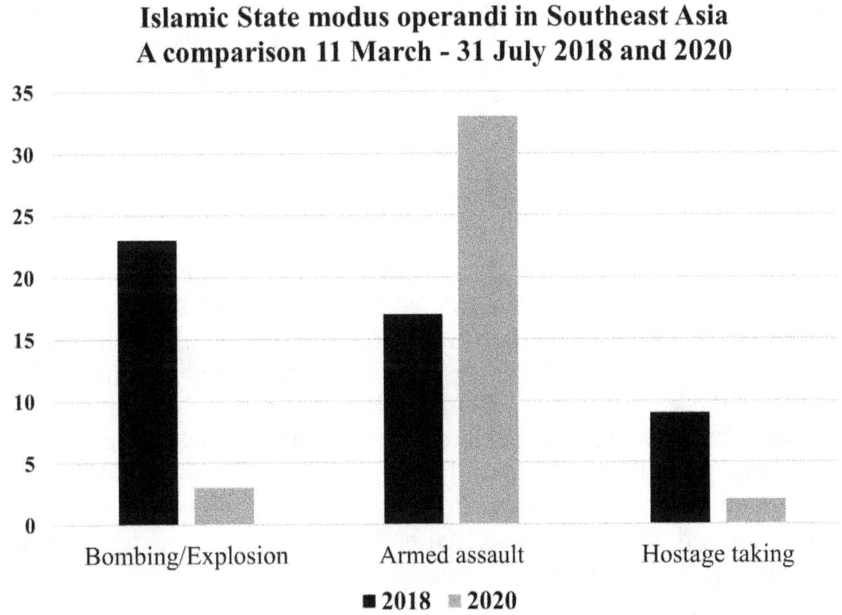

Figure 2.12. Radical Islamist terrorist targets and modus operandi in Southeast Asia. © Katalin Pethő-Kiss.

grenade, in 2020 IEDs were involved much less frequently. Apparently, armed assault became the most commonly applied modus operandi. Stabbing remained jihadists' preferred tactic, which requires less effort in terms of training, planning, and funds (Rahmah 2021). In 2018 there were nine instances in which radical Islamist operatives kidnapped their victims; this number decreased to two in 2020. This seems to contradict those predictions that suggested the chaos caused by the pandemic would exasperate the factors that contribute to kidnapping for ransom (Damora 2020).

The same radical Islamist terrorist entities were active in Southeast Asia, but their level of intensity was reduced. The previously noteworthy Bangsamoro Islamic Freedom Movement's activity in the region decreased almost three-fold. Meanwhile, the Islamic State claimed an increased number of attacks. Interestingly, there is no change with regard to Abu Sayyaf Group, which claimed responsibility for nine attacks both in 2018 and 2020. The number of attacks claimed by Jamaah Ansharut Daulah (JAD) may have dropped because of the following factors. First, by May 2020 Indonesian National Police had arrested fifty-seven individuals suspected to be members of JAD. And second, a disagreement emerged within the group, as operatives perceived the relevance of the pandemic in different ways. While one section was busy working out a contingency plan to save themselves from the pandemic, others were eager to become martyrs and incited attacks (Levenia and Sciascia 2020).

United States

An assailant at a sleepover party stabbed three people in Ballen Isles neighborhood, Palm Beach Gardens, Florida, United States in March 2018. At least one person was killed and two others injured in the assault. Corey Johnson claimed responsibility and stated that he carried out the attack because the victims made fun of how he practiced his Muslim faith. Sources also noted that Johnson allegedly contacted members of the Islamic State of Iraq and the Levant (ISIL) and showed interest in joining the group. Previously, he had shown a fascination for Nazis and white supremacists, had reportedly antagonized female classmates, and had made derogatory comments against Jews and LGBT people (Wang 2018).

A Salafi jihadist-inspired aviation student from Saudi Arabia killed three men at Naval Air Station Pensacola in Florida in December 2019 (NBC News, 8 December 2019). Religious terrorism and the threat

Table 2.1. Radical Islamist terrorism in the United States.

Radical Islamist-related terrorist incidents in the USA A comparison — 2018 and 2020 March 11–July 31		
Year	Number of terrorist attacks	
2018	1	
2020	0	
Radical Islamist targets in the USA **A comparison — 2018 and 2020 March 11–July 31**		
Type target	2018	2020
Private citizens	1	0
Radical Islamist modus operandi in the USA **A comparison - 2018 and 2020 March 11–July 31**		
Modus operandi	2018	2020
Armed assault	1	0
Radical Islamist groups in the USA **A comparison — 2018 and 2020 March 11–July 31**		
Terrorist groups	2018	2020
Radical Islamist	1	0

posed by Salafi jihadists remain a concern in the United States because of the following factors. First, al-Qaeda and Islamic State incitements to conduct lone offender-type attacks are continuous. Second, there are still a considerable number of radical Islamist fighters in Syria and Iraq. At the same time, AQ and IS-aligned groups operating in Yemen, Nigeria, Somalia, and Afghanistan also constitute an ongoing serious threat (Jones, Doxsee, and Harrington 2020).

How Has the Radical Islamist Threat Evolved in the United States?

Within the examined time period, in 2020 no radical Islamist-inspired terrorist incident was reported. In 2018 right-wing extremists were responsible for 90 percent of extremist-related killings (ADL Center on Extremism 2020). In 2020 the Department of Homeland Security confirmed that home-grown white supremacist and neo-Nazi terrorists are the greatest security concern. In 2020 Boogaloo movement activists conducted most of the terrorist incidents in the United States (Hoffman and Ware 2020).

The Role of Ramadan

One-third or 600 million of the world's Muslim population is from or lives in South Asia. They also form a significant immigrant diaspora in the west and east, with a presence in North America, Europe, Southeast Asia, Australia, and New Zealand. Islam is the dominant religion in Afghanistan (35 million), Bangladesh (150 million), Maldives (550,000), and Pakistan (200 million), and the dominant religion after Hinduism in India (200 million) and Buddhism in Sri Lanka (2 million) and Nepal (1.3 million) (Pew Research Center 2020). While South Asia hosts the world's largest regional population of Muslims, Southeast Asia hosts 242 million adherents, or 42 percent of the population. From the eighth century, Islam grew in South Asia, starting with India and Sri Lanka through maritime trade. After adapting to local traditions, Islam flourished in South and Southeast Asia. However, reformist, revivalist, and radical Islamic movements, most notably Wahhabism, challenge local and traditional Islam today (Nationsonline 2015).

The most sacred month for Muslims is Ramadan. In the ninth month of the Islamic calendar, Muslims mark that Allah gave the first chapters of the Qu'ran to the Prophet Muhammad in 610. Muslims around the world abstain from pleasures and pray to get closer to God. Ramadan is also a powerful symbol of unity; fasting brings together family and friends without geographic restrictions (Ross 2018).

On 23 April 2020, the beginning of the Holy month of Ramadan, Islamic State-aligned groups and supporters shared in multiple languages across their channels well wishes together with guidelines to remain safe. As the rewards are multiplied for an attack during Ramadan, there were supposed to have been more attacks in conflict areas (Iraq, Syria, Afghanistan, Mindanao, Poso). Radical Islamist posters called Ramadan the "month of invasions and jihad" (SITE Intelligence Group [2020)]. IS-linked groups posted a litany of material, including praise of the alleged IS supporter who carried out a vehicular attack in Paris. They called for further attacks during the pandemic and expressed joy for those who had died from the virus in the United States and Italy. In conjunction with the destabilization of law and security enforcement caused by COVID-19 around the world, the potential for an increase in attacks and incitements posed a heightened threat (SITE Intelligence Group 2020).

With the dawn of Ramadan, Islamic State began its campaign by mounting two attacks in which policemen and intelligence personnel were injured in France and Iraq respectively. An IS lone wolf conducted a vehicle ramming attack against police during an identity check on 27 April 2020. A 29-year-old Frenchman drove his car into police cars and motorcycles, injuring three officers in the northwestern Paris suburb of Colombes. The driver had a knife in his car along with a letter pledging allegiance to IS and claiming that he wants to impose Islamic sharia law around the world (Reuters, 28 April 2020). In response to the call, both operatives and supporters threatened attacks in retaliation for closing the mosques. Two Islamic State supporters in Tunisia attempted to infect police officers by coughing and deliberately contaminating a busy precinct (Middle East Eye, 17 April 2020).

During Ramadan 2020, IS media output from the "Battle of Attrition" military campaign in the form of provincial photo reports spiked to the highest monthly levels since November 2019, with the majority coming from Iraq for the second consecutive month. Feature video output remained on pace with the 1–2 average seen in the last six months, with a piece from Iraq Province, while unofficial Amaq News Agency videos totaled six, down from eight in April 2020. Islamic State claimed its first suicide operation in Iraq in nearly a year. An IS suicide attacker with explosive belts detonated himself on 28 April 2020 while attempting to penetrate Kirkuk's intelligence headquarters. The security guards at the entrance started to shoot him, making him detonate himself, which resulted in injuries to the security guards (Abdul-Zahira 2020). Islamic State's remnants regrouped and initiated a series of attacks on both Peshmerga forces as well as the Iraqi army. Islamic State's Al-Naba Issue 235 included an infographic of statistical breakdowns of IS operations in Iraq during Ramadan 2020. Accordingly, group fighters killed and wounded 426 in 266 attacks in the holy period (SITE Intelligence Group 2020).

In addition to the release of the third issue of the Indian Subcontinent-focused magazine "The Voice of Hind" (2020), Islamic State-linked, India-centric Islamist groups increased calls for attacks in India. "The Voice of Hind" suggested multiple ways to mount attacks in India and also promoted past incidents in Afghanistan, Bangladesh, Maldives, and Sri Lanka. Referring to the latest plot in the Maldives, Islamic State said: "May Allah accept all your efforts and operations you have executed such as the burning of a hotel and two of their boats and the stabbing of an Australian Kaafir. May it be worse for the apostate democratic government so that Allah punishes them by your hands." It suggested lone wolves in India use kitchen knives, axes, hammers to stab and bludgeon, ropes and belts to choke, vehicles to run over people, petrol bombs to "wreak the havoc," and bare hands to throw heavy objects from rooftops in order to maim and kill (The Voice of Hind 2020).

Indonesian Islamic State supporters on Telegram celebrated previous attacks carried out by jihadist fighters and incited attacks against Indonesian National Police counterterrorism squad Densus 88's newly appointed chairman, along with other high-ranking officials. They called for operations during the holy month of Ramadan targeting Christian churches in particular (SITE Intelligence Group 2020).

We have detected a clear difference between trends during Ramadan in conflict and nonconflict zones. The novel circumstances of being on the battlefield provided terrorists with more beneficial conditions, and accordingly a heightened level of intensity characterized radical Islamist operations. Meanwhile, restrictions on social gatherings off the battlefields resulted in a decrease in the frequency of radical Islamist attacks.

Conclusion

This chapter has attempted to better understand emerging trends in Islamist terrorism between 11 March and 31 July 2020, which have been contrasted with incidents reported in the same period in 2018. The comparison has been based on four perspectives, namely the number of attacks, their targets together with their modus operandi, and the active radical Islamist terrorist groups in the respective geographic regions. Finally, the role of Ramadan 2020 has been evaluated.

Note

1. Hadith of Prophet Muhammad:
   COVID-19
   1) *QUARANTINE* is a Prophetic advice.
   "Run away from the leper (the one with contagious ailment) as you would run away from a lion." (Bukhari Volume 7, Book 71, Number 608)
   2) *SOCIAL DISTANCING* is a Prophetic command. "Those with contagious diseases should be kept away from those who are healthy." Bukhari (6771) and Muslim (2221)
   3) *TRAVEL BAN* is a Prophetic teaching. "Do not enter a land where the plague (contagious ailment) has broken out; don't leave from where it has broken out." Bukhari (5739) and Muslim (2219)
   4) *DON'T HARM OTHERS* if you have symptoms. The Prophet said: "Do not cause harm or return harm." Sunan Ibn Mājah (2340)
   5) *STAYING HOME* is a Prophetic teaching. "Those who stay at home to protect themselves and others are under the protection of Allah." Musnad Ahmed, Saheeh

6) If necessary, *HOUSE IS A MASJID*. The Prophet said: "The entire earth has been made a Masjid, except graveyards and washrooms." Tirmidhi (al-Salaah, 291)
7) *THERE'S CURE*; patience is the virtue. The Prophet said: "There is no disease that Allah sent without sending for it a cure." Bukhari (Volume 7, Book 71, Number 582)
8) Let's *TREAT; ALLAH WILL CURE*. The Prophet said: "Every disease has a cure. If a cure is applied to the disease, it is relieved by the permission of Allah." Muslim (2204)
9) *FACE MASKING* is a Prophetic teaching. Prophet while sneezing would cover his face with his hand or with his garment." Abu Dawud; Tirmidhi (Book 43, Hadith 2969), Sahih
10) *WASH HANDS* every time you enter home. The Prophet said: "Cleanliness is half of faith." Muslim (223)
11) *HOME QUARANTINE* is a Prophetic advice. "The plague (contagion) patient who remains in his home with patience and expectation of reward, knowing that nothing will befall him other than Allah's decree will attain the reward or a martyr." Musnad Aḥmad, Sahih also Bukhari (2829) and Muslim (1914)

References

Abdul-Zahira, Qassim. 2020. "Iraq Officials Say IS Targets Intelligence Bureau; 3 Wounded." *AP News*, 28 April.

Alexander, Audrey. 2020. "The Security Threat COVID-19 Poses to the Northern Syria Detention Camps Holding Islamic State Members." *CTC Sentinel* 13: 6.

Al-Hashimi, Husham. 2020. "ISIS in Iraq: From Abandoned Villages to the Cities." Newlines Institute for Strategy and Policy website. Retrieved September 2022 from https://newlinesinstitute.org/isis/isis-in-iraq-from-abandoned-villages-to-the-cities/.

Al-Khateb, Khaled. 2020. "Islamic State Spreading Terror Once Again in Syrian Desert." *Al-Monitor*, April.

Al-Lami, Mina. 2020. "Africa's Sahel Becomes Latest al-Qaeda-IS Battleground." *BBC*, 11 May.

Azani, Eitan, Michael Barak, and Lorena Atiyas-Lvovsky. 2020. "ISIS' Threat Assessment to Israel Threat Assessment in Light of ISIS' Spokesman's Call to Foil the 'Plan of the Century' and Attack Israel." International Institute for Counter-Terrorism website. Retrieved September 2022 from https://www.ict.org.il/images/ISIS%E2%80%99%20Threat%20Assessment%20to%20Israel.pdf.

Barak, Michael. 2020. "ISIS Strengthens in Iraq." International Institute for Counter-Terrorism website. Retrieved May 2022 from https://ict.org.il/isis-strengthens-in-iraq/.

Broches, Emma. 2020. "Southeast Asia's Overlooked Foreign Fighter Problem." *Lawfare* 5 June.

"Call for Violence to Reopen Philippine Mosque Closed by COVID-19 Restrictions." 2020. Retrieved May 2022 from SITE Intelligence Group.

Campbell, John. 2020. "Niger Attack Demonstrates Islamic State in West Africa's Growing Reach." Council on Foreign Relations. Retrieved May 2022 from https://www.cfr.org/blog/niger-attack-demonstrates-islamic-state-west-africas-growing-reach.

"Contending with ISIS in the Time of Coronavirus." 2020. International Crisis Group website. Retrieved May 2022 from https://www.crisisgroup.org/global/contending-isis-time-coronavirus.

Cordesman, Anthony H. 2020. "The Real World Capabilities of ISIS: The Threat Continues." CSIS website. https://www.csis.org/analysis/real-world-capabilities-isis-threat-continues.

"Corona: It Is the Prayer of the People of al-Baghouz, Whom You Burned Alive, It Has Killed You So Reap the Results of Your Actions." 2020. TRAC Terrorism Research and Analysis Consortium website. Retrieved May 2022 from https://www.trackingterrorism.org/chatter/cgi-green-b1rds-unofficial-islamic-state-corona-it-prayer-people-al-baghouz-whom-you-burned-/.

Cruickshank, Paul. 2020. "ISIS Exploiting Coronavirus Security Gaps to Relaunch Insurgency, UN Report Warns." *CNN*, 23 July.

Damora, Brittany. 2020. "COVID-19: Impact on Kidnap for Ransom Activity." *Security Magazine*, 13 April.

"European Union Terrorism Situation and Trend Report 2020." 2019. Europol website. Retrieved May 2022 from https://www.europol.europa.eu/activities-services/main-reports/european-union-terrorism-situation-and-trend-report-te-sat-2020.

Gartenstein-Ross, Daveed, Emelie Chace-Donahue, and Colin P. Clarke. 2020. "The Threat of Jihadist Terrorism in Germany." International Centre for Counter-Terrorism website. Retrieved May 2022 from https://icct.nl/publication/the-threat-of-jihadist-terrorism-in-germany/.

Grierson, Jamie, Dan Sabbagh, Matthew Weaver, Simon Murphy, and Molly Blackall. 2020. "Libyan Held over Reading Multiple Stabbing 'Known to Security Services.'" *The Guardian*, 21 June.

Hanna, Andrew. 2020. "What Islamists Are Doing and Saying on COVID-19 Crisis." Wilson Center website. Retrieved May 2022 from https://www.wilsoncenter.org/article/what-islamists-are-doing-and-saying-covid-19-crisis.

Hoffman, Bruce, and Jacob Ware. 2020. "The Terrorist Threat from the Fractured Far Right." *Lawfare*, 1 November.

"Imam in Hamas TV Friday Sermon a Day before Coronavirus Cases Confirmed in Gaza: 'This Virus Is a Soldier of Allah.'" 2020. Memri website. Retrieved May 2022 from https://www.memri.org/tv/gaza-friday-sermon-palestinian-sheikh-jamil-mutawa-coronavirus-allah-soldier-praise-victims.

"Indonesia." 2020. International Crisis Group website. Retrieved May 2022 from https://www.crisisgroup.org/crISwatch/database?location percent5B percent 5D = 44&date_range = last_6_months&from_month = 01&from_year = 2020&to_month = 01&to_year = 2020.

"Indonesian IS-Aligned Account Urges Supporters Carry Out Attacks during COVID-19 Pandemic." 2020. Retrieved May 2022 from SITE Intelligence Group.

"Interactive Data Table: World Muslim Population by Country." 2019. Pew Research Center website. Retrieved May 2022 from https://www.pewforum.org/chart/interactive-data-table-world-muslim-population-by-country/.

"IS-Aligned Group Mocks 'Disbelieving' Countries over Inability of Scientific Progress to Stop COVID-19." 2020. Retrieved May 2022 from SITE Intelligence Group.

"IS-Aligned Maldivian Channel Urges for Attacks during COVID-19 Crisis." 2020. Retrieved May 2022 from SITE Intelligence Group.

"Islamic World." Nations Online website. Retrieved May 2022 from https://www.nationsonline.org/oneworld/muslim-countries.htm.

Jackson, Ashley. 2020. "For the Taliban, the Pandemic Is a Ladder." *Foreign Policy*, 6 May.

"Jihadist Threat Alert IS-aligned Group Portrays COVID-19 Pandemic as Revenge for Muslims of Baghuz." 2020. Retrieved May 2022 from SITE Intelligence Group.

Johnson, Bridget. 2020. "ISIS Lauds 'Death and Terror' of Coronavirus Outbreak." *Homeland Security Today*, 27 January.

Jones, Seth G., Catrina Doxsee, and Nicholas Harrington. 2020. "The Escalating Terrorism Problem in the United States." CSIS Briefs. Retrieved May 2022 from https://csis-website-prod.s3.amazonaws.com/s3fs-public/publication/200612_Jones_DomesticTerrorism_v6.pdf.

Joscelyn, Thomas. 2020. "How Jihadists Are Reacting to the Coronavirus Pandemic." Foundation for Defense of Democracies website. Retrieved May 2022 from https://www.fdd.org/analysis/2020/04/06/how-jihadists-are-reacting-to-the-coronavirus-pandemic/.

Knights, Michael, and Alex Almeida. 2020. "Remaining and Expanding: The Recovery of Islamic State Operations in Iraq in 2019–2020." *CTC Sentinel* 13: 5.

Kruglanski, Arie W., Rohan Gunaratna, Molly Ellenberg, and Anne Speckhard. 2020. "Terrorism in Time of the Pandemic: Exploiting Mayhem." *Global Security: Health, Science and Policy* 5(1): 121–32.

Levenia, Ultra, and Alban Sciascia. 2020. "How COVID-19 Is Reshaping Terror Threats in Indonesia." *The Diplomat*, May.

Lurie, Devin. 2020. "ISIS in the Philippines: A Cause for Concern." American Security Project website. Retrieved May 2022 from https://www.americansecurityproject.org/isis-in-the-philippines-a-cause-for-concern/.

Mashal, Mujib, and Najim Rahim. 2020. "Taliban Stage a Major Attack, as Violence Intensifies in Northern Afghanistan." *The New York Times*, 13 July.

Meek, James Gordon. 2020. "Terrorist Groups Spin COVID-19 as God's 'Smallest Soldier' Attacking West." *ABC News*, 2 April.

Millward, James, and Dahlia Peterson. 2020. "China's System of Oppression in Xinjiang: How It Developed and How to Curb It." *Brookings*, September.

"Murder and Extremism in the United States in 2019." 2020. ADL Center on Extremism website. Retrieved May 2022 from https://www.adl.org/media/14107/download.

Perkins, Brian M. 2020. "IS-CAP Attack Claims in DRC Increase, but Capabilities Largely Remain the Same." *Terrorism Monitor* 18(14).

"Philippines." 2019. International Crisis Group website. Retrieved May 2022 from https://www.crisisgroup.org/asia/south-east-asia/philippines.

Pikulicka-Wilczewska, Agnieszka. 2020. "The Islamic State Remains Alive in Afghanistan." *The Diplomat*, April.

Rahmah, Unaesah. 2021. "Southeast Asia, Indonesia, Philippines, Malaysia, Myanmar, Thailand, Singapore." *Counter Terrorist Trends and Analyses* 13(1).

"Recent Global Jihadist Updates on the COVID-19 Pandemic April 1–7, 2020." 2020. Retrieved May 2022 from SITE Intelligence Group.

"Recent Jihadist Updates on the COVID-19 Pandemic April 28–May 6, 2020." 2020. Retrieved May 2022 from SITE Intelligence Group.

Rolbieczki, Tomasz, Pieter van Ostaeyen, and Charlie Winter. 2020. "The Islamic State's Strategic Trajectory in Africa: Key Takeaways from Its Attack Claims." *CTC Sentinel* 13(8).

Ross, Rachel. 2018. "What Is Ramadan?" Live Science website. Retrieved May 2022 from https://www.livescience.com/61815-what-is-ramadan.html.

Rubin, Alissa J., Lara Jakes, and Eric Schmitt. 2020. "ISIS Attacks Surge in Iraq Amid Debate on U.S. Troop Levels." *The New York Times*, 10 June.

Rubio, Pablo. 2020. "Egypt a Recurrent Target of Jihadist Terrorism." Atalayar website. Retrieved May 2022 from https://atalayar.com/en/content/egypt-recurrent-target-jihadist-terrorism.

Schmid, Alex P. 2012. "The Revised Academic Consensus Definition of Terrorism." *Perspectives on Terrorism* 6: 2.

"Security Council Press Statement on Terrorist Attack in Afghanistan." 2020. United Nations Security Council.

"Security Situation in Somalia." 2019. ECOI.NET website. Retrieved May 2022 from https://www.ecoi.net/en/countries/somalia/featured-topics/security-situation/.

Seldin, Jeff. 2020. "Pushed to the Brink Again, Islamic State's Afghan Affiliate Claims Deadly Attacks." *VOA News*, 12 May.

"Situation in West Africa, Sahel 'Extremely Volatile' as Terrorists Exploit Ethnic Animosities, Special Representative Warns Security Council." 2020. United Nations Security Council website. Retrieved May 2022 from https://www.un.org/press/en/2020/sc14245.doc.htm.

"Spotlight on Global Jihad March 12–18, 2020." 2020. Retrieved May 2022 from The Meir Amit Intelligence and Terrorism Information Center.

"Spotlight on Global Jihad March 19–25, 2020." 2020. Retrieved May 2022 from The Meir Amit Intelligence and Terrorism Information Center.

"Spotlight on Global Jihad March 26–April 1, 2020." 2020. Retrieved May 2022 from The Meir Amit Intelligence and Terrorism Information Center.

"Spotlight on Global Jihad April 2–6, 2020." 2020. Retrieved May 2022 from The Meir Amit Intelligence and Terrorism Information Center.

"Spotlight on Global Jihad April 7–22, 2020." 2020. Retrieved May 2022 from The Meir Amit Intelligence and Terrorism Information Center.

"Spotlight on Global Jihad April 23–30, 2020." 2020. Retrieved May 2022 from The Meir Amit Intelligence and Terrorism Information Center.

"Spotlight on Global Jihad May 1–6, 2020." 2020. Retrieved May 2022 from The Meir Amit Intelligence and Terrorism Information Center.

"Spotlight on Global Jihad May 7–13, 2020." 2020. Retrieved May 2022 from The Meir Amit Intelligence and Terrorism Information Center.

"Spotlight on Global Jihad May 14–20, 2020." 2020. Retrieved May 2022 from The Meir Amit Intelligence and Terrorism Information Center.

"Spotlight on Global Jihad May 21–26, 2020." 2020. Retrieved May 2022 from The Meir Amit Intelligence and Terrorism Information Center.

"Spotlight on Global Jihad May 27–June 3, 2020." 2020. Retrieved May 2022 from The Meir Amit Intelligence and Terrorism Information Center.
"Spotlight on Global Jihad June 4–10, 2020." 2020. Retrieved May 2022 from The Meir Amit Intelligence and Terrorism Information Center.
"Spotlight on Global Jihad June 11–17, 2020." 2020. Retrieved May 2022 from The Meir Amit Intelligence and Terrorism Information Center.
"Spotlight on Global Jihad June 18–24, 2020." 2020. Retrieved May 2022 from The Meir Amit Intelligence and Terrorism Information Center.
"Spotlight on Global Jihad June 25–July 1, 2020." 2020. Retrieved May 2022 from The Meir Amit Intelligence and Terrorism Information Center.
"Spotlight on Global Jihad July 2–8, 2020." 2020. Retrieved May 2022 from The Meir Amit Intelligence and Terrorism Information Center.
"Spotlight on Global Jihad July 9–15, 2020." 2020. Retrieved May 2022 from The Meir Amit Intelligence and Terrorism Information Center.
"Spotlight on Global Jihad July 16–22, 2020." 2020. Retrieved May 2022 from The Meir Amit Intelligence and Terrorism Information Center.
"Spotlight on Global Jihad July 23–29, 2020." 2020. Retrieved May 2022 from The Meir Amit Intelligence and Terrorism Information Center.
"Spotlight on Global Jihad July 30–August 5, 2020." 2020. Retrieved May 2022 from The Meir Amit Intelligence and Terrorism Information Center.
"Syria Security Situation." 2020. European Asylum Support Office website. Retrieved May 2022 from https://coi.easo.europa.eu/administration/easo/PLib/05_2020_EASO_COI_Report_Syria_Security_situation.pdf.
"The Voice of Hind." 2020. Issue 3.
Umar, Haruna, and Sam Olukoya. 2020. "In Nigeria, an Islamic State-Linked Group Steps Up Attacks." *AP News*, 26 June.
"Virus Fears Spread at Camps for ISIS Families in Syria's North East." International Crisis Group website. Retrieved May 2022 from https://www.crisisgroup.org/middle-east-north-africa/eastern-mediterranean/syria/virus-fears-spread-camps-isis-families-syrias-north-east.
Von Hein, Matthias. 2020. "'Islamic State' Exploiting Coronavirus and Conflict to Rise Again." *DW*, 22 May.
Wang, Amy B. 2018. "A Teen with Former Neo-Nazi Ties Claims His 'Muslim Faith' Led Him to Stab Three, Police Say." *The Washington Post*, 22 March.
"Weekly Report on the Islamic State, April 22–28, 2020." 2020. Retrieved May 2022 from SITE Intelligence Group.
"Weekly Report on the Islamic State, April 29–May 5, 2020." 2020. Retrieved May 2022 from SITE Intelligence Group.
"Weekly Report on the Islamic State, May 6–12, 2020." 2020. Retrieved May 2022 from SITE Intelligence Group.
"Weekly Report on the Islamic State, May 20–26, 2020." 2020. Retrieved May 2022 from SITE Intelligence Group.
"Weekly Report on the Islamic State, May 27–June 2, 2020." 2020. Retrieved May 2022 from SITE Intelligence Group.
"Weekly Report on the Islamic State, June 3–9, 2020." 2020. Retrieved May 2022 from SITE Intelligence Group.

"Weekly Report on the Islamic State, June 17–23, 2020." 2020. Retrieved May 2022 from SITE Intelligence Group.

"Weekly Report on the Islamic State, July 1–7, 2020." 2020. Retrieved May 2022 from SITE Intelligence Group.

"Weekly Report on al-Qaeda Branches and Linked Groups July 16–22, 2020." 2020. Retrieved May 2022 from SITE Intelligence Group.

"Weekly Report on al-Qaeda Branches and Linked Groups, July 23–29, 2020." 2020. Retrieved May 2022 from SITE Intelligence Group.

"Weekly Report on the Islamic State, July 30–August 4, 2020." 2020. Retrieved May 2022 from SITE Intelligence Group.

Weiss, Caleb. 2020. "Islamic State in Somalia Suffers Setbacks Despite Uptick in Claimed Activity." *Long War Journal*, 1 June.

Zenn, Jacob. 2020. "ISIS in Africa: The Caliphate's Next Frontier." Newlines Institute for Strategy and Policy website. Retrieved May 2022 from https://newlinesinstitute.org/isis/isis-in-africa-the-caliphates-next-frontier/.

CHAPTER 3

How Far Right Extremists Exploited the Coronavirus Crisis

Introduction

COVID-19 has offered a unique opportunity for far right entities to capitalize on the pandemic and thereby advance their malicious agenda. Accordingly, lockdown protests provided the extreme right-wing a convenient avenue to recruit new members, amplify its presence, and agitate public unrest. There has been a continued interest in bioterrorism, resulting in threats against ethnic minorities, and at the same time, these threat groups have aimed to exacerbate pressure on healthcare and other critical services. Arson attacks on 5G infrastructure, misinformation campaigns, and circulated conspiracy theories were all part of their strategy to take advantage of the extraordinary crisis and aggravate social instability.

To gain a better understanding of how the associated threat has evolved since the pandemic outbreak, this chapter examines far right operations, incitements, and propaganda activities between 11 March and 31 July 2020 on both the European and the American continent. Our understanding is based on an investigation of extremist right-wing narratives, which provide insights into the very recent operational circumstances and strategies far right threat groups have employed. Proceedings in the Australian and New Zealand-based right-wing extremists' activities are detailed in the concluding section of this chapter.

Far Right Operations

One extreme right-wing operation occurred on both the European and the American continent that had direct links to the pandemic. Timothy R. Wilson, a neo-Nazi from Missouri, was suspected of planning to attack a Missouri hospital and was killed during a shootout with FBI agents on 26 March 2020. Later, on 29 June 2020, German anarchists targeted a vehicle belonging to WISAG, a German service company in

Berlin, claiming that it had assisted government "repression" during the pandemic (SITE Intelligence Group 2020).

Far Right Incitements

From March until July 2020, far right extremists operating on the European continent disseminated twelve posts inciting violence. Meanwhile, those on the American continent incited eighteen pandemic-related violent acts. Investigating the temporal distribution of these incitements, March and April were the most active periods for the European entities, while their American counterparts showed more activity in April and May 2020.

Most of these incidents urged followers to commit armed assault. Accordingly, in March 2020, neo-Nazi posts called for violent acts on cities, critical infrastructure, members of the military force, and black Americans (SITE Intelligence Group 2020). In accordance with a far right belief in the "FEMA Camp" conspiracy theory, threats against FEMA agents were disseminated. The theory, which dates back to the 1980s, postulates that the United States Federal Emergency Management Agency (FEMA) intends to imprison US citizens in concentration camps following a major crisis (SITE Intelligence Group 2020). Simultaneously, neo-Nazi discussions on 4chan—an anonymous imageboard website—and Telegram—an encrypted instant messaging service—encouraged armed resistance in the face of the government pandemic

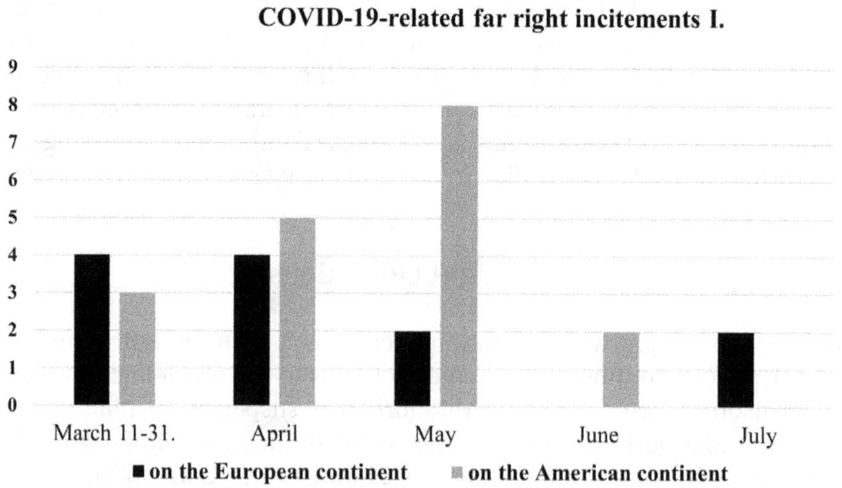

Figure 3.1. COVID-19-related far right incitements I. © Katalin Pethő-Kiss.

crackdown. Meanwhile, white supremacists urged supporters to conduct acts of violence and infrastructural sabotage as an accelerationist response to authorities enforcing coronavirus mitigation and lockdown procedures across the United States. The anarchist group Contra Media issued a statement that called for Argentineans to take up arms and "embrace revolutionary action" because of COVID-19 restrictions on 29 June 2020. Later, in July 2020, a user on Telegram group chat affiliated with the neo-Nazi group "VR" posted messages claiming to have attended recent protests in Belgrade and engaged in a violent confrontation with law enforcement (SITE Intelligence Group 2020).

A slightly lower number of incitements encouraged members either to organize or to participate in lockdown protests. A 28 April 2020 Telegram post was disseminated among alt-right and far right channels promoting a series of "massive anti-lockdown protests across the US on 1 May 2020." Andrew Anglin, a prominent white nationalist, praised armed demonstrators in Michigan's state capitol. In May the Philadelphia chapter of the Proud Boys promoted upcoming quarantine protests in the city. A video was released on 15 May 2020 by the Russian far right organization "Nation and Freedom" Committee (KNS) in which a masked individual discussed the potential for protest actions in Novosibirsk, Russia (SITE Intelligence Group 2020).

Besides the aforementioned, outlets intended to encourage members to prepare for violent acts. In line with this, far right forums urged supporters to organize militias in major US cities, and videos were propagated showing members engaged in various types of training to encourage others to "develop new skills." The Russian white nationalist group Imperial Legion posted a statement on its official VK page on 7 April 2020 urging its members to "[pray, train, and prepare]" for the crisis (SITE Intelligence Group 2020).

Only a minor fraction of incitements called for deliberate infections. On 1 April 2020, neo-Nazi Telegram channels ("NAR" and "SMS") distributed a statement that asserted a "hypothetical 28-year-old lone wolf domestic terrorist" could ship coronavirus-infected products to countries with "high population densities and large but unstable economies" as a biological weapon to "expedite worldwide economic collapse." Drawing on the devastation of the Black Plague, on 11 July 2020 the accelerationist neo-Nazi Telegram channel "SSS," with almost 4,300 subscribers, claimed that the coronavirus would be capable of similar havoc. This communication contained an image detailing the necessary materials and instructions to build a "poison fragmentation grenade," which would be more effective if deployed "in countries with lower hygiene standards, less developed healthcare facilities, and a higher population density." In a call for acts of bioterrorism, a recruitment poster was released on 18 May 2020 by the neo-Nazi "Waldkrieg Division" urging followers to intentionally infect "non-whites" with COVID-19 (SITE Intelligence Group 2020).

Far right communications also offered alternative ways to accelerate public strains. Accordingly, prominent neo-Nazi Telegram channels urged their followers in 5 May 2020 posts to avoid lockdown protests and encouraged alternative ways to "stoke tensions." Simultaneously, an image depicting toxic combinations of household chemicals was distributed by a neo-Nazi Telegram channel suggesting that toxic gases should be released in busy grocery stores. Symptoms resulting from the attack would mimic COVID-19 and send hundreds of people into an already overburdened healthcare system (SITE Intelligence Group 2020).

The overwhelming majority of far right incitements involved targeting public spaces and the general public. Calls for armed assault and anti-lockdown protests all aimed to induce public fear and intensify the general panic.

On the American continent, Michigan's state governor and the Argentinean government were the targets against which extremists articulated incitements. Additionally, biowarfare was planned against Trump

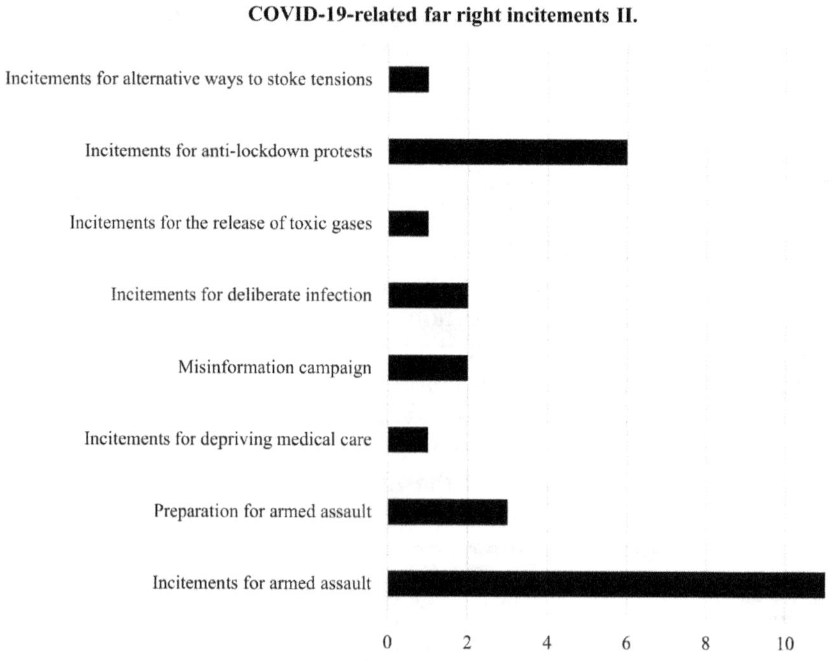

Figure 3.2. COVID-19-related far right incitements II. © Katalin Pethő-Kiss.

rally events in Tulsa, with a Telegram post that called for COVID-positive individuals to "assemble" outside Tulsa's BOK Convention Center. A supposed "parody" poster distributed by "The Fellow Nationalist" neo-Nazi Telegram channel showed an edited image of *Kill Bill* actress Uma Thurman with a far right-styled facemask and illuminated eyes. The text read "KILL BILL GATES" and was followed up with "IN MINECRAFT" (SITE Intelligence Group 2020).

Following the declared COVID-19 national emergency, on 25 March 2020 neo-Nazi Telegram channel "EFC" posted several statements inciting violence against members of the military and law enforcement. In May 2020, far right discussions on 4chan and Telegram channels called for direct action against law enforcement officials (SITE Intelligence Group 2020).

There were also inciteful statements calling for attacks on critical infrastructure. A March post by the neo-Nazi group "Vorherrschaft Divi-

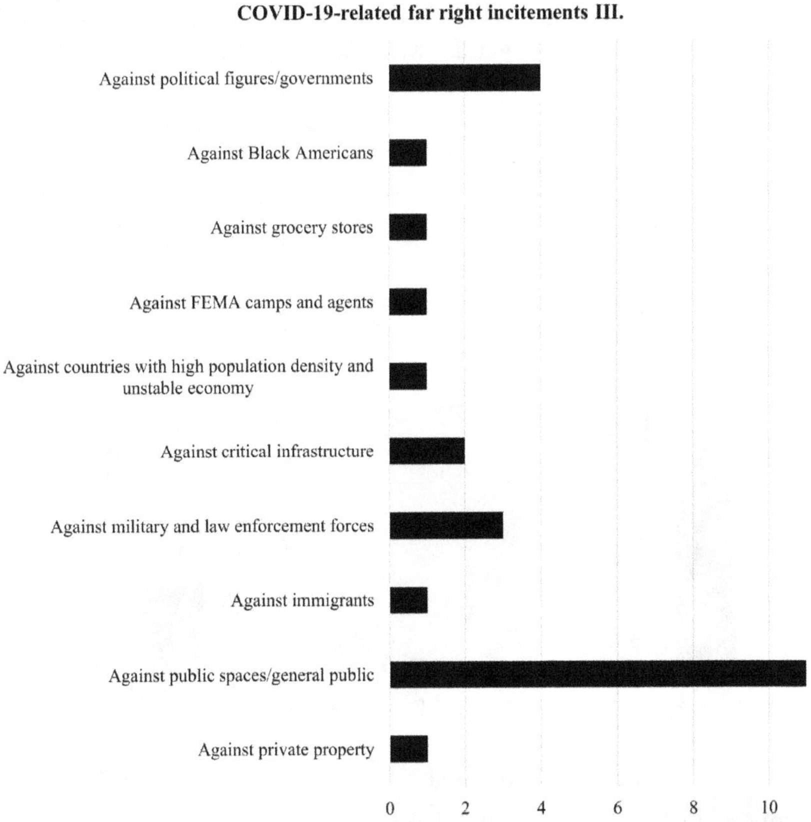

Figure 3.3. COVID-19-related far right incitements III. © Katalin Pethő-Kiss.

sion" (VD) incited followers to attack "transportation structures, power lines, water towers, bridges, railroads, and grocery stores." The prominent neo-Nazi Telegram channel "SSS" encouraged acts of violence and infrastructural sabotage as an accelerationist response to US authorities on 22 May 2020 (SITE Intelligence Group 2020).

In addition, private property, immigrants, countries with a high population density but unstable economy, FEMA camps and agents, grocery stores as well as black Americans were addressed by other far right incitements (SITE Intelligence Group 2020).

Far Right Propaganda Activities

In total, far right entities operating on the American continent disseminated altogether twenty-six posts, while Europeans only eighteen posts. Figure 3.4 indicates that the overwhelming majority of propaganda activities were related to spreading conspiracy theories. Only a very small amount of far right propaganda was explicitly about recruiting new

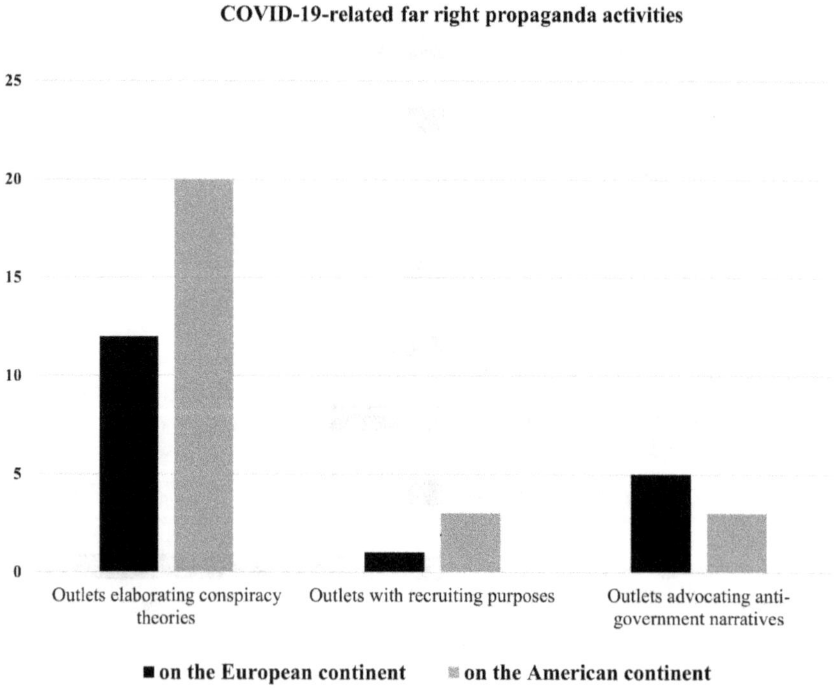

Figure 3.4. COVID-19-related far right propaganda activities.
© Katalin Pethő-Kiss.

members. Interestingly, an insignificant number of outlets advocated straightforward antigovernment narratives.

Communication Outlets Elaborating Conspiracy Theories

After investigating far right accounts, the following main narratives were propagated on the examined forums. Firstly, concerted anti-Chinese propaganda occurred. In March a forum on the 8chan successor site 8kun urged users to accelerate existing Sinophobic slurs. Some posts on the thread insisted that the Chinese deliberately spread the virus to compromise "western" states (SITE Intelligence Group 2020).

Secondly, the coronavirus was claimed first as "an invention of the elites" by neo-Nazi WhatsApp group "NSRD" (National Socialist Regime Germany) in its April 2020 post. Consequently, a user known as SPF stated that global corporate elites used the coronavirus to intentionally induce the current economic crisis to "wipe out [their] competition" and to "purge and consolidate" power (SITE Intelligence Group 2020).

Thirdly, other circulated propaganda blamed capitalism for the emergence of the virus. Prominent German neo-Nazi figure Frank Kraemer advocated in his 7 April 2020 podcast that the current economic crisis was not caused by the pandemic but was rather the result of "the longstanding failures of capitalism and free-market systems." He also asserted that the "globalist elite" was using the virus "to distract populations from the imminent global financial collapse" (SITE Intelligence Group 2020).

In another narrative in May, various far right groups criticized the censorship of Plandemic, a movie that promoted their conspiracy theories. Far right political ideology was also glorified when extreme right-wing Italian Telegram channel "ID" asserted that the pandemic could have been managed better along far right political ideology. It claimed that the present European liberal policy is the source of Italy's economic, political, and social difficulties (SITE Intelligence Group 2020).

The United Nations was targeted by far right propaganda when Mundo Viperino and Miguel Blasco, director of neo-Nazi media group "Aqui la Voz de Europa," argued that the pandemic is the UN's secret agenda aimed at achieving population control by "replacing cultures from the Third World" (SITE Intelligence Group 2020).

In May "Aqui la Voz de Europa" raised conspiracy issues such as the uncertainty over vaccines. On 8 July 2020, a far right "Boogaloo" channel claimed that the military would be deployed to force Americans to take the COVID-19 vaccine, possibly during the fall US election (SITE Intelligence Group 2020).

5G remained a core coronavirus conspiracy topic for actors on the far right. They posit that cell towers are part of a plan by the faceless "elite" to spread COVID-19. An April 2020 post from a prominent neo-Nazi Telegram channel urged people to "shoot down Amazon delivery drones" and "strap ridiculous amounts of explosives to their drones [and fly] them toward 5G towers then detonate them" (SITE Intelligence Group 2020). US neo-Nazi groups were striving to "amplify the fear" of the public and capitalize on "5G hysteria." In April far right Telegram channels celebrated recent attacks against 5G infrastructure as a means of pressuring "foreign occupation governments" to unveil their oppressive pandemic agendas, and they called on followers to "cut down a couple of 5G towers to force the System to make the first move." Neo-Nazi videos were disseminated that documented alleged arson attacks against 5G infrastructure (SITE Intelligence Group 2020).

Antisemitic posts were very common among far right narratives. A post citing the news that a Jewish man was selling a stockpile of medical supplies to doctors at a 700 percent markup claimed the incident as evidence of a broader "anti-white" sentiment within the Jewish community and described Baruch as a "parasite," since his actions were part of a broader effort to "keep [non-Jewish whites] from protecting themselves while his coethnics spread [the illness]." The decades-old, United States-based neo-Nazi group National Socialist Movement (NSM) also targeted Jews with harassment efforts. Antisemitic and other racial narratives were circulated in the Spanish neo-Nazi group Aqui la Voz de Europa's video, released as a reaction to the George Floyd protests in the United States. The video blamed Jews and globalists for what was alleged to be their agenda to destroy European culture with a "virus" worse than COVID-19. Whites in Europe and elsewhere have allegedly been "mentally conditioned to hate themselves, to hate their history, their culture, and their traditions." On 29 April 2020, a message from Neo-Nazi group "ML88" posted to their Telegram channel "F" urged that "the time is now" for the far right to organize and seize power. The message was presented as a caption attached to an antisemitic cartoon (SITE Intelligence Group 2020).

In April the previous "FEMA Camp" conspiracy theory resurfaced among far right Telegram users. Consequently, incitements to violence against FEMA agents were disseminated. In addition, a US-based neo-Nazi group called for a "Psychological Warfare Campaign" during the pandemic. It encouraged the spread of coronavirus conspiracy theories and far right propaganda and symbols. The goal of these initiatives was to “amplify fear” among the public and capitalize on “5G hysteria.” Far right media services also published a seven-part series of posts claiming that the pandemic is a hoax (SITE Intelligence Group 2020).

Right-wing extremist groups in South America were engaged in various doxxing incidents. On 20 May 2020, Anarchists Worldwide released the date and birthplace of Brazilian politician Antonio Fontinele along with his residential addresses and his cell phone number in retaliation for the government’s alleged failures in addressing the COVID-19 pandemic. Anarchists Worldwide issued a second “doxxing action” in June when the personal information of Roberto Jefferson Monteiro Francisco, a Brazilian Labor Party (PTB) politician, was disseminated. Jefferson, who was expelled from Brazil’s Congress in 2005 and banned from being elected to public office for ten years, currently has a strong social media presence and is vocal in his support of President Jair Bolsonaro. In a third act of retaliation for the government’s alleged failures in managing the COVID-19 pandemic, Anarchists Worldwide distributed Almino Monteiro Álvares Affonso’s personal information, calling him “corrupt” and accusing him of acquiring “enormous personal wealth stolen from the Brazilian people.” Consequently, an anarchist blog by NOS released the purported personal information of Nílton de Albuquerque Cerqueira, a General of the Brazilian army. The military executive was doxxed to warn members of the army and police to withdraw their support for Bolsonaro otherwise they will be targeted (SITE Intelligence Group 2020).

Social media accounts in German, Spanish, Russian, and English circulated a conspiracy theory that claimed AstraZeneca had begun producing the COVID-19 vaccine in 2018, more than a year before the pandemic outbreak. The posts concluded: “Their end goal has been to depopulate humans; you are the carbon they want to reduce.” Other conspiracy theorists on social media sites linked the AstraZeneca vaccine to adverse reactions “such as blood clots, including some that required amputations, drawing claims that the vaccines were a tool of depopulation and a bioweapon” (SITE Intelligence Group 2020). After sharing Pfizer’s news that immunity from its COVID-19 vaccine may wane after six months and require a booster, conspiracy theory social media channels encouraged firing squad execution for pharma executives and attacks against vaccine facilities. Social media users expressed anger and skepticism against combination vaccines, claiming that they are more lethal than traditional therapeutics. As a response to the claims of the COVID-19 vaccine’s adverse effects, a user in a Boogaloo group called for the destruction of vaccine centers, stating: “Burn vaccination centers with all faggots inside.” As a response to news of North Carolina's "Doses-to-Doors" COVID-19 vaccination campaign, "far right and QAnon groups threatened to rape, murder, and even deploy biological agents against the health department workers delivering shots: with one writing, 'I'll go "shot" for "shot" with these communist assholes'" (SITE Intelligence Group 2020).

Conspiracy theorists incited violence against Joe Biden and his administration in response to the news that the United States government will mandate COVID-19 vaccines for active-duty servicemen. The United Kingdom government was also threatened with violence over the possible vaccination of children. Social media users claimed, "If you go for the kids with the vaccines, trust me, we're coming for you," with commenters supporting him: "With you, all the way, leave our kids alone." QAnon and conspiracy theorist social media posts threatened violence over what was alleged to be Moderna's vaccine experiment on children in Australia. Condemning pandemic restrictions, a Russian white nationalist organization "called for guerrilla warfare and resistance against the colonial regime." Neo-Nazi and QAnon social media groups spread the European addresses of Pfizer, Moderna, AstraZeneca, and Johnson & Johnson vaccine producers, stating that "these companies must disappear" (SITE Intelligence Group 2020).

Table 3.1. Communication outlets propagating conspiracy theories. © Katalin Pethő-Kiss.

Conspiracy theories	**European far right groups**	**American far right groups**
Anti-Chinese propaganda	Yes	Yes
Coronavirus as an invention of the elites	Yes	Yes
Anti-capitalism	Yes	No
Plandemic, the movie	Yes	Yes
Far right political ideology	Yes	No
Narratives against the United Nations	Yes	No
5G conspiracy theories	Yes	Yes
Uncertainty over vaccines	Yes	Yes
Antisemitic narratives	Yes	Yes
FEMA Camp conspiracy theories	No	Yes
The pandemic is a hoax	Yes	Yes
Doxxing	No	Yes

The introduction of vaccine passports and other restrictive countermeasures announced in 2021 further amplified social media account activities. Online far right conspiracy theorist campaigns called on supporters to boycott companies requiring employees to vaccinate themselves. Social media users heavily defended unvaccinated United Airlines staff, who were to be placed on unpaid leave. An anti-COVID-19 channel organized demonstrations across France against vaccine passports. A white nationalist organization based in the Netherlands and Belgium promoted an Amsterdam protest against the vaccine passport program. Their motto was "Say no to the QR society!" Rallies against COVID-19 passports were also scheduled for Glasgow, Scotland, and England, Italy, and Australia (SITE Intelligence Group 2020).

Outlets with Recruiting Purposes

Lockdown protests were a central pillar in right-wing extremists' strategy, as extremists could gain favor with protestors. White nationalists and neo-Nazis used this kind of demonstration to recruit and amplify their presence amid the COVID-19 crisis. Additionally, the influential neo-fascist hate group Proud Boys engaged in various small protests on its Telegram channel, not just for media attention and recruitment but also to expand their political influence. The Philadelphia branch of the same entity proposed using a large, widely publicized gathering as a means of gaining recognition for their organization. To incite further tensions around such mass demonstrations, extremists disseminated misinformation about protesters being arrested, thereby urging violent acts against law enforcement. After novel epidemic restrictions were introduced in Australia and New Zealand in 2021, conspiracy theorists called for anti-lockdown protests at several local government locations. In England and Spain, COVID-19 conspiracy channels urged European followers to participate in anti-lockdown demonstrations too. Reportedly, a prominent neo-Nazi group based in Switzerland took part in a demonstration against vaccine mandates and handed out its promotional material among those who were present. Following the 20 March 2021 demonstrations against pandemic restrictions, an international anti-lockdown group issued an announcement urging a third round of global protests in forty-five countries on 24 July 2021 (SITE Intelligence Group 2021).

Far right extremists attempted to misuse cyberspace for their purposes in innovative ways. An example is a 6 May 2020 Telegram channel "BMW," which encouraged its followers to "raid" an online seminar hosted by the political organization known as Turning Point USA (SITE Intelligence Group 2020).

Outlets Advocating Antigovernment Narratives

Spanish and French far right communities were the most active in disseminating anti-government content. "Pugilato," a Spanish-language neo-Nazi heavy metal band, released a music video on 8 May 2020 representing antigovernment voices condemning Spain's pandemic lockdown. Democracia Nacional (DN) agreed with the journalists' standpoint condemning the Sánchez government's state of emergency for COVID-19 and warning that the country was moving toward a dictatorship. A released DN poster accused the government of being the real virus. In an 11 May 2020 blogpost, French neo-Nazi Blanche Europe (BE) claimed that authorities have been using the COVID-19 crisis as means of controlling the population. Previously, in April, the same extremist group accused officials of taking advantage of the pandemic situation to enforce "repressive" measures against the public. French white nationalist blog Jeune Nation shared an article from the far right publication Militant, adding that the pandemic had been used as a tool to control the public. The paper suggested that official information channels were deliberately overplaying the effects of the disease to justify restrictive social measures (Ariza 2020). Jeune Nation also shared information about a rally being organized by Les Nationalistes, a French far right group, on 22 May 2020. The event called for the reopening of religious spaces and lifting of the restrictive measures put in place during the quarantine (SITE Intelligence Group 2020).

Far Right Activities in Australia and New Zealand

Right-wing extremist movements in Australia and New Zealand had a concerted focus on anti-Chinese and anti-Asian narratives. In a collaboration between the association of Being Asian Australian and the Asian Australian Alliance, a tool was created to facilitate the reporting of racist incidents as a result of the pandemic (Baker 2020). Chinese Australians were reported to have experienced an increase in hostility, both online and in person. Social media posts, racists interactions, and bullying incidents at schools exacerbated the fear of Chinese people in Australia. Propaganda was disseminated by the neo-Nazi Telegram channel "BTL" that included photos of banners blaming Chinese immigrants for the spread of the coronavirus. According to Christina Ariza at the Tony Blair Institute, there was a huge spike in COVID-19-related anti-Chinese and anti-Asian racism in Australia. Importantly, it is unfortunate that confirming the far right groups behind these activities is still particularly challenging (SITE Intelligence Group 2020).

Similar to United States-based far right extremists, fellow Australian radicals also exploited Black Lives Matter protests. These demonstrations offered unique opportunities for white supremacists to mobilize themselves and misuse these events for their recruiting purposes. In both the US and Australia, posts on Telegram discussed extremists' attendance at these rallies (SITE Intelligence Group 2020).

Regarding far right activities in New Zealand, on 21 March 2020, a user commented in support of a neo-Nazi Vorherrschaft Division (VD) statement that incited followers to target critical infrastructure. One of the most prominent New Zealand-based far right groups is Action Zealandia. This white nationalist group was established shortly after Brenton Tarrant's Christchurch attack in March 2019. Its members adhere to a Pan-European Identitarian ideology that has hostile views of Western governments, media corporations, immigrants, people of color, and religious minorities. A week before the anniversary of Tarrant's Christchurch attack, neo-Nazi Telegram channel "BTL" shared a selfie taken by a masked individual outside Al Noor mosque in Christchurch accompanied by a threat to repeat the 2019 shooting attack that killed fifty-one people and injured at least forty. The attack was foiled and the individual, a member of Action Zealandia (AZ), arrested. During June and July, AZ activists hung banners with slogans articulating "White Lives Matter" at frequently visited public spaces. A video that was posted about these activities concluded with the message "Join Us" and encouraged those who intended to join to provide donations by visiting the contact page of the group (SITE Intelligence Group 2020).

Conclusion

Radical right-wing extremists mobilized themselves in a timely manner in response to the COVID-19 pandemic. Accordingly, this chapter has examined far right operations, incitements, and propaganda activities between 11 March and 31 July 2020 to better understand how these radical groups capitalized on the crisis situation. Europe-, Americas-, Australia-, and New Zealand-based far right groups' operational activities and narratives have been the subject of our analysis.

References

"Anarchists Call for Action against Argentinian Government for COVID-19 Measures." 2020. Retrieved May 2022 from SITE Intelligence Group.

"Anti-COVID-19 Demonstration Channel Announces September 18 Vaccine Passport Protests across France." 2020. Retrieved May 2022 from SITE Intelligence Group.

Ariza, Cristina. 2020. "From the Fringes to the Forefront: How Far Right Movements across the Globe Have Reacted to Covid-19." Tony Blair Institute for Global Change website. Retrieved May 2022 from https://institute.global/policy/fringes-forefront-how-far-right-movements-across-globe-have-reacted-covid-19.

"AstraZeneca COVID-19 Vaccine Allegedly Produced in 2018 Purported by Conspiracy Theorists." 2020. Retrieved May 2022 from SITE Intelligence Group.

"Australian Conspiracy Group Announces October 18, 2021 Strike Against COVID-19 Vaccinations and Vaccine Passports." 2020. Retrieved May 2022 from SITE Intelligence Group.

"Australian White Nationalists Target Immigrants with Propaganda Referencing Coronavirus." 2020. Retrieved May 2022 from SITE Intelligence Group.

Baker, Nick. 2020. "A New Tool Has Been Launched to Report Anti-Asian Racism in Australia during the COVID-19 Outbreak." *SBS News*, 3 April.

"Biden, US Government Threatened Following Alleged Forced Vaccinations for Military." 2020. Retrieved May 2022 from SITE Intelligence Group.

"'Bioweapon 100 percent': AstraZeneca COVID-19 Vaccine Alleged to Cause Clots, Amputations; Conspiracy Theorists React." 2020. Retrieved May 2022 from SITE Intelligence Group.

"Bombings, Firing Squads Incited Following Pfizer Vaccine Immunity Announcement." 2020. Retrieved May 2022 from SITE Intelligence Group.

"Brazilian Anarchist Group Doxxes Third Politician over COVID-19 Government Failures." 2020. Retrieved May 2022 from SITE Intelligence Group.

"Brazilian Anarchists Dox Army General over Government COVID-19 Failures." 2020. Retrieved May 2022 from SITE Intelligence Group.

"Brazilian Politician Doxxed by Anarchist Group Vowing Retaliation for Government's COVID-19 Response." 2020. Retrieved May 2022 from SITE Intelligence Group.

"'Burn Vaccination Centers' Incited in Boogaloo Discussion on Vaccine Side Effects." 2020. Retrieved May 2022 from SITE Intelligence Group.

"Capitalizing on COVID-19 Crisis, Neo-Nazi User Incites Attacks on Critical Infrastructure." 2020. Retrieved May 2022 from SITE Intelligence Group.

"Claiming Military Will Force COVID-19 Vaccinations, 'Boogaloo' Channel Urges Networking and Preparations." 2020. Retrieved May 2022 from SITE Intelligence Group.

"Conspiracy Groups Threaten Violence over Alleged Moderna Vaccine 'Experiment' on Children in Australia." 2020. Retrieved May 2022 from SITE Intelligence Group.

"Conspiracy Theorist Issues Video Calling for Anti-lockdown Protests at Local Governments across Australia, New Zealand." 2020. Retrieved May 2022 from SITE Intelligence Group.

"COVID-19 Conspiracy Channel Announces September 25 Vaccine Passport Protests across Italy." 2020. Retrieved May 2022 from SITE Intelligence Group.

"COVID-19 Conspiracy Channels Announce September 19, 25 Anti-Lockdown Protests in Essex, Newcastle, England." 2020. Retrieved May 2022 from SITE Intelligence Group.

"'Destroy Big Pharma': Conspiracists Claim Combination Vaccines More Lethal than Traditional Therapeutics." 2020. Retrieved May 2022 from SITE Intelligence Group.

"Far Right Chat Discusses Plans to 'Trash' Protest, Organize with White Men 'Willing to Shed Blood' in US and Australia." 2020. Retrieved May 2022 from SITE Intelligence Group.

"Far Right Forum Discusses Organizing Militias in New York City, Other Major U.S. Cities amidst Coronavirus Shutdowns." 2020. Retrieved May 2022 from SITE Intelligence Group.

"Far Right Group Accuses Spanish Government of Using COVID-19 to Establish a Dictatorship." 2020. Retrieved May 2022 from SITE Intelligence Group.

"Far Right Italian Telegram Channel Releases Statement on COVID-19, Advocates for Proliferation of Identitarian Politics." 2020. Retrieved May 2022 from SITE Intelligence Group.

"Far Right, QAnon Pledge Killing Healthcare Workers Conducting Door-to-Door Vaccination Campaign." 2020. Retrieved May 2022 from SITE Intelligence Group.

"Forum Calls for Far Right Community to Push Coronavirus-Inspired Sinophobic Propaganda Campaign." 2020. Retrieved May 2022 from SITE Intelligence Group.

"French Neo-Nazi Blog Accuses Authorities of Using COVID-19 as Population Control." 2020. Retrieved May 2022 from SITE Intelligence Group.

"French White Nationalist Blog Rebukes Government Response to COVID-19, Espouses Conspiracy Theories." 2020. Retrieved May 2022 from SITE Intelligence Group.

"German Company Targeted in Anarchist Arson Attack for COVID-19 'Repression.'" 2020. Retrieved May 2022 from SITE Intelligence Group.

"'Global Massacre': Spanish Far Right Video Claims COVID-19 Accelerating 'UN Agenda 2030' Conspiracy." 2020. Retrieved May 2022 from SITE Intelligence Group.

"In Response to COVID-19 Crisis, French Neo-Nazi Blog Promotes Violence against Immigrants and Minorities." 2020. Retrieved May 2022 from SITE Intelligence Group.

"International Protests against COVID-19 Restrictions in 45 Countries Announced for July 24, 2021." 2021. Retrieved May 2022 from SITE Intelligence Group.

"Member of Neo-Nazi Group Discusses Participation in Serbia's Protests against COVID-19 Lockdown and Government." 2020. Retrieved May 2022 from SITE Intelligence Group.

"Movie-Styled Neo-Nazi Poster Calls to 'Kill' Leading Figure in COVID-19 Fight." 2020. Retrieved May 2022 from SITE Intelligence Group.

"Neo-Nazi Channel Promotes Use of COVID-19 as Biological Weapon against Vulnerable Nations." 2020. Retrieved May 2022 from SITE Intelligence Group.

"Neo-Nazi Chat Users Call Corona Virus 'Invention of the Elites' Target German Chancellor." 2020. Retrieved May 2022 from SITE Intelligence Group.

"Neo-Nazi Group Encourages Combat Preparation during COVID-19 Crisis, Releases Training Video." 2020. Retrieved May 2022 from SITE Intelligence Group.

"Neo-Nazi, QAnon Groups Spread Addresses of Pfizer, Moderna, AstraZeneca, Johnson & Johnson." 2020. Retrieved May 2022 from SITE Intelligence Group.

"Neo-Nazi Telegram Channel Threatens Another Attack on Christchurch Mosque." 2020. Retrieved May 2022 from SITE Intelligence Group.

"Neo-Nazi User Promoted Using COVID-19 for Acts of Bioterrorism." 2020. Retrieved May 2022 from SITE Intelligence Group.

"Neo-Nazis Circulate Advertisement Calling for COVID Patients to Attend Trump Rally." 2020. Retrieved May 2022 from SITE Intelligence Group.

"Neo-Nazis Encouraged to Incite Panic during Coronavirus Pandemic." 2020. Retrieved May 2022 from SITE Intelligence Group.

"New Zealand-Based White Nationalist Group Publishes Activism Report." 2020. Retrieved May 2022 from SITE Intelligence Group.

"Recent Far Right Updates on the COVID-19 Pandemic March 25–April 1, 2020." 2020. Retrieved May 2022 from SITE Intelligence Group.

"Recent Far Right Updates on the COVID-19 Pandemic April 2–7, 2020." 2020. Retrieved May 2022 from SITE Intelligence Group.

"Recent Far Right Updates on the COVID-19 Pandemic April 8–15 2020." 2020. Retrieved May 2022 from SITE Intelligence Group.

"Recent Far Right Updates on the COVID-19 Pandemic April 22–28, 2020." 2020. Retrieved May 2022 from SITE Intelligence Group.

"Recent Far Right Updates on the COVID-19 Pandemic April 29–May 5, 2020." 2020. Retrieved May 2022 from SITE Intelligence Group.

"Recent Far Right Updates on the COVID-19 Pandemic May 6–12, 2020." 2020. Retrieved May 2022 from SITE Intelligence Group.

"Recent Far Right Updates on the COVID-19 Pandemic May 13–26, 2020." 2020. Retrieved May 2022 from SITE Intelligence Group.

"Russian Far Right Organization Shares Video Assessing Prospects of Protest Actions during COVID-19 Crisis." 2020. Retrieved May 2022 from SITE Intelligence Group.

"Russian White Nationalist Group Responds to COVID-19 'Armageddon', Encourages 'Training and Preparation.'" 2020. Retrieved May 2022 from SITE Intelligence Group.

"'Say No to the QR Society': Dutch White Nationalist Group Promotes October 3 Amsterdam Protest against Vaccine Passport Program." 2020. Retrieved May 2022 from SITE Intelligence Group.

"Second Brazilian Politician Doxxed by Anarchist Group for Government Failure to Respond to COVID-19 Demands." 2020. Retrieved May 2022 from SITE Intelligence Group.

"Spanish Neo-Nazi Video Declares US and European Protests a Symptom of 'Virus' Worse than COVID-19." 2020. Retrieved May 2022 from SITE Intelligence Group.

"'Sue Them All': United States Far Right Conspiracy Theorists Curate List, Call for Boycott against Companies Requiring COVID-19 Vaccine." 2020. Retrieved May 2022 from SITE Intelligence Group.

"Swiss White Nationalist Group Attends, Capitalizes on Anti-Vaccination Protest for Recruitment Purposes." 2020. Retrieved May 2022 from SITE Intelligence Group.
"UK Far Right Conspiracy Theory Groups Announce Additional Rallies for September 25." 2020. Retrieved May 2022 from SITE Intelligence Group.
"United Airlines Threatened with Boycotts, Lawsuits, Execution Following Announcement of Unpaid Leave for Unvaccinated Employees." 2020. Retrieved May 2022 from SITE Intelligence Group.
"'We Are Being Killed': Russian White Nationalist Organization Calls for Action, War against COVID-19 Measures." 2020. Retrieved May 2022 from SITE Intelligence Group.
"'We're Coming for You': UK Government Threatened over Possible Vaccination of Children." 2020. Retrieved May 2022 from SITE Intelligence Group.

CHAPTER 4

Beyond the Radical Islamist and Right-Wing Threat

Introduction

Violent extremist groups exploit times of uncertainty to advance their agendas and inevitably have been seeking to take advantage of the disruption caused by COVID-19 (EU Radicalisation Awareness Network 2020). Extremists have integrated coronavirus into their propaganda (UN CTED 2020), and the pandemic has been used to bolster narratives across all extremist ideologies. Religious extremists, radical left-wing groups, and white supremacists have been determined to raise tensions within society to facilitate the failure of existing political systems and realize their nefarious objectives (ISD Global 2020). These terrorist groups all strive to fit the pandemic situation into their ideological context regardless of whether their commentaries are consistent or logical (Burchill 2020).

Narratives Circulated among Extremists beyond Radical Islamists and Far Right Entities

Antigovernmental narratives have been at the forefront of extremist movements since the pandemic outbreak. Alarming surges in extremism occurred in France, Italy, and Spain, where misinformation campaigns on social media encompassed conspiracy theories and pseudoscience (Lichfield 2020). The relevance of radical Islamists and white supremacists may have been subsiding, but the economic consequences of the coronavirus crisis offered a unique opportunity for these entities to revive (The Soufan Center 2020). Left-wing activists pursue an economic reading of the crisis (Bröning 2020) and contend that the worsening post-pandemic economic situation will deepen economic disparities in society. In line with this, citizen anger emerging from these inequalities may push people to get their voices heard by engaging in violent acts

(The Soufan Center 2020). Interestingly, left-wing participants of a 2020 study claimed a decrease in patriotism and a "more positive attitude toward immigration and welfare policies" (Rigoli 2020), while right-wing supporters reported higher patriotism and a more negative attitude toward immigration and welfare policies. Left-wing agendas may derive strength from state-centric national actions in managing the pandemic crisis. At the same time, the economic consequences of COVID-19 have led to a revival of conflict over redistribution, which may be bolstering far left narratives (Bröning 2020). While the far right in the United States accuses migrants and refugees of bringing in the virus (Kildiş 2020), the far left blames the healthcare system and calls on government to compensate minority groups for the economic inequality that makes them more at risk of the serious health consequences of infection (Bowden 2020; Gaffney 2020). Extreme left activists also protested on the streets. In Paris, they demonstrated to demand better working conditions for healthcare workers (BBC, 16 June 2020), and Antifa's far left supporters participated in antiracism protests after the death of George Floyd (Sardarizadeh and Wendling 2020).

The global pandemic crisis unequivocally shed light on climate change and associated environmental deterioration. Violent extremist groups have exploited the symptoms of climate change as an effective argument to attract new supporters (Dene 2020). Witnessing the disruption COVID-19 has caused, climate change and its consequences can be deemed to be that powerful as well. The destabilizing effect of both crises inherently paves the way for extremist efforts to endeavor to take advantage of the catastrophe these phenomena may end up creating (Sinan Siyech 2020). Environmental refugees who have already migrated from natural disasters may be the subject of future extremist hatred. In line with this, the threat of ecoterrorism will likely push extremists to exploit the crisis for their recruiting purposes (The Soufan Center 2020). A noteworthy example was Islamic State's incitements that called on supporters to engage in bushfire terrorism in Australia at the beginning of 2020 (Zimmerman 2020). Leveraging a natural phenomenon and creating a well-timed manmade catastrophe out of it would be highly beneficial for terrorists and would have serious consequences for society. Terrorists will capitalize on future environmental catastrophes; therefore, the associated national security threat should be acknowledged and preparedness should be enhanced (Dene 2020). We need to draw lessons from managing the COVID-19 pandemic, which as a global problem like climate change demands collective action. Effective communication of scientific standpoints has been given the utmost significance during challenging pandemic times. The correction of false information and the trust in expert opinion is also critically important with regard to climate change (Bellamy 2020). This implies the need for a multiagency coordination and disaster response together with a proactive approach to future natural or manmade disasters (Tin, Hertelendy, and Ciottone 2020).

At the same time, supporters of ecoterrorism ideology blame over-population, immigration, and over-industrialization for climate change (Siegel 2021). Followers think that the mass murder of refugees in Western countries could remedy environmental damage (Kamel, Lamoureux, and Makuch 2020). They cite scientific arguments for finite planetary boundaries and claim a race-based natural aristocracy for white Europeans (Allison 2020). Their social media rhetoric uses nature-themed photos, logos, and emojis, which look harmless at first sight (Owen 2019). Their narratives depicting COVID-19 as the "Earth's vaccine" have gone viral since the outbreak (Newton 2020). On the news website Common Dreams, the pandemic has been perceived as "nature's response to human transgression" (Klare 2020). *The Guardian* cited the UN's environment Chief, Inger Anderson, as asserting that the virus is "nature sending us a message" (Carrington 2020). An article in *Psychology Today* referred to coronavirus as "a gift" and mother nature as "turning it up a notch" after the failure of humans to listen to earth's other warnings (Goldman-Wetzler 2020). Earlier in the year, an ecoterrorist group shared on its Telegram channel a guidebook titled "Ecodefense: A Field Guide to Monkeywrenching," detailing techniques for damaging property, subverting industrial development, and sabotaging critical infrastructure. In July 2020, an ecoterrorist channel on a prominent online platform encouraged its followers to obtain weapons and capitalize upon the political unrest in the United States (SITE Intelligence Group 2020). Articles titled "Sopa de Wuhan" (Wuhan Soup) suggested racist allegations that "unnatural" eating may be a catalyst for COVID-19 (Fraser 2020). The Telegram account of "Eco-Fascist Central" also refortified traditional antisemitic and Islamophobic narratives with fallacious theories related to the pandemic. The group advocated spreading the virus in countries "with large populations or high levels of pollution" (UNICRI 2020). Therefore, it is of great importance to identify those malevolent interests that aim to support violent measures as "necessary, natural or inevitable" (Anson 2020) to heal the environment. Well-trusted climate justice activists should be provided with platforms to condemn these fallacies (Almonte 2021). At the same time, economic difficulties will force governments to reallocate resources, thereby potentially decreasing amounts devoted to green programs. This disillusionment may add further impetus for eco-extremist violence (Pauwels 2020). In the end, allow us to remind our readers that Patrick Crusius the El Paso murderer, Brenton Tarrant the Christchurch shooter, and Anders Breivik the perpetrator of the 2011 Norway terrorist attack all shared ecoterrorist views in their manifestos (Darby 2019).

Another worrisome, entwined link can be identified between far right groups and green nationalist activists. Jacob Chansley, known as the "QAnon Shaman," was arrested in the Capitol riot on January 6. As one of the most visible participants in the riot, he "engages in energy healing, psychedelic ceremonies, requested organic food while in detention and is against chemical pollution of the environment" (NHPR, 22 January 2021). Far right movements can undoubtedly attract new supporters by adopting these environmental elements in their populist narratives. Right-wing environmentalist ideas can be tracked, for instance, in Marine Le Pen's "patriotic ecology" concept (Patin 2021).

It was suggested that once the pandemic is perceived as an impetus for increased interest in automation and the application of robotics, ideologies that plant aversion toward technology in some people's minds would be revived (Romei 2020). For such individuals, instead of advocating the benefits of technological advances such as artificial intelligence and machine learning, they regard these novelties as a threat to job opportunities (The Soufan Center 2020). Previous attacks against 5G towers (Brodkin 2020) suggest that technological advances can provide fertile ground for violent incitements.

Conclusion

In sum, we can speak about an elevated level of intensity with regard to the activities of extremist groups other than those that are radical Islamist and right-wing since the pandemic outbreak. Nevertheless, experts agree that the threat of jihadists or white supremacists and their acts of terrorism in the near future is considerably higher than that of left-wing or ecoterrorist actors (The Soufan Center 2020).

References

Allison, Marcia. 2020. "'So Long, and Thanks for All the Fish!': Urban Dolphins as Ecofascist Fake News during COVID-19." Intellect website. Retrieved May 2022 from https://www.intellectbooks.com/so-long-and-thanks-for-all-the-fish-urban-dolphins-as-ecofascist-fake-news-during-covid-19.

Almonte, Samara. 2021. "COVID-19 Is Exposing the Green Side of Fascism." *Platform Magazine*.

Anson, April. 2020. "No One Is a Virus: On American Ecofascism." *Environmental History Now*, 21 October.

Bellamy, Jackson. 2020. "Lessons Learned from COVID-19: Insights for Climate Change Mitigation." North American and Arctic Defence and Security Network website. Retrieved May 2022 from https://www.naadsn.ca/wp-content/uploads/2020/12/20-dec-Bellamy-Lessons-Learned-From-COVID-19-that-can-be-Applied-to-Climate-Change.pdf.

Bowden, Ebony. 2020. "AOC Wants Coronavirus 'Reparations' for Minority Communities." *New York Post*, 3 April.

Brodkin, Jon. 2020. "Cell-Tower Attacks by Idiots who Claim 5G Spreads COVID-19 Reportedly Hit US." Ars Technica website. Retrieved May 2022 from https://arstechnica.com/tech-policy/2020/05/prepare-for-cell-tower-attacks-by-5g-covid-19-conspiracy-theorists-us-warns/.

Bröning, Michael. 2020. "A Revival of the Left in the Age of Coronavirus?" *Berlin Policy Journal*, 16 July.

Burchill, Richard. 2020. "Extremism in the Time of COVID-19." Bussola Institute website. Retrieved May 2022 from https://papers.ssrn.com/sol3/papers.cfm?abstract_id=3693293.

Carrington, Damian. 2020. "Coronavirus: 'Nature Is Sending Us a Message', Says UN Environment Chief." *The Guardian*, 25 March.

"COVID-19 Disinformation Briefing No. 1." 2020. ISD Global website. Retrieved May 2022 from https://www.isdglobal.org/isd-publications/covid-19-disinformation-briefing-no-1/.

Darby, Luke. 2019. "What Is Eco-Fascism, the Ideology behind Attacks in El Paso and Christchurch?" GQ website. Retrieved May 2022 from www.gq.com/story/what-is-eco-fascism.

Dene, Margaret. 2020. "Rising Tides of Terrorism." Foreign Policy Research Institute website. Retrieved May 2022 from https://www.fpri.org/article/2020/07/rising-tides-of-terrorism/.

"Eco-fascist Group Shares Infrastructural and Environmental Sabotage Guidebook." 2020. Retrieved May 2022 from SITE Intelligence Group.

"Eco-fascists Tell Supporters to Arm Themselves." 2020. Retrieved May 2022 from SITE Intelligence Group.

Fraser, Jay. 2020. "Eco-fascism: The Rhetoric of the Virus." Organize website. Retrieved September 2022 from https://organisemagazine.org.uk/2020/04/24/eco-fascism-the-rhetoric-of-the-virus-theory-and-analysis/.

Gaffney, Adam. 2020. "America's Extreme Neoliberal Healthcare System Is Putting the Country at Risk." *The Guardian*, 21 March.

Goldman-Wetzler, Jennifer. 2020. "The Gifts of the Coronavirus." *Psychology Today*, 12 March.

"Intelbrief: The Coronavirus Will Increase Extremism across the Ideological Spectrum." 2020. The Soufan Center website. Retrieved May 2022 from https://thesoufancenter.org/intelbrief-the-coronavirus-will-increase-extremism-across-the-ideological-spectrum/.

Kamel, Zachary, Mack Lamoureux, and Ben Makuch. 2020. "'Eco-fascist' Arm of Neo-Nazi Terror Group, The Base, Linked to Swedish Arson." *Vice*, 29 January.

Kildiş, Hüseyin Pusat. 2020. "Horseshoe Theory and Covid-19." *E-International Relations*, 23 July.

Klare, Michael T. 2020. "Is the Covid-19 Pandemic Mother Nature's Response to Human Transgression?" *Common Dreams*, 2 April.

Lichfield, John. 2020. "The Next Epidemic: Resurgent Populism." *Politico*, 6 April.

Newton, Deja. 2020. "The Dark Side of Environmentalism: Ecofascism and COVID-19." Office of Sustainability website. Retrieved May 2022 from https://usfblogs.usfca.edu/sustainability/2020/04/15/the-dark-side-of-environmentalism-ecofascism-and-covid-19/.

Owen, Tess. 2019. "Eco-fascism: The Racist Theory that Inspired the El Paso and Christchurch Shooters." *Vice*, 6 August.

Patin, Katia. 2021. "The Rise of Eco-fascism." Coda website. Retrieved May 2022 from https://www.codastory.com/waronscience/the-rise-of-eco-fascism/.

Pauwels, Annelies. 2020. "How Europe's Terrorists Take Advantage of the Pandemic." EU Observer. Retrieved May 2022 from https://euobserver.com/opinion/148173.

Rigoli, Francesco. 2020. "Opinions about Immigration, Patriotism, and Welfare Policies during the Coronavirus Emergency: The Role of Political Orientation and Anxiety." *The Social Science Journal*, 11 September.

Romei, Valentina. 2020. "Pandemic Boosts Automation and Robotics." *Financial Times*, 19 October.

Sardarizadeh, Shayan, and Mike Wendling. 2020. "George Floyd Protests: Who Are Boogaloo Bois, Antifa and Proud Boys?" *BBC*, 17 June.

Siegel, Sarah. 2021. "Beware of Ecofascism: COVID-19 Will Not Cure Our Environmental Issues." The Daily Clog website. Retrieved May 2022 from https://www.dailycal.org/2021/04/08/beware-of-ecofascism-covid-19-will-not-cure-our-environmental-issues/.

Sinan Siyech, Mohammed. 2020. "Learning from Covid-19: Preparing for the Impact of Climate Change on Conflict and Terrorism." Observer Research Foundation website. Retrieved May 2022 from https://www.orfonline.org/expert-speak/learning-covid19-preparing-impact-climate-change-conflict-terrorism/.

"Stop the Virus of Disinformation: The Risk of Malicious Use of Social Media during COVID-19 and the Technology Options to Fight It." 2020. UNICRI website. Retrieved September 2022 from https://unicri.it/sites/default/files/2020-11/SM%20misuse.pdf.

"The Impact of the COVID-19 Pandemic on Terrorism, Counter-terrorism and Countering Violent Extremism." 2020. United Nations Security Council Counter-Terrorism Committee Executive Directorate website. Retrieved May 2022 from https://www.un.org/securitycouncil/ctc/news/impact-covid-19-pandemic-terrorism-counter-terrorism-and-countering-violent-extremism-update.

Tin, Derrick, Alexander Hertelendy, and Gregory R. Ciottone. 2020. "What We Learned from the 2019–2020 Australian Bushfire Disaster: Making Counter-terrorism Medicine: A Strategic Preparedness Priority." *American Journal of Emergency Medicine* 46: 742–43.

"Violent Right-Wing Extremism in Focus." 2020. EU Radicalisation Awareness Network website. Retrieved May 2022 from https://ec.europa.eu/home-affairs/sites/homeaffairs/files/what-we-do/networks/radicalisation_awareness_network/docs/ran_brochure_violent_right_wing_extremism_in_focus_en.pdf.

Zimmerman, Augusto. 2020. "Jihad by Fire?" *Spectator Australia*, 29 January.

CHAPTER 5

Novel Terrorist Tactics and Targets

Introduction

The pandemic has disrupted economies and public healthcare systems and has obviously introduced new factors into violent extremists' operational circumstances. Both radical Islamists (Islamic State and al-Qaeda) and the far right have sought to exploit times of uncertainty as well as the social isolation of people facing the crisis, using it as an opportunity to expand their activity by spreading conspiracy theories, calling for attacks, and deliberately infecting others. Extremists have integrated coronavirus into their propaganda, and the pandemic has been used to bolster narratives across all ideologies. Interestingly, right-wing groups have discussed weaponizing the COVID-19 virus more often compared to their radical Islamist counterparts.

After a careful assessment of changes both in the radical Islamist and the far right terrorist threat landscape, this chapter aims to elaborate on how COVID-19 has changed extremists' operational tactics and targets.

Observations with Regard to the Radical Islamist Threat

The pandemic's impact on jihadist terrorism has been highly complex and multifaceted. It has varied also in the short, medium and long term. It may yet be too early to identify what effects the coronavirus will have on violent extremism in the long run. Nevertheless, there is a considerable amount of information suggesting that violent nonstate actors have made operational changes since the pandemic outbreak. Research in the previous chapters was based upon a quantitative assessment of recent radical Islamist-inspired terrorist incidents to provide a snapshot view of new trends. These include, first, the decrease in the number of radical Islamist terrorist attacks both in Europe and in Southeast Asia, which indicates that restrictive epidemiological measures caused undue difficulties for jihadist endeavors. Their operational circumstances had to be changed because of factors such as less crowded places, an elevated authority presence, and the unreliability of their supply chains amidst lockdowns. These factors all may have contributed to the challenge of mounting attacks. It is, however, particularly difficult to identify only one factor that explicitly hindered or delayed radical Islamist terrorist groups' operations in nonconflict zones. Still, there has not yet been a significant decrease in the number of completed terrorist attacks. Authorities therefore cannot disregard the associated threat but should rather devote enough resources for countermeasures even during a pandemic crisis. The situation is different in conflict zones, where the outbreak brought solely advantageous circumstances for jihadist fighters. On the battlefields, because of the risk of contagion, international troops were withdrawn. Local military forces struggled to counter terrorist operations without their support, thus it is important to make sure international cooperation continues uninterrupted in future crisis situations. With this in mind, training and technological capabilities should be reconceptualized in line with applicable epidemiological restrictions.

Second, as the analyses revealed, in conflict zones, military personnel and facilities have become the most prominent radical Islamist targets since the pandemic outbreak. Not only is there a heightened military presence but the army's symbolic value has also been elevated since the pandemic outbreak. Accordingly, Islamic State operatives in Syria, Iraq, Afghanistan, and Africa continued to strike military compounds and personnel together with police checkpoints and their officers, while the number of attacks on private citizens and businesses markedly decreased. Lockdowns eliminated crowds of civilian soft targets; therefore, attacking citizens may have been more difficult for jihadist fighters. These observed changes in radical Islamist targets should urge authorities to strategically reorganize their counter-terrorism operations in accordance with regular threat assessments. Another noteworthy example here is Mozambique, where a significant change in modus operandi has emerged since the pandemic outbreak. While Islamic State operatives previously ambushed government institutions and military compounds, after March 2020 the jihadist groups attacked cities, towns, and critical infrastructure, supposedly taking advantage of the pandemic crisis situation (Meir Amit Intelligence 2020).

Third, as recorded, radical Islamist activities in Europe suggest jihadi-inspired individuals may have operated as they did under normal circumstances but mounted unsophisticated attacks. Resorting to armed assault instead of deploying improvised explosive devices may suppose that the movement of goods was restricted and terrorists' access to operational resources was maybe limited. These findings could be of great importance for counterterrorism agencies to map and better understand radical Islamist supply systems.

Changes in Far Right Threat Groups' Operational Environment

The virus drew the attention of threat groups across the political and religious spectrum. Contrary to public perception, far right groups exploited the virus more than politico-religious formations. The extreme right-wing discourse painted national governments and international institutions as either responsible for or complicit in the spread of COVID-19. Far right commentators from France, Italy, and Spain all claim that official responses to the pandemic have been driven by a supposedly sinister ulterior motive (SITE Intelligence Group 2020). Directed at the private sector, the far right released a clip titled Plandemic to engender public mistrust in health institutions. From disobeying quarantine regulations to organized protests, the extreme right-wing exclamations criticize government measures to impose "authoritarian" control over populations. In addition to vandalizing healthcare workers' vehicles, the far right encouraged those infected to cough on healthcare workers and for nails to be placed in hospital parking lots. Capitalizing on fears, disillusionment, and social tensions, these threat groups shared disinformation with their supporters and potential future recruits on both the deep and dark web.

Harnessing antiestablishment and social discontent, far right groups and supporters targeted Muslims, Jews, and Asians—especially ethnic Chinese—at lockdown protests. Singaporean law student Jonathan Mok suffered a coronavirus-related racist attack by a group of boys in London on 24 February 2020. After calling Mok "Corona virus" and shouting "I don't want your Corona virus in my country," one of the boys punched him in the face (The Straits Times, 6 March 2020). Neo-Nazi activists encouraged followers to deliberately infect groups, including Jewish minorities (Dearden 2020b), while a forum urged those who were diagnosed with the virus to cough into their hands and touch "things that will have high contact traffic [such as] door handles, handrails, restrooms, sink taps, etc." Others suggested infected individuals withdraw hundreds of dollars in small bills, contaminate them, and then "hit up major stores in lots of different cities." To expand their base, most far right groups promoted white nationalism (SITE Intelligence Group 2020).

In February 2020, an online content aggregator published the following on a far right Telegram channel: "the black swan event" is an opportunity "to destabilize the kike economy [implying a Jewish-controlled economy]." It urged supporters to create "the necessary conditions under which revolution is possible." "The glorious Happening is upon us," read the post, referring to a race war and stoking racism toward "Asians" (CoronaChan 2020). The far right channel published a list of "accelerationist goals" to be achieved by pushing racial and political narratives about the outbreak. "We need to #1 racialize it and #2 politicize it. In the coming weeks I anticipate hundreds of chinks racial slurs for a person of Chinese descent and urbanites to be confirmed infected in the USA" (CoronaChan 2020). The far right identifies its accelerationism goals as:

1. Praise the arrival of the WuFlu Pandemic loudly so the Jew media takes notice;
2. Stigmatize Asians to exacerbate racial tensions and create fear;
3. Celebrate the climbing death counts and laugh at the suffering of the shitlibs in the cities;
4. Make comparisons to the End Times to further spread panic;
5. Encourage making necessary preparations so the store shelves clean out and the markets crash. (CoronaChan 2020)

Extreme far right activists also discussed how to turn the virus into a bioweapon.

"What to do if you get COVID-19 . . . Visit your local Mosque!, visit your local synagogue!; spend time in diverse neighborhoods! spend the day on public transport!" (ADL 2020).

Motivated by "racial, religious and anti-government animus" (Levine 2020), Timothy Wilson, a 36-year-old white supremacist, planned to detonate an explosives-laden vehicle in the parking lot of Belton Regional Medical Center in Cass County, Missouri, United States. Two days earlier, Wilson visited the hospital property and conducted a dry run. Starting 30 January, he bought explosives—two five-pound bags of urea and sixty pounds of ammonium nitrate and another type of fertilizer. Wilson also planned to hit an elementary school with African American students, a power grid, bridges, a nuclear plant, Islamic centers in Missouri, a synagogue in Arkansas, the Walmart headquarters, and the University of Kansas Hospital in Kansas City. Wilson committed suicide on 24 March 2020 as FBI agents attempted to arrest him. Notably, Wilson had served in the navy and had received the "E" Ribbon, Good Conduct Medal, National Defense Service Medal, Iraq Campaign Medal, Global War on Terrorism Service Medal, and Coast Guard Special Operations Service Medal (Kosnar and Helsel 2020).

After the Christchurch attack in 2019, the number of far right violent attacks in the West had surpassed the number carried out by Muslim threat groups (Nguyen and Miller 2020). With the social dislocation and radicalization that the pandemic brought, the far right sought to exploit COVID-19 to grow its support base, from North America to Europe and Australia. To garner media attention, right-wing extremists publicly identified COVID-19 as a "Chinese Virus" and welcomed the pandemic.

In continental Europe, the uncertainty surrounding coronavirus led to a boom in conspiracy theories on social media. With people spending more time online, there was a rise in engagements with Telegram groups spreading conspiracy theories about vaccines, contactless payment, and 5G masts (The Straits Times, 1 May 2020). "5G has remained a core Corona virus conspiracy topic for actors on the far right and far left alike, who posit that the cell towers are part of a plan by the faceless 'elite' to spread COVID-19" (SITE Intelligence Group 2020).

Far right movements exploited the pandemic for their malevolent purposes using all possible means. Firstly, they promoted their ideology to recruit new members. Secondly, in the chaos caused by the pandemic, one associated Telegram channel incited its members to racialize and politicize the crisis to destabilize the economy and accelerate the collapse of society. By mobilizing their members, their endeavor was to spread fear. The British far right, as well as neo-Nazi activists, called on their members diagnosed with COVID-19 to deliberately infect certain minority groups (Jews and Muslims) by targeting their houses of worship and other frequently visited places. Besides the calls for physical attacks, right-wing activists misused cyberspace in another innovative way with so-called Zoombombing. Far right Telegram channels in the United Kingdom also attempted to organize an anti-lockdown protest. Simultaneously, antigovernment and anti-law enforcement narratives have been constantly at the forefront of far right propaganda.

We can observe that certain narratives keep reoccurring and have been used in support of a wide variety of ideological objectives. Right-wing extremists and white supremacists draw attention to ethnic minorities as the source of the disease. Neo-Nazis in Germany accelerated the spread of conspiracy theories with regard to COVID-19 and put themselves forward as a defender of the deprived by providing assistance for the elderly. Meanwhile, radical groups in Europe torched 5G telephone towers, falsely believing that radiation from these telecommunication masts may play a role in spreading the virus.

Protests are right-wing extremists' main arena for recruiting new members. The far right managed to adapt to the consequences of lockdowns and stay-at-home practices in a timely manner. Accordingly, they increased their presence in cyberspace to bolster conspiracy theories and reach out to vulnerable individuals. The general restrictions on mass gatherings may have seriously disrupted their efforts to maintain their international relationships with other right-wing extremist entities, with cross-border links of crucial importance in spreading their ideologies, inciting violent acts, making acquaintance with new members, and obtaining funding sources.

Emerging Organized Crime Threat

The pandemic has yielded another important criminogenic factor that requires particular attention. With the approval and global distribution of COVID-19 vaccines, new organized criminal networks emerged. Criminal organizations have attempted to "infiltrate and disrupt supply chains" (INTERPOL 2020) by the falsification, theft, and illegal advertising of these vaccines. Mexican organized crime groups have reportedly established manufacturing laboratories for fake vaccines (Sullivan 2021). Pfizer confirmed that it had identified bogus COVID-19 vaccines in Mexico and Poland (Miles 2021). The number of advertisements for stolen or counterfeit vaccines on the dark web increased by 300 percent in the first three months of 2021 (CNN, 23 March 2021), while the sale of fake vaccines grew by 400 percent (Miao 2021).

This vibrant black market has created an acute problem in countries with a lower availability of COVID-19 vaccines (Alarabiya, 10 April 2021; Williams 2021). In a joint operation with INTERPOL, South African and Chinese Police disrupted an international fake vaccine criminal network in early March 2021. The trafficking incident involved a shipment of approximately 2,400 doses of counterfeit vaccines across continents. During the raid in China, 80 suspects were arrested at the manufacturing premises (Craig 2021); meanwhile, two people were arrested in South Africa. Counterfeit vaccines were also being distributed underground in the Philippines (Cabato 2021). According to a study by the Economist Intelligence Unit (2021), widespread vaccination in developing countries may not be achieved until 2023. In line with this, people under the control of armed groups need to be taken into account (Gillard 2020). It is hoped that in India lessons learnt from the dire shortages of vaccines (ABC News, 28 April 2021) mean the government will make efforts to fortify its stockpiles in future and in accordance with the ever-changing threat landscape.

The demand for proof of vaccine status generated an elevated level of interest in acquiring counterfeit vaccine cards. These cards were created to order upon the buyer providing the necessary personal data to the vendors (CNN, 23 March 2021). Additionally, INTERPOL's Cybercrime Unite revealed that of "3,000 websites associated with online pharmacies suspected of selling illicit medicines and medical devices, around 1,700 contained cyber threats, especially phishing and spamming malware" (INTERPOL 2020). Additionally, three Baltimore men were detained in February 2021 for operating a fraudulent Moderna website (De León 2021). A "global standardized system for traceability, from product manufacture to patient treatment" for vaccines may be an applicable guarantee of authenticity (Stone 2021). Experts have also urged upgrading the security arrangements around coronavirus vaccination centers, considering the elevated level of terrorist threat at such facilities (Dearden 2020a).

New Threats to the Food Industry

COVID-19 severely disrupted the global food system (Committee on World Food Security High Level Panel of Experts 2020; Stirling Haig et al. 2020). Travel bans, economic restrictions and reduced food purchasing power due to job losses resulted in fundamental changes (Howard and Simmons 2020). Food insecurity led to protests in multiple regions (Hayden 2020). Although transmission is most likely to occur through close contact with infected people, concerns emerged over contaminated food (Food Safety Authority of Ireland 2020) as a result of terror groups. Infected radicals were encouraged to deliberately contaminate food and drink by coughing in supermarkets (Elliott 2020). Threat groups urged people infected with coronavirus to lick fruit and vegetables in the local grocery store and put them back (Janes 2020). A Neo-Nazi group proposed infecting items, possibly food, and shipping them to a country with a "high population density . . . like China." They also suggested cutting the cooling system and power lines of grocery stores, putting cyanide in soda, and "cough[ing] into the potato salad at whole foods." Another Neo-Nazi group suggested infected supporters walk through the supermarket coughing, specifically on kosher items (SITE Intelligence Group 2020). Likewise, Islamic State urged Indian fighters to poison the food and drinks of "nonbelievers."

Taking all this into consideration, risks should be re-evaluated (Nakat and Bou-Mitri 2021) and counterstrategies applied to address these novel implications.

Conclusion

The discussion in this chapter has attempted to summarize the changes COVID-19 has introduced into radical Islamist and far right violent extremists' operational circumstances. By looking at the dynamics in the threat landscape, trends in their operational tactics and targets have been identified.

References

Cabato, Regine. 2021. "A Black Market for Illegal Coronavirus Vaccines Is Thriving in the Philippines." *The Washington Post*, 16 January.

"CoronaChan." 2020. Retrieved May 2022 from Telegram https://t.me/s/CoronaChanNews?before = 229.

"COVID-19 (Coronavirus)." 2020. Food Safety Authority of Ireland website. Retrieved May 2022 from https://www.fsai.ie/faq/coronavirus.html.

Craig, Nathan. 2021. "SA Fertile Ground for Covid-19 Vaccine Black Market." *IOL News*, 28 March.

Dearden, Lizzie. 2020a. "Counter-terror Protection for Covid Vaccination Centres." *Independent*, 23 December.

———. 2020b. "Neo-Nazis Telling Followers to 'Deliberately Infect' Jews and Muslims with Coronavirus, Report Warns." *Independent*, 6 July.

De León, Concepción. 2021. "Three Men Are Accused in Scheme to Sell Covid-19 Vaccines." *The New York Times*, 12 February.

Elliott, Josh K. 2020. "Woman Facing Terror Charges over Coronavirus Coughing 'Prank' at Grocery Store." *Global News*, 26 March.

Gillard, Emanuela-Chiara. 2020. "COVID-19 Vaccine: Reaching People in Areas Controlled by Armed Groups." Chatham House website. Retrieved May 2022 from https://www.chathamhouse.org/2020/12/covid-19-vaccine-reaching-people-areas-controlled-armed-groups.

Hayden, Sally. 2020. "Activists Protest at Coronavirus-Related 'Hunger Pandemic' in Uganda." *The Irish Times*, 18 May.

Howard, Julie, and Emmy Simmons. 2020. "Covid-19 Threatens Global Food Security: What Should the United States Do?" Center for Strategic and International Studies website. Retrieved May 2022 from https://www.csis.org/analysis/covid-19-threatens-global-food-security-what-should-united-states-do.

"Impacts of COVID-19 on Food Security and Nutrition: Developing Effective Policy Responses to Address the Hunger and Malnutrition Pandemic." 2020. Committee on World Food Security High Level Panel of Experts website. Retrieved May 2022 from http://www.fao.org/3/cb1000en/cb1000en.pdf.

Janes, Chelsea. 2020. "Coughing 'Attacks' May Be Prosecuted as Terrorism in War on Coronavirus." *The Washington Post*, 8 April.

Kosnar, Michael, and Phil Helsel. 2020. "FBI Says Man Killed in Missouri Wanted to Bomb Hospital amid Coronavirus Epidemic." *NBC News*, 27 March.

Levine, Mike. 2020. "FBI Learned of Coronavirus-Inspired Bomb Plotter through Radicalised US Army Soldier." *ABC News*, 26 March.

Miao, Hannah. 2021. "WHO Warns Against Sales of Counterfeit Covid Vaccines on the Dark Web." *CNBC*, 26 March.

Miles, Frank. 2021. "Pfizer Confirms Fake COVID Vaccines Found in Mexico, Poland Black Markets." *Fox News*, 21 April.

"More Than 85 Poor Countries Will Not Have Widespread Access to Coronavirus Vaccines before 2023." 2021. The Economist Intelligence Unit website. Retrieved May 2022 from https://www.eiu.com/n/85-poor-countries-will-not-have-access-to-coronavirus-vaccines/#: ~ :text = vaccines percent20before percent202023-,More percent20than percent2085 percent20poor percent20countries percent20will percent20not percent20have,to percent20coronavirus percent20vaccines percent20before percent202023&text = For percent20most percent20middle percent2Dincome percent20countries,before percent202023 percent2C percent20if percent20at percent20all.

Nakat, Zeina, and Christelle Bou-Mitri. 2021. "COVID-19 and the Food Industry: Readiness Assessment." Food Control. Retrieved May 2022 from https://www.ncbi.nlm.nih.gov/pmc/articles/PMC7523550/.

Nguyen, Kevin, and Barbara Miller. 2020. "Christchurch Shooting Inspired Global Efforts to Tackle Far Right Extremism: Experts Say It's Still a Problem." *ABC News*, 14 March.

"Orange Notice INTERPOL Warns of Organized Crime Threat to COVID-19 Vaccines." 2020. INTERPOL website. Retrieved May 2022 from https://www.interpol.int/News-and-Events/News/2020/INTERPOL-warns-of-organized-crime-threat-to-COVID-19-vaccines.

"Recent Far Right Updates on the COVID-19 Pandemic March 25–April 1, 2020." 2020. Retrieved May 2022 from SITE Intelligence Group.

"Recent Far Right Updates on the COVID-19 Pandemic April 2–7, 2020." 2020. Retrieved May 2022 from SITE Intelligence Group.

"Recent Far Right Updates on the COVID-19 Pandemic April 16–21, 2020." 2020. Retrieved May 2022 from SITE Intelligence Group.

"Recent Far Right Updates on the COVID-19 Pandemic April 29–May 5, 2020." 2020. Retrieved May 2022 from SITE Intelligence Group.

"Recent Far Right Updates on the COVID-19 Pandemic May 6–12, 2020." 2020. Retrieved May 2022 from SITE Intelligence Group.

"Recent Far Right Updates on the COVID-19 Pandemic, May 13–26, 2020." 2020. Retrieved May 2022 from SITE Intelligence Group.

"Spotlight on Global Jihad April 7–22, 2020." 2020. Retrieved May 2022 from The Meir Amit Intelligence and Terrorism Information Center.

Stirling Haig, Christian, Habiba Ahmed, Henry Newton, and Samuel Brannen. 2020. "Covid-19 Reshapes the Future." Center for Strategic and International Studies website. Retrieved May 2022 from https://www.csis.org/analysis/covid-19-reshapes-future.

Stone, Judy. 2021. "How Counterfeit Covid-19 Vaccines and Vaccination Cards Endanger Us All." *Forbes*, 31 March.

Sullivan, Shane. 2021. "Liquid Gold – False COVID-19 Vaccines Emerge in Latin America." *InSight Crime*, 18 January.

"White Supremacists Respond to Coronavirus with Violent Plots and Online Hate." 2020. ADL website. Retrieved May 2022 from https://www.adl.org/blog/white-supremacists-respond-to-coronavirus-with-violent-plots-and-online-hate.

Williams, Clive. 2021. "Covid-19 Vaccines Hit the Black Market." *The Strategist*, 22 February.

CHAPTER 6

Future Trajectories for Emerging Radical Islamist and Far Right Trends

Could Violent Extremists Weaponize COVID-19?

Since the beginning of the contemporary wave of international terrorism in 1968, there has never been so much chatter on a virus. Terrorist groups worldwide have expressed interest in capitalizing on COVID-19. The virus is hard to weaponize in order to cause mass casualties, but deliberate infection is still a serious concern. There have been instances recorded where nonstate actors engaged in the malicious spread of coronavirus, particularly within law enforcement and medical research facilities. For instance, in the United Kingdom, infected assailants used spit as a weapon on police officers (Weaver and Dodd 2020). Similarly, Belly Mujinga, a 47-year-old British railway ticket office worker, died after a man deliberately coughed on her (DW, 12 May 2020). In Belgium, where several cases of spitting were reported, offenders could be fined up to €2,400 and could face prison terms of up to two years. If claiming to be infected to scare others, the offenders will be subjected to the same penalties (The Brussels Times, 31 March 2020). A Pennsylvania woman, Margaret Cirko, aged 35, coughed and spat on US $35,000 worth of produce and merchandise at a grocery store. She was arrested and charged with two felony counts of terrorist threats, one felony count of threats to use a "biological agent" and one felony count of criminal mischief (Halpin and Kalinowski 2020).

Regardless of the aforementioned handful of attempts at deliberate infection, SARS-CoV-2 has not yet proved stable enough for violent extremist purposes for two reasons. First, the virus loses its ability to infect after a relatively short period of time. We have learnt the virus causes serious or fatal consequences mostly in the elderly generation and has been shown to be mild or even asymptomatic in younger generations. Second, restrictions on mass gatherings as well as newly adopted sanitary habits such as wearing masks in public spaces have all undermined malicious intentions to infect groups of people. Ultimately, it is looking more likely that people will learn to live with the virus, reducing the virus vulnerabilities violent extremists aim to exploit. This may be the best-case future scenario barring a more fatal mutation. A future dangerous and highly infectious disease may revive violent extremists' motivations for bioterrorism.

The Future Radical Islamist Threat

The Islamic State has already declared they will have a role in paving the way for the future (Islamic State quoted by SITE Intelligence Group 2020):

> As we all know, the corona virus Pandemic has cast its gloomy, painful shadow over the entire world. Across the globe, there appears to be no light at the end of the dark tunnel that the world finds itself in. People are stuck in their homes, and shops and businesses are being forced to shut down. The global economy is paralyzed and the world is utterly perplexed by this predicament. Everything that was once taken for granted lies now in grave jeopardy. Economies of major nations lie in ruin as they find their entire state apparatus, including army and security [,] pinned down by an invisible enemy. Norms of social behavior, lifestyles, everything is being redefined. Allah alone knows what the coming days hold in store. In the midst of this unprecedented crisis, we consider it our duty to console our Muslim brothers and sisters and discuss the way forward for the Muslim world specifically and humanity in general.

With Afghanistan emerging as an alternative base to Syria, the strategy of the Islamic State is to radicalize the Muslim population in South Asia (Mines and Jadoon 2020). Having declared Wilayat (provinces of the caliphate) in India and Pakistan, Islamic State propaganda claims that attempts to eradicate jihad in Afghanistan failed and instead spread to other regions of the subcontinent. Referring to Prime Minister Narendra Modi as "the Pharaoh of India," the Islamic State says that the recent attack against the Sikh temple in Kabul was to avenge Indian actions in Kashmir (Mir 2020).

> And if the Hindu Polytheists today have begun to bother the Muslims who testified Tawheed and live in India by arresting them, lynching them, and introducing new laws to evict them, then soon they will begin to take them away either dead, imprisoned, or homeless. Allah said: "And they will continue to fight you until they turn you back from your religion if

> they are able" [2:217]. So, remember they will not leave anyone amongst you except the one who apostates from his religion and follows theirs. The only cure to it is Jihad as Shaykh Abu Musab az-Zarqawi said: "Verily after Tawheed the best antidote to the problems of this Ummah is Jihad for the sake of Allah." (Mir 2020)

With the decentralization of the Islamic State, it is creating regional capabilities. The focus of the Islamic State is to expand throughout South Asia by spreading its ideology among the Muslims of the region (Business World 2020).

> Thus, the barren lands which had become devoid of Jihad turned fertile after being nourished by the blood of Shuhadah. The patrons of the creed of al-Wala'a wal Bara'a rose against the enemies of Allah and reaffirmed that they will not cease their Jihad until the word of Allah becomes the Highest. The Knights of Wilayah Hind, on one hand, have marched forth with this blessed caravan and on the other hand, the Mujahideen of Wilayah Pakistan are exerting all efforts to intensify the flames of war. Striking the enemies of Allah, they are supreme by their aqeeda and tawheed, not through themselves. They are defiant by their certainty that victory, strength, and triumph are for them by the grace of Allah not by their weapons nor numbers. (Business World 2020)

Islamic State's South Asia issue of The Voice of Hind (issue 6) was designed and developed to radicalize South Asian territorials and its diaspora. One of the articles focused on "Prison, The University of Yusuf." The article called for prisoners to reflect on their religious education and be supported and freed. "It is from the utmost responsibilities of the Muslims that he removes the distress from the other oppressed Muslim brothers and sisters and more so when someone from the Muslimeen is in the prisons of the kuffar. Therefore, we must try every possible way to free them and comfort them" (The Voice of Hind 2020). Governments should pay special attention to attempts at prison infiltration to connect with terrorists, prison breaks to free terrorists, and radical and violent groups supporting families of terrorists.

The message of the Islamic State is essentially Islamic domination or Islamic supremacy of the subcontinent.

> And prior to that, your brothers in Sri-Lanka have also glorified the Khilafah by shedding the filthy blood of crusaders while they refused humiliation and subservience and offered their blood and lives for their religion. And so, have the lions of the Khilafah in Bangladesh, who trod the path of honor and dignity and have been carrying out attacks against the apostate regime. We also congratulate the brothers from the Maldives for carrying out the blessed arson attack against the apostate regime, a first of its kind

> officially announced by the Khilafah. O Muwahideen in Pakistan, Kashmir, Bangladesh, Maldives, Sri-Lanka, and India we bring you glad tidings of Ghazwa e Hind. So, thank Allah and praise Him for He has provided us a chance for being among those who have been promised the conquest of Hind by Imam of Mujahideen and last messenger Muhammad SAW. . . . The Messenger of Allah (blessings and peace of Allah be upon him) said: "There are two groups of my ummah whom Allah will protect from the Fire: a group who will conquer India, and a group who will be with 'Eesaa ibn Maryam' (peace be upon him)." (Narrated by an-Nasaa'i (no. 3175) and Imam Ahmad in al-Musnad (37/81)) (SITE Intelligence Group 2020)

Muslim radicals advocating Shariah (Islamic law) are nearly 10 percent of Indonesia's population. Although they are small, they exercise disproportionate power (Indonesia Investments 2020). They have the capacity to mobilize on current issues and conduct massive and at times aggressive campaigns. The radicals do not agree with the "new normal" policy, which they present as one of the capitalist systems that does not benefit society. Increasingly, there is support from the youth; a survey by Universitas Islam Negeri (UIN) found that 10 percent of millennials agree to Khilafah. Every year, there is growing support for the implementation of Islamic law (Beach and Suhartono 2020).

In East Asia, where the Islamic State created a province, the Philippines is the center of gravity (Zenn 2019). There has been an increase in terrorist incidents in the Southern Philippines since the new counterterrorism bill was passed in parliament and signed into law as the Anti-Terrorism Act (Business and Human Rights Resource Centre 2020). In response to this Act, which was approved by Philippine President Rodrigo Duterte, a Facebook post on 4 July 2020 said that the new legislation will not stop IS from mounting attacks. Threatening members of the Armed Forces of the Philippines in Mindanao, the English-language post said:

> A Message to the Crusader forces of the Philippines the "ally Dog of Coalition of forces" wanted to defeat the Islamic State. The head of the Crusader Forces Duterte signed Anti-Terror Bill yesterday to Intimidate the Mujahideen and its supporters and Followers to stop their fight towards the Crusader forces and its Devilish Democratic governance. Indeed, your terror bill is just a piece of junk paper that will not intimidate us or make us stop what we are doing. But it will surely motivate us to do more for the sake of Allah. Oh, crusader forces this is a dire warning to all of you living among our City and land, Surrender and pack your things up and go back to your own city, or else one way or another, the sword of the Islamic state will be on your neck Bi'idnillah. What is happening in Sulu, Cotabato, and in Lanao Del Sur for this past month is just the beginning. The more you force Muslims to be afraid of you the more blood of your

Crusader forces will spill on our soil. (Abu Musa Mashriqi) (SITE Intelligence Group 2020)

Twenty-six days after twin bombings that killed fourteen people and hurt seventy-five others in Jolo, Sulu province on 24 August 2020, Islamic State attempted to mount another plot demonstrating its capacity to attack. Reportedly, the terrorist operation was disrupted when a concerned citizen alerted the authorities. The military's Western Mindanao Command (Westmincom) coastguardsmen found a package containing explosives at Jolo pier between the offices of the harbormaster and the maritime police at Barangay Walled City. Westmincom chief Lt. Gen. Corleto Vinluan Jr. said personnel of the PCG (Philippine Coast Guard) explosives and ordnance division (EOD) were conducting paneling operations at the pier when they stumbled upon the package a little past 6 PM on Saturday. The package contained a rifle grenade, two electric blasting caps, a spark plug, and concrete nails. Troops of the 35th infantry battalion were immediately deployed to cordon off the area while an EOD team from the Sulu provincial police office and personnel from the Jolo police station responded to the site. The improvised explosive device was promptly disarmed and safely disposed of (Peralta-Malonzo 2020).

To counter the emerging threat in South Asia, it is paramount to counter both the operational and ideological networks and dismantle them. If the threat is not adequately countered, the ideology will spread to South Asian Muslims living outside the subcontinent, and they too will support or stage attacks. The South Asian male and female Muslim population and its diaspora and migrant communities are a huge reservoir of potential support for Islamic State's radicalization and recruitment.

In 2020, Islamic State took control of one of the world's largest natural gas reserves at the strategic port of Mocimboa da Praia in Cabo Delgado Province, Mozambique (BBC News, 12 August 2020). Since 2017, there had been many battles between government forces and the local terrorist group, which was known previously as Al-Sunna wa Jama'a (ASWJ) before reinventing itself as the Islamic State. The fighting in 2020 killed more than 1,500 people and displaced at least 250,000 (Machado 2020). At the time, the Islamists publicized that they had accomplished two great feats in Mozambique "by the grace of Allah, through which they changed the course of events and cut off the ambitions of major countries in the resources of Muslims there" (BBC News, 18 September 2020). The second of these feats was taking control of the two islands of Metundo and Vamizi, which lie in the Indian Ocean off the northeast of Mozambique. This had a great impact on the region, as the two islands are located close to the middle of the sea corridor between Mozambique and Madagascar, the width of which does not exceed 460 km. Control over these islands was a disruption of all movement in this corridor.

Islamic State had occupied the port twice before, and after the first occupation all the international newspapers were abuzz due to the amount of natural gas that had been discovered there, estimated at 1,000 billion cubic meters. We can tell the value of this discovery from the number of investments made in the field. The most prominent company that has invested is the US energy firm Anadarko, with a value of $25 billion. Transport vessels that are contracted with this company have been attacked twice since the start of their investment (DW, 13 July 2020). Other investors include the French company Total, at a value of $20 billion, and the Japanese government, at a value of $14 billion. Also, several other countries such as Britain, the Netherlands, Italy, South Africa, and Vietnam have contributed approximately $14.9 billion (Darby 2020). African nations and the international community responded decisively to support Mozambique to retake the port.

Discovery of the giant gas field (as well as a huge ruby deposit) in Cabo Delgado in 2009–10 did not improve the quality of life of the people. Both Christian and Muslim clerics and preachers from religious international aid agencies competed to convert local people. A majority Muslim hub, both East Africans and Mozambicans trained in Saudi Arabia introduced their version of Islam. One year after the Islamic State in Iraq and Syria proclaimed a caliphate, violent confrontations started in 2015, where traditional Muslim leaders supported by the police tried to block the Islamists (Morier-Genoud 2020).

The Islamic State strategy in Africa suggests that they think it preferable to spread over wide geographical areas with mobile armed groups and thus not concentrate on any one particular place. IS is still committed to keeping the war on the move and responsive, and to starting qualitative work by targeting the important economic and military centers in Africa, in addition to inciting Muslims to pursue jihad (Gargard 2020).

In the spectrum of Muslim threat groups, the Islamic State (IS) remains the most dominant movement. However, al-Qaeda (AQ) poses a long-term strategic threat (Mueller and Stewart 2016). While the Islamic State poses the most imminent operational threat to governments and societies worldwide, the AQ movement is deepening its capabilities and expanding its networks appreciably (Fitton-Brown 2020). A vacuum created by IS in Syria is being rapidly filled by AQ. In the past few years,

AQ as a movement has grown manifold. With the loss of Baghouz, the last territorial stronghold of the IS in Syria, its rival Hay'at Taḥrīr al-Shām (HTS), the AQ branch in Syria, has emerged as the single biggest group in the Syrian theatre (CSIS 2020). HTS is now building a global network. It is co-opting many AQ affiliates and working with them ideologically and operationally. The AQ movement has emerged stronger (Taylor 2019) for three reasons. First, the global counterterrorism focus is on the IS and not on AQ (UN News, 24 August 2020). Second, IS suffered significantly both in its core in Syria and Iraq and in the periphery in its wilayats (provinces). Third, there has been stepped-up covert support from Arab and non-Arab regimes for HTS to fight the Russian and Iran-backed President Bashar al-Assad regime (Ajjoub 2020).

HTS has built significant alliances worldwide, increasing its strength, size, and influence. As the most active AQ branch, HTS is providing new capabilities to AQ affiliates worldwide (CSIS 2020). In addition to the AQ core in Afghanistan and HTS, the other branches of AQ are the Afghan Taliban, al-Shabaab in Somalia, AQ in the Islamic Maghreb, AQ in Arabian Peninsula, Turkistan Islamic Party in China, AQ in the Indian Subcontinent, Abu Sayyaf Group, and Jemaah Islamiyah in Southeast Asia. The HTS has a growing presence in Asia—northeast Asia, Central Asia, South Asia and Southeast Asia. As the Southeast Asian fighters have been integrated into the other fighting formations, HTS has not identified the dedicated Southeast Asian group. Through its Indonesia-based Abu Ahmed Foundation, Jemaah Islamiyah funded the HTS training capability Malhama Tactical (Soliev 2020).

In the future, AQ will have two global epicenters—in Afghanistan, with the AQ core until 2020 led by Dr Ayman al Zawahiri (Congressional Research Service 2020; Schmitt 2020), and in Syria, with Abu Mohammad al-Julani (Schmitt 2020). With Ayman al-Zawahiri now deceased, Abu Mohamed al Jolani is likely to provide global leadership to AQ affiliates. The resurgent AQ movement is likely to eclipse the global threat posed by the Islamic State in the coming months and years (Schmitt 2020). At the same time, the HTS, threatened by Russian- and Iranian-backed Syrian forces, face a split within. The HTS and its AQ-linked groups face rivalry. To consolidate its strength, the HTS invited several groups to sign a statement reaffirming their allegiance (CSIS 2020). In the coming years, it is very likely that the threat group as a semi-conventional military force will be defeated by the Syrian forces. However, HTS will survive as an underground insurgent and terrorist organization. If the HTS core in Syria maintains its alliance with other AQ-aligned groups, the fledgling HTS global network will pose a formidable and continuing threat to global security (Al-Tamimi 2020).

Unless and until world leaders find the resolve to work together, the AQ and IS global footprint is likely to grow in the coming decades. Global command structures of AQ and the IS stretch from Africa to the Caucasus and from the Middle East to Asia. Both AQ and IS have successfully co-opted local groups and built capabilities to expand their influence. Through these means, they will disseminate propaganda, raise funds, and recruit more people to their cause. The outcome of such efforts is likely twofold. These groups are likely to launch attacks in their home and neighboring countries while encouraging individuals, cells, and networks in the West to carry out attacks in their name. Although their local affiliates may cooperate on some occasions, competition between the IS and AQ for leadership of the other's affiliates—and the global movement as a whole—is likely to encourage more competition than cooperation in the long run. Nevertheless, temporary pressure arising from the deaths of incumbent leaders and ideological similarity between both movements renders short-term cooperation likely in at least some theatres, particularly where friendly or noncompetitive relationships have already existed between their local affiliates. If there is a long-term fusion or merger of these movements, the global threat to governments and communities can be expected to increase exponentially.

Instead of allowing geopolitical egos to harm their long-term security, governments should work together to address security challenges common to all. On 9 October 2019, Turkey launched Operation Peace Spring to secure its borders north of Syria and east of the Euphrates River (Uras 2019). As a sequel to past operations such as Euphrates Shield and Olive Branch, the aim of this operation was to fight the Kurdish groups who had played a pivotal role in the military defeat of IS. Coupled with the US withdrawal, a power vacuum exists that has been filled by Turkey, Russia, Iran, and threat groups such as the IS and local AQ affiliates such as HTS. If the geopolitical agendas of both distant and regional governments continue to take a priority over these pressing security concerns, it is likely that the IS will reconstitute itself in the short term—approximately over one to two years—and reemerge as a formidable threat within five years. Unless governments work together to fight both a resurgent al-Qaeda (Zimmerman 2021) and a presently weakened IS (Tarallo 2020), this threat is sure to return with a greater vengeance.

Despite its territorial losses in 2019, IS has remained resilient. There has been an upsurge of attacks in Iraq, Syria, and across Africa. The terrorist organization could yet capitalize on the pandemic by exploiting the security vacuum in Iraq and Syria left by the reduced military presence. After Europol removed jihadist online content from Telegram in November 2019, supporters identified new platforms for spreading propaganda, indicating a persistence that might not be directed by IS leadership (Azman 2021). AQ, however, has suffered the loss of many chief commanders. This is reflected in their network, which is more focused on local conflicts and cannot advance the group's core aspirations (Pantucci 2020b). Both IS and AQ used social media to provide "a broad strategic narrative to guide the actions of a widely scattered global network of affiliates and cells" (Ramakrishna 2021).

Experts agree that despite the progress in eliminating the Islamic State progress in Syria and Iraq, the radical Islamist threat will not cease to exist in the future. Africa is of most concern in this regard. Likewise, Afghanistan "must not be allowed to be used as a safe haven for terrorists or threaten the stability of neighboring countries" (UN Security Council 2022). The Islamic State's Afghanistan-Pakistan chapter (Islamic State Khorasan) carried out the deadliest attacks in the area. IS Khorasan fighters attacked a maternity ward in a predominantly Shi'ite neighborhood of Kabul in 2020, killing sixteen mothers and mothers-to-be. Despite its high-profile attacks, the terrorist organization has suffered serious losses from Taliban and US-led military operations. Therefore, it cannot hold any territory in the region and operates in smaller covert cells. Unlike other radical Islamist terrorist organizations in the region, IS-Khorasan did not accept the Taliban takeover in Afghanistan and highlighted that the Taliban "betrayed jihadists with the US withdrawal deal and vowed to continue its fight" (India Today, 26 August 2021). Importantly, a 2021 US Department of the Treasury report stated that the finances of the richest jihadist organization have significantly shrunk. Islamic State's revenue generated from its illicit financial activities, together with its cash reserves, is claimed not to be enough to establish a new caliphate in the region. Experts argue that because of the security vacuum in Syria and Iraq, IS will remain present in the area and will try to consolidate its position, but it may not pose "a strategic threat on an international or even regional level" (Holleis and Knipp 2022).

The Future Far Right Threat

There are also worrisome factors when considering the right-wing extremism-related future threat. To begin with, the number of live streaming audiences has drastically increased since the lockdowns in the spring of 2020.[1] This socially isolated audience were tending to engage with misinformation campaigns, propagandistic speeches on conspiracy theories, and incitements to hatred. It is alarming that for instance on the DLive platform the most popular content has included racial justice protests, antivaccine propaganda, conspiracies linking 5G networks to the spread of COVID-19, and calls to make more white babies while quarantined. Lone actors who obtain tactical inspiration and gain social support in online communities have been given utmost significance within right-wing extremist entities (Bjørgo and Ravndal 2019). We have already witnessed certain tragic incidents that testify to the impact of online radical propaganda on unstable individuals. Both the New Zealand and German attackers were radicalized in cyberspace and were streamlining their malevolent actions. In March 2019, a Florida man who had been radicalized by online conspiracy theorists was arrested after sending pipe bombs to the critics of Donald Trump. Still in that spring, four people were shot dead at the Poway synagogue by a gunman who had beforehand posted racist content on 8chan. In August 2019, a man who had previously made publicly available a racist manifesto killed twenty-three people at the El Paso Walmart (Bergengruen 2020). Challenges associated with detecting lone wolf actors remain for intelligence and law enforcement agencies (Aasland and Bjørgo 2018).

While major social media platforms like YouTube, Facebook, or Twitter have targeted hate speech with focused strategies, less-regulated channels are more concerned about their income to survive and therefore care less about content that should be banned. For platforms like DLive, becoming what their users consider "free speech" and "uncensored" alternatives can be lucrative. More speech also means more money for the platform, and less content moderation means less expense. Another pull factor for radical propagandists lies in finances. Twitch and YouTube take a 45 and 50 percent cut respectively from live streamers' earnings, while sites like DLive ask for only 10 percent of creators' profit (Bergengruen 2020).

The impact of radical online content may be even more concerning for members of the younger generation. Numerous recent examples show that teenagers—spending hours daily on platforms where extremist content is circulated—are ready to share Black Lives Matter messages illustrated in racist cartoons. These all substantiate that bigger efforts are necessary to better understand "this new extremist ecosystem" (Bergengruen 2020). Another noteworthy factor here is the potential long-term effect of the pandemic's economic consequences on radicalization. The pool of hopeless and unemployed people will likely increase because of the crisis situation, and in parallel a more susceptible audience is about to be established. This enhanced online recruited base may considerably heighten the risk of offline extremist activities in the long term (Ariza 2020).

One promising avenue may be the tracking of emerging platforms. Extreme right-wing groups have become increasingly sophisticated in using social media platforms, and the internet in general, to recruit and radicalize (UN CTED 2020). These entities are eager to adopt new technologies that can be easily exploited, to bolster their narratives and advance their agenda. Effective counterpolicies should be the endeavor of governments and law enforcement agencies together with experts in civil society. Violent extremists are on the edge of seeking new forums, and such intentions should be recognized and abolished in a timely manner (Bergengruen 2020).

Lockdowns and epidemiological restrictions on public gatherings arguably gave extraordinary power to right-wing extremist demonstrations (Dave et al. 2020). Ignited by the killing of George Floyd by a police officer, the 2020 Black Lives Matter movement became an international phenomenon (Westerman, Benk, and Greene 2020). These protests (Hill et al. 2020) induced social tension and unrest (Eligon 2020) and further challenged law enforcement capabilities. Far right entities enhanced their online social media activities to capitalize on the turmoil. White supremacist propaganda increased by more than 65 percent in 2020 compared to the previous year.[2] The far right managed to unite the fragmented, more moderate extremist groups (Murdoch 2020). The Boogaloo movement, which includes loosely far right individuals, also increased its visibility during the surge in protests (Cohen 2020). Anti-lockdown demonstrations provided a handy platform for these antigovernment extremists. First, they rallied at protests organized by other groups. Later in May, however, their "Blue Igloo" section called for participation in their own gatherings in North Carolina. Boogaloo supporters took relatively passive roles at these demonstrations, emerging since May 2020 as armed protectors of local businesses who countered lockdown measures (ADL 2020), but have become increasingly violent in their actions. Several members of the Boogaloo movement were arrested for firing guns at police personnel (Campbell 2020) and possessing materials for Molotov cocktails (Blankstein 2020). Members of Proud Boys, a far right, anti-immigrant, all-male group (Sardarizadeh and Wendling 2020), clashed with left-wing activists at Black Lives Matter demonstrations in Seattle, Washington, and Portland, Oregon over the summer of 2020 (McEvoy 2020). The group was particularly active in spreading conspiracy theories regarding the pandemic (Wilson 2020).

There was also a heightened risk of political violence and instability in the United States around the 2020 general election (Armed Conflict

Location and Event Data Project 2020). The Department of Homeland Security's assessment identified "white supremacist extremists" as the biggest physical threat to the democratic elections (Klippenstein 2020) and that they remain the "most persistent and lethal threat in the homeland" (US Department of Homeland Security 2020). A mob of protesters attacked the United States Capitol on 6 January 2021. In the unrest, five individuals were killed and over 100 people were injured (Wilber 2021). Federal authorities arrested almost 300 individuals (NPR, 19 January 2021) who participated in the 6 January riot. Members of various extremist groups throughout the country coalesced in the storm of the US Capitol. They were allegedly affiliated with organizations such as The Three Percenters, The Oath Keepers, Proud Boys, and Texas Freedom Force (Schmidt 2021). Several followers of the QAnon online conspiracy theory were also arrested (Lewis 2021). Two Proud Boys supporters were charged, one with conspiracy and the other one with leading a mob of 100 people (Benner and Feuer 2021). Rioters arrived at the siege from over 180 counties throughout the United States (The George Washington University Program on Extremism 2021). It was an unprecedented event, where disparate extremist groups mobilized themselves together. It is of great concern whether these violent extremists have established links with each other and will mobilize themselves in the future (Selsky 2021).

The bulletin issued by the FBI, the Department of Homeland Security, and the National Counterterrorism Center predicted that in 2021 the "anti-government specifically militia violent extremists will likely pose the greatest domestic terrorism threat" (Tomazin 2021). The United States Capitol Police Department issued a statement on 3 March 2021 about threats made toward members of Congress and the Capitol complex. Security arrangements were accordingly upgraded at the venue (United States Capitol Police 2021).

A 16-year-old boy was the first detainee. Inspired by far right extremist ideology in Singapore, he was arrested for allegedly planning to knife Muslims in two nearby mosques on the Christchurch attacks anniversary. Inspired by Brenton Tarrant, the detained boy intended to live stream his attack. Because of the strict gun-control rules in Singapore, he planned to use a machete instead of a rifle like Tarrant (Mahmud 2021). The boy intended to steal his father's credit card to rent a car and drive between the two mosques. The Ministry of Home Affairs claimed that he was a Protestant Christian of Indian ethnicity and had been motivated by a strong antipathy toward Islam and a fascination with violence. "He was watching Islamic State propaganda videos and falsely believing that IS represents Islam. He prepared a manifesto for dissemination prior to the attack" (BBC News, 28 January 2021). While in detention, he will receive a comprehensive program of religious, psychological, and social rehabilitation (Mahmud 2021).

The extreme far right consists of loosely affiliated organizations with the same ideological settings. The porous nature of these relationships substantially heightens their associated threat as compared to traditional terrorist organizations because it is more challenging to track or predict their actions (White 2020). This challenge can only be addressed by the joint effort of authorities, society, and the tech industry (ADL 2020). Currently, the complexity of national legislation makes the disruption of these networks fragmented (Janik and Hankes 2021; Pantucci 2020a).

Conclusion

The purpose of this chapter was twofold. First, the discussion has attempted to identify future trajectories for emerging radical Islamist and far right trends. Secondly, the challenges associated with novel threats have been taken into account.

Note

1. In 2019, 2,724; in 2020 more than 4,500 incidents of white supremacist propaganda were distributed. ADL Center on Extremism, "A Report from the Center on Extremism Murder and Extremism in the United States in 2020" February 2021. https://www.adl.org/media/15825/download.

References

Aasland, Jacob, and Tore Bjørgo. 2018. "Investigating Terrorism from the Extreme Right: A Review of Past and Present Research." *Perspectives on Terrorism* 12(6).

Ajjoub, Orwa. 2020. "HTS and al-Qaeda in Syria: Reconciling the Irreconcilable." MEI website. Retrieved May 2022 from https://www.mei.edu/publications/hts-and-al-qaeda-syria-reconciling-irreconcilable.

"Al Qaeda and Islamic State Affiliates in Afghanistan." 2020. Congressional Research Service website. Retrieved May 2022 from https://crsreports.congress.gov/product/pdf/IF/IF10604.

Al-Tamimi, Aymen Jawad. 2020. "From Jabhat al-Nusra to Hay'at Tahrir al-Sham: Evolution, Approach and Future." Konrad Adenauer Stiftung website. Retrieved May 2022 from https://www.kas.de/c/document_library/get_file?uuid=8cfa4cdb-e337-820d-d0bd-4cd998f38612&groupId=252038.

"A Report from the Center on Extremism Murder and Extremism in the United States in 2020." 2021. ADL Center on Extremism website. Retrieved May 2022 from https://www.adl.org/media/15825/download.

Ariza, Cristina. 2020. "From the Fringes to the Forefront: How Far Right Movements across the Globe Have Reacted to Covid-19." Tony Blair Institute for Global Change website. Retrieved May 2022 from https://institute.global/policy/fringes-forefront-how-far-right-movements-across-globe-have-reacted-covid-19.

Azman, Nur Aziemah. 2021. "The Islamic State (IS): Maintaining Resilience in a Post-caliphate, Pandemic Environment." *Counter Terrorist Trends and Analyses* 13(1).

Beach, Hannah, and Muktita Suhartono. 2020. "Faith Politics on the Rise as Indonesian Islam Takes a Hard-Line Path." *The New York Times*, 15 April.

Benner, Katie, and Alan Feuer. 2021. "Justice Department Unveils Further Charges in Capitol Riot." *The New York Times*, 3 February.

Bergengruen, Vera. 2020. "How Far Right Personalities and Conspiracy Theorists Are Cashing in on the Pandemic Online." *Time*, 20 August.

Bjørgo, Tore, and Jacob Aasland Ravndal. 2019. "Extreme-Right Violence and Terrorism: Concepts, Patterns, and Responses." International Centre for Counter-Terrorism website. Retrieved May 2022 from https://icct.nl/publication/extreme-right-violence-and-terrorism-concepts-patterns-and-responses/.

Blankstein, Andrew, Tom Winter, and Brandy Zadrozny. 2020. "Three Men Connected to 'Bogaloo' Movement Tried to Provoke Violence at Protests, Feds Say." *NBC News*, 2 June.

Campbell, Josh. 2020. "Suspected Boogaloo Bois Member Arrested and Charged with Erioting." *CNN*, 23 October.

"Capitol Police Increase Security Following Threat." 2021. United States Capitol Police website. Retrieved May 2022 from https://www.uscp.gov/media-center/press-releases/capitol-police-increase-security-following-threat.

Cohen, Seth. 2020. "Civil War 2.0? The 'Boogaloo' Movement Is a Wake-up Call for America." *Forbes*, 16 June.

Darby, Megan. 2020. "Seven Countries Back Africa's Biggest Investment, a $20 Billion Gas Project." *Climate Home News*, 20 July.

Dave, Dhaval, Andrew Friedson, Kyutaro Matsuzawa, Joseph J. Sabia, and Samuel Safford. 2020. "Black Lives Matter Protests, Social Distancing and COVID-19." Institute of Labor Economics website. Retrieve May 2022 from http://ftp.iza.org/dp13388.pdf.

"Demonstrations and Political Violence in America: New Data for Summer 2020." 2020. Armed Conflict Location and Event Data Project. Retrieved May 2022 from https://acleddata.com/2020/09/03/demonstrations-political-violence-in-america-new-data-for-summer-2020/.

"Despite Islamic State Leader's Death, Defeating Threat of Terrorist Group, Affiliates Remains 'Long-Term Game', Top Counter-Terrorism Official Warns Security Council." 2022. UN Security Council website. Retrieved May 2022 from https://reliefweb.int/report/world/despite-islamic-state-leader-s-death-defeating-threat-terrorist-group-affiliates.

Eligon, John. 2020. "Black Lives Matter Grows as Movement while Facing New Challenges." *The New York Times*, 28 August.

Fitton-Brown, Edmund. 2020. "The Persistent Threat from the Islamic State and al-Qaeda: The View from the UN." The Washington Institute website. Retrieved

May 2022 from https://www.washingtoninstitute.org/policy-analysis/view/the-persistent-threat-from-the-islamic-state-and-al-qaeda-the-view-from-the.

Flanagan, Jane. 2020. "Stars' Paradise Isle Taken over by Insurgents Linked to ISIS." *The Times*, 17 September.

Gargard, Geebio. 2020. "How Islamic State Could Utilize COVID-19 Woes as Catalyst for African Resurgence." *The Defense Post*, 9 July.

Gunaratna, Rohana. 2020. "Contention, Escalation and Cycles of Vengeance: Reflections on the Global Threat Landscape." In *United by Violence, Divided by Cause?* ed. La Toya Waha, 101–16. Baden-Baden: Nomos.

Halpin, James, and Bob Kalinowski. 2020. "Hanover Township Woman Charged in Gerrity's Supermarket Coughing Episode." *The Times-Tribune*, 9 June.

"Hay'at Tahrir al-Sham (HTS)." 2020. Center for Strategic and International Studies website. Retrieved May 2022 from https://www.csis.org/programs/transnational-threats-project/terrorism-backgrounders/hayat-tahrir-al-sham-hts.

Hill, Evan, Ainara Tiefenthäler, Christiaan Triebert, Drew Jordan, Haley Willis, and Robin Stein. 2020. "8 Minutes and 46 Seconds: How George Floyd Was Killed in Police Custody." *The New York Times*, 24 January.

Holleis, Jennifer, and Kersten Knipp. 2022. "In Syria and Iraq IS Is Still Capable, but No Global Threat." *DW*, 26 January.

"Homeland Threat Assessment October 2020." 2020. US Department of Homeland Security website. Retrieved May 2022 from https://www.dhs.gov/sites/default/files/publications/2020_10_06_homeland-threat-assessment.pdf.

"Islamic State Expanding Its Presence in South Asia under Pakistan's Patronage, Say Experts." 2020. *Business World*, 30 September.

Janik, Rachel, and Keegan Hankes. 2021. "The Year in Hate and Extremism 2020." SPL Center website. Retrieved May 2022 from https://www.splcenter.org/news/2021/02/01/year-hate-2020.

Klippenstein, Ken. 2020. "White Supremacists Are a Threat to Elections, Says The DHS." *The Nation*, 18 September.

Lewis, Sophie. 2021. "Capitol Police Warns of 'Possible Plot to Breach the Capitol' by Militia Group." *CBS News*, 3 March.

Machado, Zenaida. 2020. "Mozambique Should Protect Civilians during Insurgent Fight." Human Rights Watch website. Retrieved May 2022 from https://www.hrw.org/news/2020/08/14/mozambique-should-protect-civilians-during-insurgent-fight.

Mahmud, Aquil Haziq. 2021. "16-year-old Singaporean Detained under ISA after Planning to Attack Muslims at 2 Mosques." *Channel News Asia*, 27 January.

McEvoy, Jemima. 2020. "Who Are the Proud Boys, the Group Behind the Controversial Portland Rally?" *Forbes*, 26 September.

"Member States Concerned by the Growing and Increasingly Transnational Threat of Extreme Right-Wing Terrorism." 2020. UN CTED website. Retrieved May 2022 from https://www.un.org/securitycouncil/ctc/sites/www.un.org.securitycouncil.ctc/files/20200401_press_release_trends_alert_extreme_right-wing_terrorism.pdf.

Mines, Andrew, and Amira Jadoon. 2020. "Can the Islamic State's Afghan Province Survive Its Leadership Losses?" *Lawfare*, 17 May.

Mir, Shakir. 2020. "#NotInMyName, Say Kashmiris after ISIS Claims Kabul Attack Was Revenge for Kashmir." *The Wire*, 26 March.

Morier-Genoud, Eric. 2020. "The Jihadi Insurgency in Mozambique: Origins, Nature and Beginning." *Journal of Eastern African Studies* 14(3): 396–412.

Mueller, John, and Mark G. Stewart. 2016. "Misoverestimating ISIS: Comparisons with al-Qaeda." *Perspectives on Terrorism* 10(4): 30–39.

Murdoch, Simon. 2020. "Patriotic Alternative Uniting the Fascist Right?" HOPE Not Hate website. Retrieved May 2022 from https://www.hopenothate.org.uk/wp-content/uploads/2020/08/HnH_Patriotic-Alternative-report_2020-08-v3.pdf.

Pantucci, Raffaello. 2020a. "Cooperating in Tackling Extreme Right-Wing Ideologies and Terrorism." *RUSI Commentary*, 18 December.

———. 2020b. "End of Al Qaeda Era?" *RSIS Commentary*, 3 December.

Peralta-Malonzo, Anne. 2020. "Explosive Found on Jolo Roadside." *Sun Star Manila*, 20 September.

"Philippines: President Signs Controversial Anti-terror Bill into Law, Giving Government More Room to Act against Critics & Opponents." 2020. Business and Human Rights Resource Centre website. Retrieved May 2022 from https://www.business-humanrights.org/en/latest-news/philippines-president-signs-controversial-anti-terror-bill-into-law-giving-govt-more-room-to-act-against-critics-opponents/.

"PROTECT Plan to Fight Domestic Terrorism." 2020. ADL Center on Extremism website. Retrieved May 2022 from https://www.adl.org/protect-plan.

"Radical Islam in Indonesia." 2020. Indonesia Investments website. Retrieved May 2022 from https://www.indonesia-investments.com/business/risks/radical-islam/item245.

Ramakrishna, Kumar. 2021. "Global Threat Landscape." *Counter Terrorist Trends and Analyses* 13(1).

"Recent Global Jihad Updates on COVID-19 Pandemic March 25–April 1 2020." 2020. Retrieved May 2022 from SITE Intelligence Group.

"Recent Global Jihad Updates on the COVID-19 Pandemic April 22–28, 2020." 2020. Retrieved May 2022 from SITE Intelligence Group.

Sardarizadeh, Shayan, and Mike Wendling. 2020. "George Floyd Protests: Who Are Boogaloo Bois, Antifa and Proud Boys?" *BBC*, 17 June.

Schmidt, Roberto. 2021. "Members of Right-Wing Militias, Extremist Groups Are Latest Charged in Capitol Siege." *NPR*, 19 January.

Schmitt, Eric. 2020. "Al Qaeda Feels Losses in Syria and Afghanistan but Stays Resilient." *The New York Times*, 27 October.

Selsky, Andrew. 2021. "Capitol Attack Reflects US Extremist Evolution over Decades." *AP News*, 23 January.

"SITE Intelligence Weekly Report on the Islamic State July 1–7, 2020." 2020. Retrieved May 2022 from SITE Intelligence Group.

Soliev, Nodirbek. 2020. "Charity for 'Jihad' in Syria: The Indonesian-Uyghur Connection." *RSIS Commentary*, 12 March.

Tarallo, Mark. 2020. "After Setbacks, ISIS Ramps Up Attacks." *Security Management*, August.

Taylor, Christian. 2019. "Al-Qaida Is Stronger Today Than It Was on 9/11." *The Conversation*, 1 July.
"The Boogaloo Movement." 2020. ADL Center on Extremism website. Retrieved May 2022 from https://www.adl.org/boogaloo.
"The Voice of Hind." 2020. Issue 6.
"This Is Our House! A Preliminary Assessment of the Capitol Hill Siege Participants." 2021. The George Washington University Program on Extremism website. Retrieved May 2022 from https://extremism.gwu.edu/sites/g/files/zaxdzs2191/f/This-Is-Our-House.pdf.
Tomazin, Farrah. 2021. "Inspired by the Capitol Siege, Extremists Remain Top of Terror List." *The Sydney Morning Herald*, 20 January.
"Treasury Targets ISIS Financial Facilitators in Syria and Turkey." 2021. US Department of the Treasury website. Retrieved May 2022 from https://home.treasury.gov/news/press-releases/jy0179.
Uras, Umut. 2019. "Turkey's Operation Peace Spring in Northern Syria: One Month On." *Al Jazeera*, 8 November.
Weaver, Matthew, and Vikram Dodd. 2020. "Coronavirus Outbreak, Police Examine CCTV Footage of Suspect Who Spat at UK Rail Worker Who Later Died." *The Guardian*, 13 May.
Westerman, Ashley, Ryan Benk, and David Greene. 2020. "In 2020, Protests Spread across the Globe with a Similar Message: Black Lives Matter." *NPR*, 30 December.
White, Jessica. 2020. "Far Right Extremism Steals the Show in 2020." *RUSI Commentary*, 26 November.
Wilber, Del Quentin. 2021. "FBI Director Says Capitol Riot Was 'Domestic Terrorism'." *Los Angeles Times*, 2 March.
Wilson, Jason. 2020. "Proud Boys Are a Dangerous 'White Supremacist' Group Say US Agencies." *The Guardian*, 1 October.
Zenn, Jacob. 2019. "The Islamic State's Provinces on the Peripheries: Juxtaposing the Pledges from Boko Haram in Nigeria and Abu Sayyaf and Maute Group in the Philippines." *Perspectives on Terrorism* 13(1): 87–104.
Zimmerman, Katherine. 2021. "Al Qaeda & ISIS 20 Years After 9/11" Part of the Wilson Center's 20-Year Memorial of the September 11th, 2001 Attacks.

Conclusion

Policy Recommendations

Introduction

Violent extremist groups exploit times of uncertainty such as the COVID-19 pandemic to advance their agendas (EU Radicalization Awareness Network 2020). Extremists have integrated coronavirus into their propaganda (UN CTED 2020) to advance narratives across all extremist ideologies. In carefully examining both radical Islamist and far right trends, this research aimed to establish a true picture of the threat landscape since the pandemic outbreak. This could serve as a basis for policymakers to make amendments to counterterrorism strategies both in conflict and nonconflict zones. With this in mind, both academic and practitioner perspectives on future counterterrorism policies will be put forward in this concluding section.

Academic Perspectives on Counterterrorism Policies

It has been argued that the pandemic has tested "national resilience, international solidarity, and multilateral cooperation" (The Fine Globe 2020). Growing fragmentation in society and anti-racial narratives warn authorities to stay vigilant and allocate funds to prepare for potential acts of terrorism (Pantucci 2020). COVID-19 offered novel opportunities for both radical Islamist and right-wing extremists to accelerate violence against their objects of hate (Kruglanski et al. 2020). Just as terrorists are continuously adjusting to the circumstances of the pandemic, so do authorities need to make adjustments to address the associated challenges (Voronkov 2020). All government policymaking will have been impacted by the pandemic, and counterterrorism policies are no exception. In the following, we take account of the most relevant factors.

Efforts cannot be relaxed to prevent and counter the global threat of terrorism. Countries need to reaffirm their commitment to international counterterrorism coordination. The reallocation of resources to fight the pandemic together with imposed travel and trade restrictions have already had serious consequences for countering violent extremism (CVE) activities (UN CTED 2020). Efficiently preventing and countering the spread of extremist narratives in cyberspace is still important. Therefore, public and private partnerships are still required to counter terrorists' narratives and cybercrime. The United Nations has strongly articulated the need for innovative "pandemic sensitive holistic approaches" to tackle online extremist propaganda (UN News, 6 July 2020). Content moderation policies need to adapt to this new volume of worrisome online information (Counter Extremism Project 2020). Besides an elevated level of vigilance, messages of hate should be publicly discredited. With this in mind, world leaders are recommended to "disavow bigoted conspiracy theories" (Kruglanski et al. 2020).

Tracking apps that slow the spread of COVID-19 by alerting people who have been in close contact with an infected person could be a valuable asset to counterterrorism efforts. Restrictive measures have revealed terrorists' plans and tactics for attacks and redefined their supply chains, which needs to be taken into account when drafting new counterterrorism policies. Violent extremists' changing operational circumstances suggest that they will more likely misuse online financial services and virtual assets to move and conceal illicit funds. By exploiting the difficult economic times, terrorist entities in developing countries will engage in "new cash-intensive and high-liquidity lines of business" (Financial Action Task Force 2020). To tackle these new challenges, law enforcement and intelligence agencies should proactively engage with the private sector to strengthen communication on security issues. There have been various examples of radicalized individuals exploiting social media to establish international links with the clear intention of mobilizing themselves for violence. Such incitements should be addressed by more concerted and systematic counter-efforts (Ong 2020).

Practitioner Perspectives on Counterterrorism Policies

Far right movements have been exploiting the pandemic for their malevolent purposes by all possible means. Firstly, right-wing extremists used the COVID-19 crisis to recruit new members (Christodoulou 2020). Secondly, in the chaos caused by the pandemic, white supremacists advocated the "collapse of society in order to build a racially pure nation." In line with this, one associated Telegram channel incited its members to "racialize and politicize the crisis [to] destabilize the economy and accelerate the collapse of society" (Murphy, Oliver, and Maples 2020). By mobilizing their members, they endeavor to spread fear. At the same time, the British far right, as well as neo-Nazi activists, called on members diagnosed with COVID-19 to deliberately infect certain minority groups (Jews and Muslims) (Ehsan 2020; Malik 2020) by targeting their houses of worship and other frequently visited places. Besides the calls for physical attacks (Weimann and Masri 2020), far right activists misused cyberspace in another innovative way, with so-called Zoombombing (Koblentz-Stenzler 2020). This targeted harassment on Zoom involved online trolls posting obscene or hateful messages (Middle East Eye, 30 April 2020). Right-wing extremists and white supremacists drew attention to ethnic minorities as the source of the disease. Neo-Nazis in Germany accelerated the spread of conspiracy theories with regard to COVID-19 and put themselves forward as defenders of the deprived by providing assistance for the elderly (Zeit Online, 1 April 2020).

The pandemic is perceived by the Islamic State as a "divine command" (Maor-Hirsch 2020) and as an extraordinary opportunity for a new surge in terrorism. Al-Qaeda in South Asia has claimed that the West is responsible for the outbreak. In accordance with their narratives and as a punishment from God, the virus attacks Western governments "for the injustice and oppression committed against Muslims" (Wilson Center 2020). In a May video, Abubakar Shekau, leader of one Boko Haram faction, asserted that the virus is Allah's punishment for the sins of mankind. He claimed this could be proved by the fact that his group members had not been infected regardless of the fact that they had been praying in congregations without maintaining social distancing (Tony Blair Institute for Global Change 2020). With the intention to strengthen their political legitimacy, extremist groups distributed food and medical supplies in areas where the state's presence was weak (Columbo and Harris 2020). The Taliban and Hezbollah even provided public health services for the needy (Clarke 2020). There are, however, grave concerns within the Islamic State's leadership over potential infections within the group's support base. Therefore, fighters in refugee camps and prisons are given particular attention (Welby 2020). This is corroborated by the Al-Naba newsletter in which IS incited its followers to make use of the pandemic and free its members in Syrian prisons and detention camps (Reliefweb 2020).

We can observe that certain narratives keep reoccurring, and these have been used in support of a wide variety of ideological objectives, but ideology-specific interpretations are also being presented. To mention some of the commonalities, both jihadist and far right actors engage in conspiratorial concepts of COVID-19's origins, although with different explanations. Religious extremists interpreted the pandemic as "God's will" and saw the crisis as a "geopolitical opportunity" (Comerford and Davey 2020) for political and economic collapse. Meanwhile, right-wing extremists and white supremacists drew attention to ethnic minorities as the source of the disease. Radical groups in Europe torched 5G telephone towers as they falsely believed that radiation from these telecommunication masts was playing a role in spreading the virus (Reuters, 6 April 2020). It is also informative that "37 percent of a representative British target audience had heard about the 5G conspiracy theory and almost a third of (those) people found it credible" (Hermansson 2020).

As scapegoats of the pandemic, members of two communities have been specifically selected. On one hand, the Jewish community was targeted by five categories of COVID-19-related conspiracy theories. Radical groups first regarded the virus as fake and as a Jewish plot aiming to mislead the public. Another theory said that the pandemic had been deliberately manufactured for malicious purposes. Other conspiracy theories claimed that since Jews primarily spread the virus, huge numbers of Jews would die of the disease. There were also posts that encouraged readers to intentionally infect Jews with the virus (Community Security Trust 2020).

The rise in hatred toward Asian people in the UK, United States, and Australia is alarming too. A 900 percent increase in Twitter hashtags referring to hate speech toward Chinese people have been detected (L1ght 2020). A man physically and verbally assaulted a woman in a facemask who was waiting in a Chinatown subway station on 5 February 2020. He called her a "diseased expletive" (Sosa and Brown 2020). A Korean woman in Manhattan was grabbed and punched in the face in a March 2020 incident. The offender yelled at her "You've got coronavirus, you Asian expletive" (Miles 2020). At Sam's Club in Midland, Texas, a man stabbed a family from Myanmar on 14 March 2020 (Aziz 2020). As a response to hate crimes against them, Asian Americans used social media to fight back against racially motivated atrocities (VOA News, 4 April 2020).

During the pandemic, our interactive space was predominantly online, and violent extremists exploited the possibilities cyberspace offers (Ackerman and Peterson 2020), making counter-extremist operations considerably challenging. It was highly recommended that special attention be focused on these nefarious operations and new counterextremism strategies established accordingly (Commission for Countering Extremism 2020). There is a pressing need to develop effective mechanisms and collaborations to identify and counteract malevolent intentions in cyberspace (Basit 2020). Given the utmost relevance of online platforms, one of the most worrisome assertions is that—according to the Commission for Countering Extremism—90.6 percent of posts containing misinformation were not acted on by social media companies after volunteers flagged them (Center for Countering Digital Hate 2020). There are two fundamental policy response options to counter extremist exploitation of social media platforms. The first is strategic communication and the second is content moderation (Ganesh and Bright 2020).

The prevalence of fake news and misinformation campaigns during the pandemic may have truly undermined the trust in government communications. To rebuild this confidence, effective communication strategies need to be developed to improve the capacities for eliminating the spread of false information, thereby making the extremist narratives powerless (United Nations Institute for Training and Research 2020). To these ends, well-established strategic communication campaigns could clarify and negate misinformation by radical groups and could raise awareness about government policies to thwart radicalization. However, it must be recognized that the development of effective counter-narratives has prerequisites; namely, it is of great importance to gain expertise in ideological, religious, and historical settings (Rasheed 2020). World leaders should actively seek to officially discredit extremist messages of hate (Kruglanski et al. 2020). It should also be made explicitly clear that extremist content available online is radical and harmful for young people, who may feel more displaced and thus more prone to radicalization (UN CTED 2020). Youth should be taught to think critically about online radicalized content. Education programs are a central pillar to building young people's resilience to violent extremist content (UNESCO 2020). There is a stressed need for consistent dissemination of counter-narratives to debunk false extremist statements. When designing counter- or alternative narrative campaigns, the objectives and scope of this initiative should be clearly and coherently set (Radicalisation Awareness Network 2019). For the dissemination, trustworthy and genuine messengers should be selected (Zeiger and Gyte 2020).

To counter the constant indoctrinating efforts of extremists, the misinterpretations of religious doctrines should be eliminated. It should be consistently communicated that there are no religious justifications for waging armed jihad in order to establish an Islamic state or caliphate. Simultaneously, there is no place in Islam for incitements of hatred of the "other." The Qur'anic teachings do not distinguish superiority among nations and tribes. National religious authorities should have a certain degree of supervision over their local religious entities and be responsible for the accurate interpretation of religious doctrines. They are in the best position to make sure that religious teachers are well-qualified (Halimi and Sudiman 2021).

Regarding online content moderation, first we need to acknowledge the obstacles to regulating online hate speech. Legislative efforts countering terrorist content face the following problems: "the ability of users to find and effectively use mechanisms to flag illegal content, the legal verifiability of deletion requests, and the tracking of offenders, since the police and judiciary have too few qualified personnel" (Bossong 2021). To begin with, it is problematic to define what counts as extremist content; "the definition of terrorist content is broad and possibly encompasses content that may be radical, polemic or controversial, but not illegal" (Kuczerawy 2018). Without international consensus on what content is considered hate speech, when addressing such incitements, it may infringe on the freedom of speech (UN 2020). So-called "grey-zone content" constitutes another limitation to effective moderation. Such sensitive decisions may result in the excessive restriction of free speech, which can further amplify extremist counteractions (Wallner 2021). Likewise, it varies per nation which content counts as hate speech. Regardless of unanimous interpretations of fundamental liberal values, harmonizing efforts should be extended (Bossong 2021). Properly assessing content ultimately requires special expertise that may not be available within the short time proposed for removal of the content. In addition, proactive countermeasures may operate against the general monitoring obligation, with unnecessary deletions (Kuczerawy 2018). By the same token, it is questionable who is responsible for "defining an effective and enforceable regulatory framework for content moderation." Another challenge is the inconsistency in enforcing harmful content moderation (Bromell 2022).

Another concerning issue is the recommender algorithms of YouTube, Facebook, and Twitter, which may lead users to other extremist content. Because of the fact that these algorithms are kept secret, it is difficult to assess how effectively tech companies could limit these promoting tools (Agius and Barnet 2021). The consequences of removal of worrisome content may urge extremists to migrate to other less-controlled parts of the internet, making their detection even more challenging for law enforcement agencies (Whittaker 2019). With regard to right-wing extremist online content, another concerning aspect is that these actors use coded language, making it difficult to detect via automated search mechanisms.

Cooperation among multiple actors including governments and the private sector is necessary to successfully manage extremist content (Crosset and Dupont 2018). To speed up the deletion of digital extremist content, authorities have been collaborating with major online platforms. With Europol's leading role via its Internal Referral Unit and the EU Internet Forum, there is daily cooperation with companies including YouTube/Google, Facebook, Microsoft, and Twitter (EU Internet Forum 2015). A hashtag database together with a crisis protocol to block recorded terrorist acts is the most relevant tool in this collaboration. The volume of radical Islamist propaganda has been considerably reduced thanks to private sector links through the Global Internet Forum to Counter Terrorism (Global Internet Forum 2021).

To detect worrisome online content more efficiently, targeted law enforcement investigation is required, and intelligence collection efforts by interdisciplinary staff should apply automated content detection techniques.[1] Human review of these techniques can serve as a corrective measure (Keller 2018). Besides this, social media companies should be encouraged to establish self-regulation within the industry and clearly set their content standards for what is accepted or forbidden and also their moderation policies (Ring 2018). They should also provide periodic transparency reports on their content moderation activity to make better known the threat of violent extremism on tech platforms (Deverell and Janin 2020). It is recommended that technology companies develop a self-regulatory system to detect and remove extremist content (Malik 2018). Besides radicalized content removal, more coordinated cooperation is advisable between internet service providers to self-police social media platforms (Hardy 2017).

One of the most crucial steps in countering the appeal of extremism online is to strengthen digital literacy and a critical consumption of online content among young people (Briggs and Feve 2014). To prevent and combat online misinformation and disinformation campaigns, the use of technological solutions is critical (UNICRI 2020). Data science and big data visualization enable tracking of the spread of fake news and its origin. Machine-learning algorithms detect certain patterns of language in this process. Websites and platforms have been set up where the artificial intelligence-based systems verify the available infodemic. These algorithms validate news with credibility scores and help readers detect false information. Automated chatbots have been designed to debunk false information circulated on private messaging applications. The presence of these autonomous fact-checkers means that accurate information provided by accountable organizations is what remains. Web browser extensions can provide translating services, are able to review and examine the validity of available information, and also identify security threats by tracking cookies. Digital media information literacy platforms and tools strengthen readers' critical thinking, allowing them to more accurately assess misleading online content. These technology-based countermeasures are able to empower individual users of the internet by providing them with the skills and tools to make better informed decisions (UNICRI 2020).

It has already been articulated that the long-term solution to address radicalization lies in prevention (Käsehage 2020). People who are prone to engage in extremism have individual causes for engaging in these ideologies. Their multiple and intertwined influencing factors for radicalization would be better understood on a case-by-case basis. Well-trained professionals should better understand the needs of vulnerable individuals, and assistance should be provided for them accordingly (Lynch 2018). Successful prevention programs are required to be based on close collaboration with experts from academia and practitioner circles. Regular forums could facilitate the constant exchange of best practices and threat assessments within the pool of these stakeholders (City of Copenhagen Employment and Integration Administration 2015). The youth would be empowered by the appointment of young policymakers to take effective actions to prevent and respond to violent extremism (UNESCO 2015). Educational institutions should play a pivotal role in preventing violent extremism by teaching students about options for peaceful conflict resolution (Samuel 2020).

Proactive community policing has been one of the most effective strategies to address violent extremism (US Department of Justice Community Oriented Policing Services 2014). In the pandemic situation, however, the law enforcement community was busy with the enforcement of lockdowns and other epidemiological restrictions and therefore lacked the capacity to continue these strategies. The private sector made tremendous efforts to fine-tune adjustment to the "new normal." Traditional violent extremism prevention programs and countermeasures rely heavily on interpersonal connections; many interactions were moved into cyberspace, where existing networks within local communities were maintained via digital communication opportunities (Rosand, Koser, and Schmucky-Logan 2020).

As has happened with COVID-19, future pandemics too will result in reallocations of foreign aid budgets, which are fundamental financial resources for efforts to prevent and counter violent extremism. This forces NGOs operating in the field to reconceptualize programs to prevent violent extremism (ibid.). It is also of crucial importance to continue to support existing counterterrorism activities and develop remote access solutions to proceed with them by providing, for instance, online training (United Nations Institute for Training and Research 2020).

Pandemic responses to terrorism have been "state-centric" (Basit 2020) and accordingly accelerated a nation-centered approach. Engaging primarily in state-level pressing problems may demolish international collaboration and incapacitate global counteractions against violent extremism. Particular attention should be given to existing global forums to articulate the need to continue transnational efforts.

Restrictive measures may have resulted in a change of traditional terrorist targets. Because of the pandemic, certain critical infrastructures faced a heightened level of threat as potential terrorist or extremist targets. For future pandemics, security arrangements at hospitals, medical facilities, and supermarkets should be tightened. It is highly questionable, though, whether individuals will seek innovative methods to carry out acts of bioterrorism. The most feasible counteraction will remain with citizens. Once social distancing and fundamental hygiene practices become habitual, the threat posed by a deliberate infection could be lowered considerably (United Nations Institute for Training and Research 2020).

The increasing involvement of women and family networks in jihadist activities raises serious concerns. There are tight links between IS operatives and family members residing in the Al-Hawl camp, and in Southeast Asia several female terrorists were detained (GMA News Online, 11 October 2020; Cepeda and Talabong 2019). Accordingly, counterterrorist authorities should broaden the scope of their investigations to identify the impact of the direct environment on suspected jihadists.

Epidemiological restrictions and fears about infection (SITE Intelligence Group 2020) postponed or canceled general right-wing gatherings for networking and recruiting purposes, leading to an enhanced presence in cyberspace. Numerous real-life case studies underline the threat posed by self-activating individual terrorists who have been radicalized in digital subcultures. These solo terrorists may be members of white supremacist, radicalized conservative, Fascist, Neo-Nazi, or online extremist communities, making the challenge to prevent them from doing harm extremely challenging (UN CTED 2020). Consistent serious actions should be taken to remove terrorist manuals available online. At the same time, it is possible that COVID-related restrictions have resulted in disruptions to terrorist supply chains, leading to less sophisticated means of enacting violence and increased online methods of engagement to make up for it.

Conclusion

This book has proposed to provide a more accurate assessment of the terrorist threat landscape. Online content moderation has been addressed in relation to preventing and countering violent extremism, hate speech, online financial transactions, and radical Islamist and right-wing narratives.

Note

1. DANTE Project H2020-FCT-06-2015, Detecting and ANalysing TErrorist-related Online Contents and Financing Activities. Accessed August 2022 from https://ec.europa.eu/research/participants/documents/downloadPublic?documentIds=080166e5c29fb516&appId=PPGMS.

References

Ackerman, Garry, and Hayley Peterson. 2020. "Terrorism and COVID-19: Actual and Potential Impacts." *Perspectives on Terrorism* 13(3).

Agius, Christine, and Belinda Barnet. 2021. "Can Violent Extremist Content Online Be Eliminated?" *The Interpreter*, 27 May.

"APF Analysis: The Coronavirus (COVID-19) Impact on the ISIS Detention Camps in Syria." 2020. Reliefweb website. Retrieved May 2022 from https://reliefweb.int/report/syrian-arab-republic/virus-fears-spread-camps-isis-families-syria-s-north-east.

Aziz, S. 2020. "Anti-Asian Racism Must be Stopped before it is Normalized." *Al Jazeera*, 16 April.

Basit, Abdul. 2020. "How Terrorist and Extremist Groups Are Exploiting Coronavirus Cracks in Society." *SCMP*, 1 May.

Bossong, Raphael. 2021. "The Next Steps for EU Counterterrorism Policy: Evolving Threats of Jihadism, Right-Wing Extremism, and Transatlantic Cooperation." SWP Comment, 20/2021 Berlin: Stiftung Wissenschaft und Politik – SWP – Deutsches Institute für Internationale Politik und Sicherheit. Retrieved May 2022 from https://doi.org/10.18449/2021C20.

Briggs, Rachel, and Sebastian Feve. 2014. "Policy Briefing: Countering the Appeal of Extremism Online." Institute for Strategic Dialogue. Retrieved May 2022 from https://www.dhs.gov/sites/default/files/publications/Countering%20the%20Appeal%20of%20Extremism%20Online-ISD%20Report.pdf.

Bromell, David. 2022. "Challenges in Regulating Online Content." In *Regulating Free Speech in a Digital Age*. Cham: Springer.

Cepeda, Mara, and Rambo Talabong. 2019. "At Least 23 Dead in Jolo Cathedral Bombing." *Rappler*, 27 January.

Christodoulou, Mario. 2020. "ASIO Briefing Warns That the Far Right Is Exploiting Coronavirus to Recruit New Members." *ABC News*, 12 June.

"Citing Coronavirus Concerns, European Neo-Nazi Organization Postpones Upcoming Demonstration." 2020. Retrieved May 2022 from SITE Intelligence Group.

Clarke, Colin P. 2020. "Yesterday's Terrorists Are Today's Public Health Providers." *Foreign Policy*, 8 April.

Columbo, Emilia, and Marielle Harris. 2020. "Extremist Groups Stepping Up Operations during the Covid-19 Outbreak in Sub-Saharan Africa." CSIS website. Retrieved May 2022 from https://www.csis.org/analysis/extremist-groups-stepping-operations-during-covid-19-outbreak-sub-saharan-africa.

Comerford, Milo, and Jacob Davey. 2020. "Comparing Jihadist and Far Right Extremist Narratives on COVID-19." GNET Research website. Retrieved May 2022 from https://gnet-research.org/2020/04/27/comparing-jihadist-and-far right-extremist-narratives-on-covid-19/.

"Coronavirus and the Plague of Antisemitism." 2020. Community Security Trust website. Retrieved May 2022 from https://cst.org.uk/data/file/d/9/Coronavirus%20and%20the%20plague%20of%20antisemitism.1586276450.pdf.

"Coronavirus Concerns Postpone White Nationalist Music Festival." 2020. Retrieved May 2022 from SITE Intelligence Group.

"COVID-19 How Hateful Extremists Are Exploiting the Pandemic." 2020. Commission for Countering Extremism website. Retrieved May 2022 from https://www.gov.uk/government/publications/covid-19-how-hateful-extremists-are-exploiting-the-pandemic.

Crosset, Valentine, and Benoit Dupont. 2018. "Internet et Propagande Jihadiste: la Régulation Polycentrique du Cyberespace." *Critique Internationale* (1): 107–25.

Deverell, Flora, and Maygane Janin. 2020. "Covid-19: Far Right Violent Extremism and Tech Platforms' Response." Foundation pour L'Innovation Politique website. Retrieved May 2022 from https://www.fondapol.org/app/uploads/2020/12/180-maygane-ultradroite-gb-2020-11-03-w.pdf.

Ehsan, Rakib. 2020. "Weaponizing COVID-19: Far Right Antisemitism in the United Kingdom and United States." Henry Jackson Society website. Retrieved May 2022 from https://henryjacksonsociety.org/wp-content/uploads/2020/05/HJS-COVID-19-Far-Right-Report.pdf.

"EU Internet Forum: Bringing Together Governments, Europol and Technology Companies to Counter Terrorist Content and Hate Speech Online." 2015. European Commission website. Retrieved May 2022 from https://ec.europa.eu/commission/presscorner/detail/ro/IP_15_6243.

Ganesh, Bharath, and Jonathan Bright. 2020. "Countering Extremists on Social Media: Challenges for Strategic Communication and Content Moderation." Policy Studies Organization website. Retrieved May 2022 from https://onlinelibrary.wiley.com/doi/pdf/10.1002/poi3.236.

"Global Internet Forum to Counter Terrorism Expands Its Database." 2021. Digwatch website. Retrieved May 2022 from https://dig.watch/updates/global-internet-forum-counter-terrorism-expands-its-database/.

Halimi, Mahfuh Bin Haji, and Muhammad Saiful Alam Shah bin Sudiman. 2021. "Religious Extremism: Challenging Extremist and Jihadist Propaganda." *Counter Terrorist Trends and Analyses* 13(1).

Hardy, Keiran. 2017. "Hard and Soft Power Approaches to Countering Online Extremism." In *Terrorists' Use of the Internet*, ed. M. Conway et al. iOS Press.

Hermansson, Patrik. 2020. "Trust No One: Understanding the Drivers of Conspiracy Theory Belief HOPE Not Hate." HOPE Not Hate. Retrieved May 2022 from

https://hopenothate.org.uk/wp-content/uploads/2020/04/conspiracy-report-2020-04-v1-copy.pdf.
"Impact of COVID-19 on Violent Extremism and Terrorism." 2020. United Nations Institute for Training and Research website. Retrieved May 2022 from https://www.un.org/securitycouncil/ctc/sites/www.un.org.securitycouncil.ctc/files/files/documents/2021/Jan/cted_paper_the-impact-of-the-covid-19-pandemic-on-counter-te.pdf.
Käsehage, Nina. 2020. "Prevention of Radicalisation in Western Muslim Diasporas." In *Handbook of Terrorism Prevention and Preparedness*, ed. Alex P. Schmid. The Hague, NL: ICCT Press.
Keller, Daphne. 2018. "Inception Impact Assessment: Measures to Further Improve the Effectiveness of the Fight against Illegal Content Online." SSRN. Retrieved May 2022 from http://dx.doi.org/10.2139/ssrn.3262950.
Koblentz-Stenzler, Liram. 2020. "The Far Right Leverages COVID-19 Pandemic to Gain Influence and Encourage Violence." International Institute for Counter-Terrorism website. Retrieved May 2022 from https://ict.org.il/podcasts/the-far-right-leverages-covid-19-pandemic-to-gain-influence-and-encourage-violence/.
Kruglanski, Arie W., Rohan Gunaratna, Molly Ellenberg, and Anne Speckhard. 2020. "Terrorism in Time of the Pandemic: Exploiting Mayhem." *Global Security: Health, Science and Policy* 5(1): 128.
Kuczerawy, Aleksandra. 2018. "The Proposed Regulation on Preventing the Dissemination of Terrorist Content Online: Safeguards and Risks for Freedom of Expression." Center for Democracy and Technology. Retrieved May 2022 from https://ssrn.com/abstract=3296864.
"Less Radicalisation through an Effective and Coherent Effort." 2015. City of Copenhagen Employment and Integration Administration website. Retrieved May 2022 from https://strongcitiesnetwork.org/blog/themes/de-radicalisation-and-disengagement/page/3/.
Lynch, Orla. 2018. "Ex Post Paper, Methods of Evidence-Based Approaches: Assessment and CVE/PVE." *RAN Centre of Excellence*, 21 December.
Malik, Nikita. 2018. "Terror in the Dark: How Terrorists Use Encryption, the Darknet and Cryptocurrencies." The Henry Jackson Society website. Retrieved May 2022 from https://henryjacksonsociety.org/wp-content/uploads/2018/04/Terror-in-the-Dark.pdf.
———. 2020. "Self-Isolation Might Stop Coronavirus, but It Will Speed the Spread of Extremism." *Foreign Policy*, 26 March.
Maor-Hirsch, Sigal. 2020. "ISIS in the Age of COVID-19 – from Islamizing the Pandemic to Implementing the Jihadist Strategy." International Institute for Counter-Terrorism website. Retrieved May 2022 from https://www.ict.org.il/images/ISIS%20During%20Corona%205.0.pdf.
Miles, D. 2020. "'Where's Your (Expletive) Mask?': Asian Woman Attacked in Manhattan Hate Crime." *ABC News7*, 11 March.
Murphy, Philip D., Sheila Y. Oliver, and Jared M. Maples. 2020. "Online Extremists Exploit COVID-19 to Inspire Supporters." NJOHSP Intelligence Note. Retrieved May 2022 from https://static1.squarespace.com/static/54d79f88e4b0db3478a04405/t/5e76642964f35a2e2857fefc/1584817193502/Online+Extremists+Exploit+COVID-19+to+Inspire+Supporters.pdf.

Ong, Kyler. 2020. "Ideological Convergence in the Extreme Right." *Counter Terrorist Trends and Analyses* 12(5): 1–7.

"Pandemic Focuses Attention on Investing in Youth Initiatives to Prevent Violent Extremism." 2020. UNESCO website. Retrieved May 2022 from https://en.unesco.org/news/pandemic-focuses-attention-investing-youth-initiatives-prevent-violent-extremism.

Pantucci, Raffello. 2020. "Key Questions for Counter-Terrorism Post-COVID-19." Retrieved May 2022 from https://www.rsis.edu.sg/wp-content/uploads/2020/04/CTTA-April-2020.pdf.

"Partners Reaffirm Joint Commitment to Fighting Terrorism, Violent Extremism amid COVID-19, as Virtual Counter-Terrorism Week Concludes." 2020. United Nations website. Retrieved August 2022 from https://press.un.org/en/2020/pa30.doc.htm.

"Preventing Radicalisation to Terrorism and Violent Extremism Delivering Counter- or Alternative Narratives." 2019. Radicalisation Awareness Network website. Retrieved May 2022 from https://www.interior.gob.es/opencms/pdf/servicios-al-ciudadano/plan-estrategico-nacional-de-lucha-contra-la-radicalizacion-violenta/documentacion-del-plan/ran/RAN-Collection-Preventing-Radicalisation-to-Terrorism-and-Violent-Extremism.pdf.

Rasheed, Adil. 2020. "Countering the Radical Narrative." Manohar Parrikar Institute for Defence Studies and Analyses website. Retrieved May 2022 from https://www.idsa.in/book/countering-the-radical-narrative.

"Recent Far Right Updates on the COVID-19 Pandemic April 1–7, 2020." 2020. Retrieved May 2022 from SITE Intelligence Group.

Ring, Caitlin Elizabeth. 2018. "Hate Speech in Social Media: An Exploration of the Problem and Its Proposed Solutions." Ph.D. Dissertation.

"Rising Levels of Hate Speech & Online Toxicity during This Time of Crisis." 2020. L1ght website. Retrieved May 2022 from https://l1ght.com/Toxicity_during_coronavirus_Report-L1ght.pdf?fbclid=IwAR12yPh-GIi1Ur1qwwZoCuu4nP2zG5dLxs590Exli5UXYORQCWp3w_ko1MQ.

Rosand, Eric, Khalid Koser, and Lilla Schmucky-Logan. 2020. "Preventing Violent Extremism during and after the COVID-19 Pandemic." *Brookings*, 28 April.

Samuel, Thomas Koruth. 2020. "At the Crossroads: Rethinking the Role of Education in Preventing and Countering Violent Extremism." In *Handbook of Terrorism Prevention and Preparedness*, ed. Alex P. Schmid. The Hague, NL: ICCT Press.

"Snapshot How Extremist Groups Are Responding to Covid-19." 2020. Tony Blair Institute for Global Change website. Retrieved May 2022 from https://institute.global/policy/snapshot-how-extremist-groups-are-responding-covid-19-9-april-2020.

Sosa, Anabel, and Lee Brown. 2020. "Woman Wearing Face Mask Attacked in Possible Coronavirus Hate Crime." *New York Post*, 5 February.

"Stop the Virus of Disinformation: The Risk of Malicious Use of Social Media during COVID-19 and the Technology Options to Fight It." 2020. UNICRI website. Retrieved May 2022 from https://digitallibrary.un.org/record/3927039?ln=en.

"Strategy and Plan of Action on Hate Speech." 2020. United Nations website. Retrieved May 2022 from https://www.un.org/en/genocideprevention/hate-speech-strategy.shtml.

"Tech and Terrorism: Online Extremists Exploit Coronavirus Pandemic to Incite Violence and Encourage Terrorism." 2020. Counter Extremism Project website. Retrieved May 2022 from https://www.counterextremism.com/press/tech-terrorism-online-extremists-exploit-coronavirus-pandemic-incite-violence-encourage.

"The Impact of the COVID-19 Pandemic on Terrorism, Counter-terrorism and Countering Violent Extremism." 2020. United Nations Security Council Counter-Terrorism Committee Executive Directorate website. Retrieved May 2022 from https://www.un.org/securitycouncil/ctc/news/impact-covid-19-pandemic-terrorism-counter-terrorism-and-countering-violent-extremism-update.

"United Nations Security Council Counter-Terrorism Committee Executive Directorate (CTED) virtual roundtable of the Global Research Network on 'Emerging Trends in Violent Extremism Conducive to Terrorism: A Focus on Extreme Right-wing Terrorism'." 2020. The Soufan Center website. Retrieved May 2022 from https://thesoufancenter.org/emerging-trends-in-violent-extremism-conducive-to-terrorism-a-focus-on-extreme-right-wing-terrorism/.

"Using Community Policing to Counter Violent Extremism – 5 Key Principles for Law Enforcement." 2014. US Department of Justice Community Oriented Policing Services website. Retrieved May 2022 from https://www.theiacp.org/sites/default/files/all/f-h/Final%20Key%20Principles%20Guide.pdf.

"Violent Right-Wing Extremism in Focus." 2020. EU Radicalisation Awareness Network website. Retrieved May 2022 from https://ec.europa.eu/home-affairs/sites/homeaffairs/files/what-we-do/networks/radicalisation_awareness_network/docs/ran_brochure_violent_right_wing_extremism_in_focus_en.pdf.

Voronkov, Vladimir. 2020. "Countering Terrorism during the COVID-19 Pandemic." *The Jakarta Post*, 9 July.

Wallner, Claudia. 2021. "Against the Clock: Can the EU's New Strategy for Terrorist Content Removal Work?" *RUSI Commentary*, 26 January.

Weimann, Gabriel, and Natalie Masri. 2020. "The Virus of Hate: Far Right Terrorism in Cyberspace." International Institute for Counter-Terrorism website. Retrieved May 2022 from https://www.ict.org.il/images/Dark%20Hate.pdf.

Welby, Peter. 2020. "What the Virus Pandemic Means for Violent Extremists." *Arab News*, 18 April.

Whittaker, Joe. 2019. "How Content Removal Might Help Terrorists." *Lawfare*, 30 June.

"Will to Act: How Social Media Giants Have Failed to Live Up to Their Claims on the Coronavirus 'Infodemic'." 2020. Center for Countering Digital Hate website. Retrieved May 2022 from https://252f2edd-1c8b-49f5-9bb2-cb57bb47e4ba.filesusr.com/ugd/f4d9b9_17e9f74e84414524bbe9a5b45afdf77e.pdf.

Wilson Center. 2020. "What Islamists Are Doing and Saying on COVID-19 Crisis." Wilson Center website. Retrieved May 2022 from https://www.wilsoncenter.org/article/what-islamists-are-doing-and-saying-covid-19-crisis.

Zeiger, Sara, and Joseph Gyte. 2020. "Prevention of Radicalisation on Social Media and the Internet." In *Handbook of Terrorism Prevention and Preparedness*, ed. Alex P. Schmid. The Hague, NL: ICCT Press.

Annex A

Key Radical Islamist and Far Right Messages Concerning the Pandemic

Radical Islamist Posts Concerning Europe

12 March 2020

In English posts on 12 March, one jihadist wrote, "coronavirus is healing the hearts of the believers. Alhamdulillah [Praise be to Allah] . . . Corona is a divine punishment. Look who has been hit the worst, China (Arrogant atheists), Iran (Arrogant shia), & Italy (Arrogant Christians)" (SITE Intelligence Group 2020).

19 March 2020

Following IS' initial statement in Al-Naba 220 on 6 February, which stopped short of embracing supporters' calling the virus a punishment from God to China, the group shifted its tone to say just that, thus capitalizing on the spread of the virus around the world and its economic impact on Western states. In the editorial of Al-Naba 226, published on 19 March, IS urged "lone wolf" jihadists to capitalize on the paralysis and fear overtaking "Crusader" countries amid the COVID-19 pandemic by mounting attacks, specifically citing past attacks in Paris, London, and Brussels (SITE Intelligence Group 2020).

22 March 2020

Users on a pro-IS platform posted English-language news items and charts on new infection and mortality rates (especially in America, France, Germany, Italy, Spain and Switzerland) and gleefully opined on the crisis. Additionally, supporters expressed that the virus, like natural disasters, is the "bitter fruit" of enemy oppression (SITE Intelligence Group 2020).

23 March 2020

A poster published on 23 March portrayed COVID-19 as divine revenge for the Muslim victims of coalition airstrikes in Baghuz, Syria – echoing IS' official stance on the situation as declared in Al-Naba 226. The graphic showed the virus, men in hazmat suits (one of them taking the temperature of a person), a person dead on the ground, and the torn flags of various countries, including the United States and Italy (SITE Intelligence Group 2020).

24 March 2020

The pro-al-Qaeda (AQ) Thughur Media Network issued a statement on 24 March in response to the UN Secretary General's call for a global ceasefire in the face of a pandemic. The Arabic-language message declared COVID-19 had been sent to "weaken the disbelievers" both militarily and economically. The US, France, UK, Russia, Germany, and China were all noted as having their power halted by the "invisible soldier of Allah" (SITE Intelligence Group 2020).

31 March 2020

Similar to other jihadi groups in using the COVID-19 pandemic as an opportunity to proselytize, AQ Central advocated Islam to Westerners suffering because of the coronavirus while calling on Muslims to embrace religious principles and wage jihad (SITE Intelligence Group 2020).

31 March 2020

Al-Kifah Media, a French-language media unit linked to al-Qaeda, urged the French government to end its military commitments in the Sahel region of Africa and instead direct its money and energies to fighting the COVID-19 pandemic at home (SITE Intelligence Group 2020).

1 April 2020

As the COVID-19 pandemic continued to spread globally, Filipino IS supporters celebrated the rising number of deaths in Western countries, among others, and attributed the virus to Allah and his punishment for practices against Islam (SITE Intelligence Group 2020).

3 April 2020

An IS supporter called on lone wolves to capitalize on the West's preoccupation with the COVID-19 pandemic and launch attacks, giving this message on posters depicting London and Chicago (SITE Intelligence Group 2020).

6 April 2020

IS supporters continued to highlight the impact of COVID-19 on the economy of the "Crusaders" and hoped for its continued affliction (SITE Intelligence Group 2020).

13 April 2020

JNIM, the Sahel-based branch of AQ, claimed credit for the deadly raid on a military base in Bamba and continued to urge Malian President Ibrahim Boubacar Keïta to abandon his French allies and negotiate with fighters. The statement also expressed hope the COVID-19 pandemic would exhaust participants in the French-led alliance and fragment the coalition (SITE Intelligence Group 2020).

20 April 2020

An IS-aligned publishing unit called the COVID-19 pandemic a "justified punishment" on disbelievers and urged Muslims to embrace jihad and religious principles or expect a worse fate (SITE Intelligence Group 2020).

29 April 2020

Echoing the sentiment shared by other jihadi groups, an IS-aligned media unit portrayed the coronavirus as divine retribution on the US-led coalition for Muslim deaths in Mosul and Baghouz and expressed joy for COVID-19 deaths in America and Italy (SITE Intelligence Group 2020).

4 May 2020

On a poster promoting COVID-19 as divine punishment for "disbelievers," a pro-IS media unit depicted the coronavirus spread through the Colosseum in Rome, Italy (SITE Intelligence Group 2020).

5 May 2020

Jihadists promoted the vehicular attack in Colombes, a commune in Paris, France, the perpetrator of which reportedly declared that he "did it for ISIS." Amongst responses, a jihadist suggested fighters take advantage of the situation created by the COVID-19 pandemic to mount attacks in the West (SITE Intelligence Group 2020).

29 July 2020

Prominent IS-aligned Battar Media Foundation released a second examination of the state of the US economy, "Economic Paralysis and a Certain Recession," published on 29 July. It presented arguments bolstered by news media clips about not only the American economy but that of European Union countries deteriorating as the number of coronavirus infections rise. Battar remarked that America is imploding, Europe is on the brink of a depression, and in the near future political systems will collapse (SITE Intelligence Group 2020).

Jihadist Posts Concerning Asia

18 March 2020

Describing COVID-19 as a "decree of Allah," the Afghan Taliban advocated a religious approach to dealing with the coronavirus and offered humanitarian nongovernmental organizations safe passage with equipment and medicine in areas under its control. The group issued a statement on 18 March recommending Muslims to seek forgiveness from God frequently and give charity, believing that the virus descended upon mankind because of "disobedience and sins." In addition to prayer, it also urged businessmen to refrain from price hikes on essentials and asked Muslims to obey safety guidelines issued by health experts and desist "from panic, leaving Islamic injunctions or committing actions which could, Allah forbid, amount to religious rebellion or become the cause of spreading anxiety and psychological fear among the people" (SITE Intelligence Group 2020).

19 March 2020

In a statement issued on 19 March, the Afghan Taliban gave its "sincere condolences" to Iran for the suffering caused by the pandemic and at the same time requested Iranian leaders to observe "Islamic brotherhood" and not expel Afghan refugees or deny them medical attention. In turn, they advised refugees in Iran to "strictly follow the rules and guidelines issued by the said country in combating the spread corona virus" (SITE Intelligence Group 2020).

22 March 2020

In an English article published under the "weekly comment" section on its website on 22 March, the Afghan Taliban discussed the coronavirus as a microscopic organism that has instilled fear in mankind and brought the global economy and social life to a standstill. The pandemic, it stated, is an "instance of [God's] might," as it has "even forced the staunchest atheist to take refuge in religion as a last resort" (SITE Intelligence Group 2020).

25 March 2020

A pro-IS media unit published the second issue of the English-language "Voice of Hind" magazine. It featured articles urging Indian IS jihadists to capitalize on enemies' preoccupation with the COVID-19 pandemic and wage attacks, and it slammed the deal reached between the Afghan Taliban and the US (SITE Intelligence Group 2020).

26 March 2020

The Afghan Taliban portrayed itself as better able to manage the COVID-19 pandemic in Afghanistan than the country's government, arguing that regime officials only wish to loot foreign funds (SITE Intelligence Group 2020).

22 April 2020

Arguing that greedy and corrupt government officials cannot help needy Afghans afflicted by the COVID-19 pandemic, the Afghan Taliban called on wealthy countrymen to donate (SITE Intelligence Group 2020).

4 May 2020

Alleging it is the sole party abiding by the terms of the peace agreement concluded with the United States in Doha, the Afghan Taliban cautioned a top US commander in Afghanistan, General Scott Miller, against using bellicose rhetoric toward it and claimed the Afghan government was weaponizing the coronavirus to eliminate prisoners (SITE Intelligence Group 2020).

5 May 2020

As it continued to vilify the Afghan government as corrupt and portray itself as the true representatives of the people, the Afghan Taliban charged it with embezzling funds earmarked for the COVID-19 fight and intentionally destroying power pylons and public facilities (SITE Intelligence Group 2020).

8 May 2020

Concurrent with its releasing Afghan security forces taken prisoner, the Afghan Taliban demanded the government do the same and thus fulfill the terms of the US peace deal or else it and America would face consequences if inmates die from COVID-19 (SITE Intelligence Group 2020).

Jihadist Posts Concerning Asia Pacific

26 March 2020

A Bangsamoro Islamic Freedom Fighter (BIFF) faction leader called for followers to join the group to save themselves from being infected by the COVID-19 virus and argued against the closure of mosques (SITE Intelligence Group 2020).

27 March 2020

A Filipino Islamic State (ISIS/IS)-linked account accused the government of bringing COVID-19 into the country to elicit funds and called for its supporters to abandon democracy and support fighters who are "striving to fight the soldiers of the kuffar" (SITE Intelligence Group 2020).

30 March 2020

Indonesian Islamic State (IS/ISIS) supporters called for attacks targeting "apostates in big cities." A message disseminated on multiple IS-aligned Telegram channels encouraged youths to look at Muslims around the world being killed and imprisoned and called on them to carry out attacks while the enemy is distracted (SITE Intelligence Group 2020).

31 March 2020

Indonesian Islamic State (IS/ISIS) supporters on Facebook have continued to incite attacks, with one account specifically calling for the looting of "Kuffar" (SITE Intelligence Group 2020).

8 April 2020

With the COVID-19 threat growing in Indonesia, jihadists discussed plans for a coordinated group hijrah (migration) to Saudi Arabia and Syria, suggesting various meeting places for the "operation" to start (SITE Intelligence Group 2020).

9 April 2020

Following the curfew expansion by the Philippine government to slow the spread of the novel coronavirus, an active IS-linked account threatened to kill Christians if Muslims are punished for violating quarantine order (SITE Intelligence Group 2020).

10 April 2020

Indonesian jihadists on WhatsApp incited attacks against Chinese residents in the country (SITE Intelligence Group 2020).

14 April 2020

A BIFF-linked account released videos objecting to the closure of mosques because of the COVID-19 pandemic and urging the group's fighters and Muslims in the Philippines to disobey the government mandate (SITE Intelligence Group 2020).

16 April 2020

An Indonesian Islamic State (IS/ISIS) supporter claimed that the COVID-19 pandemic signals the end times and lodged a threat against the United Nations (SITE Intelligence Group 2020).

17 April 2020

A Filipino account linked to IS disseminated a video urging fighters to carry out jihad and threatening Muslims who follow government directives on COVID-19 (SITE Intelligence Group 2020).

17 April 2020

In their first claimed attack since the implementation of the Enhanced Community Quarantine (ECQ) to restrict movement and reduce the impact of the COVID-19 virus in the Philippines, the ISEAP claimed killing sixteen soldiers and wounding others in a clash in Sulu (SITE Intelligence Group 2020).

18 April 2020

Mujahidin Indonesia Timur (MIT) leader Ali Kalora threatened attacks on members of an Indonesian public order enforcement security unit, Bantuan Polisi Pamong Praja (Banpol), claiming in a video to have captured one of its members. Kalora referenced COVID-19 in the video, claiming "tyrants" would die from the virus (SITE Intelligence Group 2020).

22 April 2020

A Filipino IS Facebook account urged its followers to fight nonbelievers and take advantage of the COVID-19-induced lockdown to carry out jihad (SITE Intelligence Group 2020).

22 April 2020

Indonesian IS supporters on Telegram encouraged disobedience toward COVID-19 safety instructions in the country (SITE Intelligence Group 2020).

28 April 2020

A radical Indonesian cleric and alleged former jihadi militant stated his disapproval of the Indonesian government's closure of mosques, vowing to keep his mosque open (SITE Intelligence Group 2020).

28 April 2020

A Filipino IS-linked account accused Philippine leaders of overstating the dangers of COVID-19, glorified IS leaders, and celebrated Ramadan as a month of victory for its fighters (SITE Intelligence Group 2020).

29 April 2020

A Filipino IS account threatened to kill soldiers and politicians who implement COVID-19 measures and urged for the decapitation of spies (SITE Intelligence Group 2020).

4 May 2020

In its first documented attack during Ramadan, and two weeks after its first operation during the COVID-19 pandemic, the Islamic State's East Asia Province (ISEAP) claimed killing two soldiers in Maguindanao (SITE Intelligence Group 2020).

6 May 2020

After recruiting amid COVID-19 and ordering fighters to disobey government directives, Bangsamoro Islamic Freedom Fighters (BIFF) faction leader continued to urge followers to fight those who "oppress Muslims" and to attend mosque congregations because that is what "true believers" do (SITE Intelligence Group 2020).

9 May 2020

After the Indonesian Ulema Council (MUI), the top Muslim clerical body in the country issued fatwa number 14 of 2020 in support of COVID-19 restrictions. IS supporters warned against following the restrictions, labeling them "STUPID-20" (SITE Intelligence Group 2020).

Jihadist Posts Concerning Africa

22 March 2020

Although Shabaab al-Mujahideen Movement, the Somalia-based branch of AQ, had yet to make a formal statement on the pandemic, its Shahada News Agency reported regular updates on the spread of the novel coronavirus in the region, including Kenya's first confirmed case of COVID-19 on 28 January and Ethiopia the following day (SITE Intelligence Group 2020).

26 March 2020

The Shabaab al-Mujahideen Movement convened a "consultative forum" on jihad in East Africa, hosting over 100 members of various strata of Muslim society in areas under its control, as well as group leaders. It was to make resolutions on civil and military issues. According to the document, jihad and support to those who wage it is considered mandatory, participation in democratic elections is forbidden, caution is due because of Ethiopian Christians entering Somalia, and Muslims must safeguard against infectious diseases and viruses such as COVID-19 and HIV (SITE Intelligence Group 2020).

15 April 2020

Abu Bakr Shekau, the leader of the Nigeria-based Jama'at Ahl al-Sunnah Lil Dawa Wal Jihad, or what is known as "Boko Haram," spoke on the COVID-19 pandemic and proposed sincere faith and piety as a solution to the affliction (SITE Intelligence Group 2020).

16 April 2020

JNIM claimed killing five Burkinabe soldiers in an attack on their post in Sollé, a town in Loroum province, northern Burkina Faso. JNIM wrote about the losses caused to the enemy in tandem with the coronavirus (SITE Intelligence Group 2020).

28 April 2020

The spokesman for the Shabaab al-Mujahideen Movement suggested that foreign forces intentionally spread the novel coronavirus in the country (SITE Intelligence Group 2020).

11 May 2020

A sermon delivered in mosques in Shabaab-controlled areas in Somalia identified protective measures against COVID-19 while decrying the shutting of mosques to halt person-to-person transmission (SITE Intelligence Group 2020).

12 May 2020

A jihadist alleged that JNIM rejected the reconciliation offer from an IS official in the Sahel and that JNIM fighters later wounded him (SITE Intelligence Group 2020).

20 July 2020

In the media, Shahada News Agency continued to provide weekly updates regarding the impact of COVID-19 across East Africa (SITE Intelligence Group 2020).

Jihadist Posts Concerning the Middle East

17 March 2020

Abdullah al-Muhaysini, a prominent Syria-based jihadi cleric, released a statement on 17 March declaring the decision by Muslim countries to close mosques a "mistake." The cleric stated COVID-19 was created by Allah because of "evil deeds" and "immorality," and he criticized Western perceptions of the virus as "environmental." He then encouraged Muslims to defy orders to close mosques, calling prayer the only solution to the virus.
"My opinion in regards to closing the mosques for gatherings and groups in the Islamic countries because of Corona! What I think is that this decision is a mistake and should not be obeyed in Muslim countries. This is because the West views the coronavirus in a purely material perspective!!" However, Muhaysini did urge those exhibiting symptoms to stay at home and for those attending prayers at mosques to wear protective gear (SITE Intelligence Group 2020).

18 March 2020

Pro-AQ Thabaat News Agency released an article written by Khalid al-Saba'i titled "Corona . . . Doom for the Oppressors and Martyrdom for the Believers." Al-Saba'i described the novel coronavirus as a "soldier" unleashed by Allah on the "sects of disbelief" that will give rise to the "collapse of the polytheists and their guardians." Acknowledging that Sunni Muslims will also be afflicted by the virus, al-Saba'i declared that those who die of the virus as "Allah has fated" will be "martyrs." The author also encouraged fighters to maintain jihad and capitalize on the potential devastation of the pandemic to "hammer the final nail in the coffin of falsehood" (SITE Intelligence Group 2020).

19 March 2020

Al-Saba'i stated that COVID-19 is the "worst nightmare of the Crusaders" and during this time in which they face a bleak economic future and overcrowded hospitals, fighters should launch operations. He also alluded to past civilian casualties in the once IS-held cities of Baghuz, Mosul, and Sirte, stating coalition forces "did not show mercy" (SITE Intelligence Group 2020).

21 March 2020

The leader of the Yemen-based Shia Ansar Allah, Abdul Malik al-Houthi, gave a speech on the sixteenth anniversary of the death of group founder Husayn Badruddin al-Houthi. The Houthi leader touched on a variety of subjects including the coronavirus pandemic. In his message, he accused the US government and American companies of manufacturing the virus and its vaccine, deploying COVID-19 both as an act of war and for economic gains. He also warned that donated medical equipment and food could potentially be contaminated with the virus. According to an English report from Ansar Allah, the Houthi leader stated: "There are military means to spread germs and viruses to a specific community for an epidemic to breakout, resulting in the so-called biological warfare . . . Some experts in biological warfare have been talking about Americans working for years to take advantage of the coronavirus and work to spread it in certain societies" (SITE Intelligence Group 2020).

1 April 2020

A channel aligned with Hay'at Tahrir al-Sham (HTS) disseminated a letter allegedly from a woman in the US expressing solidarity with "sisters" in Syria and calling the pandemic and mosque closures a sign of end times (SITE Intelligence Group 2020).

2 April 2020

Just four days after Syria reported its first death from COVID-19, a photo report from Hurras al-Deen documented the group's Advocacy Office carrying out activities in a crowded Idlib mosque (SITE Intelligence Group 2020).

8 April 2020

Noting the passage of one year since the IS lost the last vestige of its "Caliphate" in Baghouz, Syria, a supporting group, in a poster, portrayed the COVID-19 pandemic as divine retribution against enemies (SITE Intelligence Group 2020).

23 April 2020

A jihadist pointed to the increase in IS attacks in Iraq during the COVID-19 pandemic to motivate fighters elsewhere to escalate the frequency of their operations (SITE Intelligence Group 2020).

24 April 2020

A prominent Syria-based Saudi jihadi cleric, Abdullah al-Muhaysini, released the first episode in a lecture series for Ramadan, calling the COVID-19 virus the "smallest of Allah's soldiers" (SITE Intelligence Group 2020).

27 April 2020

Abdullah al-Muhaysini issued three further episodes of a daily Ramadan video series inspired by the COVID-19 pandemic (SITE Intelligence Group 2020).

1 May 2020

An AQ-aligned group based in Syria issued a story of a "brother" giving the majority of his money to fighters in Syria despite his reduced salary due to the COVID-19 pandemic and urged others to follow his example (SITE Intelligence Group 2020).

Jihadist Posts Concerning the United States

10 March 2020

Shia users on social media platforms including Facebook, Instagram, and Twitter contributed to a widespread conspiracy theory accusing the US government and President Donald Trump of deploying COVID-19 as a bioweapon. The campaign aimed to highlight the alleged crimes of the US and Trump, using the hashtag # ترامب_سلاح_وروناك (Corona is Trump's weapon). Graphics utilized in the campaign included Trump firing a gun emblazoned with the word "Corona" and handling a graphic of the virus. Arabic text accompanying the campaign stated that the United States was using the virus to destroy international rivals such as China, Iran, and Italy, as well as Trump's domestic rivals in the Democratic Party and people of color. The social media campaign also perpetuated the conspiracy theory that the Islamic State is a creation of the CIA (SITE Intelligence Group 2020).

11 March 2020

On 11 March, in response to US President Donald Trump's claim of doing a "great job" fighting COVID-19, the Shia cleric al-Sadr accused the president's "reckless policies" of creating a pandemic. The cleric further called Trump a hypocrite for portraying the US as a "healer" while filling the world with "wars, occupation, poverty, and conflicts." Al-Sadr also rejected the prospect of receiving any kind of aid from the US or American companies. In another statement on 13 March, al-Sadr once again addressed Iraqi protestors, urging restraint from violence amid tensions derived from recent attacks on and by US forces and the spread of COVID-19. The cleric's proposal of restraint was because of factors affecting the Iraqi people and not a policy of peace with the "occupiers": "We are not advocates of peace with the occupier, but we are taking into account the circumstances surrounding the proud Iraqi people, and we ask Allah to relieve them from the occupier and corrupt alike. I pause at the words of Trump: 'We are doing a great job against coronavirus . . . and the situation would have been worse had we not intervened'. O Trump . . . You and others like you are accused of spreading this disease, especially as most of those suffering from it are opponents of America" (SITE Intelligence Group 2020).

26 March 2020

IS again featured COVID-19 in its Al-Naba newspaper, with issue 227 marking the third consecutive week the group focused its prime media platform on the pandemic. The issue criticized America for thinking it could quickly eradicate the disease, stating it could never protect its people from the will of Allah (SITE Intelligence Group 2020).

1 April 2020

In its latest statement on the COVID-19 pandemic, Islamic State argued that the global spread and infection of the novel coronavirus debunks the myth believed by many about American omniscience and power (SITE Intelligence Group 2020).

9 April 2020

Indonesian IS supporters on Telegram shared a series of messages celebrating the deaths of "crusaders" in the West due to the spread of COVID-19 and hoped for a war between the US and China (SITE Intelligence Group 2020).

16 April 2020

Iraq-based Shia cleric Muqtada al-Sadr criticized US President Donald Trump for cutting funding to the World Health Organization (WHO) and declared that he is ineffective in managing the COVID-19 pandemic domestically and globally (SITE Intelligence Group 2020).

21 April 2020

After the precipitous drop in crude oil prices and the effect of the COVID-19 pandemic on multiple levels in the United States, Shia social media users launched a coordinated campaign to highlight what they perceived as the "collapse" of America (SITE Intelligence Group 2020).

22 April 2020

A pro-AQ media outlet tallied nearly 20,000 operations by fighters on three continents in a 500-day period, and regarding the COVID-19 pandemic and particularly its impact in the United States, it remarked that coronavirus might be the "final nail in America's coffin" (SITE Intelligence Group 2020).

8 May 2020

IS created a video on the COVID-19 pandemic debunking the myth of American omniscience and power for an Al-Naba editorial (SITE Intelligence Group 2020).

Far Right Posts Concerning Europe

11 March 2020

Defend Europe 2020, a two-day white nationalist music festival in Northern Italy, announced via the event's Telegram channel that the show would be "postponed to a later date." Veneto Fronte Skinheads

Cultural Association, who organized the event, said that the "complicated health situation" and consequent "logistical difficulties" for organizers and attendees led them to the decision to reschedule (SITE Intelligence Group 2020).

16 March 2020

A neo-Nazi media group advocating accelerationism—or terrorist acts committed with the goal of destabilizing society—encouraged its audience to pursue actions that would incite panic amidst the coronavirus outbreak. Posted to the Telegram channel "TR" on 16 March 2020, they incited subscribers to fire guns into cities and put bullet-sized holes in car windows to stoke tensions as populaces pursue or practice social isolation. "TR" issued the incitement in the form of a hilarious joke so as not to attract attention from the law. "It's almost as if it's time for all of you to go out in the night and (safely) pop off rounds at metropolitan areas where you're sure you won't get caught," said "TR," and they further encouraged readers to "do a magazine or two." The post also suggested "using a tennis racket and small to medium sized pebbles" to put holes in the windows of expensive cars in "ethnic and wealthy subdivisions . . . making sure no BMW has a sunroof at the end of the night" (SITE Intelligence Group 2020).

18 March 2020

On 18 March 2020, the French neo-Nazi blog Blanche Europe published an article commenting on the ongoing crisis caused by the spread of the coronavirus in France. Blanche Europe blamed China's supposed culture of "poor hygiene" for the initial outbreak but went on to condemn President Emmanuel Macron for exacerbating the situation in France by not acting quickly. One central policy the blog advocated was the physical removal of immigrants from the country or, alternatively, "extermination" of the immigrant population. Medical aid, according to the article, should be given primarily to "white" families, while treatment and care for ethnic minorities ought to be considered only after the white population is accounted for. Ultimately, the article claimed that "the best remedy for COVID-19 [was] the swastika." (SITE Intelligence Group 2020).

23 March 2020

A false infographic was disseminated by far right users on Facebook and Telegram that at first glance appeared to contain information from accredited health organizations but actually promoted deliberately infecting public spaces with COVID-19. The poster, containing the header "What to do if you get COVID-19," urged those infected with the novel coronavirus to visit mosques, synagogues, and diverse neighborhoods, as well as "spend the day on public transport!" Logos representing the Centers for Disease Control and Prevention (CDC) and the World Health Organization (WHO) were found forged onto the infographic, making it seem as if the information was supplied or endorsed by the organizations (SITE Intelligence Group 2020).

24 March 2020

On 24 March 2020, user "YR" in the Telegram chat room for members and affiliates of the neo-Nazi "Vorherrschaft Division" (VD) posted a statement urging followers to take advantage of the instability resulting from the COVID-19 pandemic by targeting powerlines, water towers, bridges, railroads, and grocery stores while "wear[ing] a breathing mask to hide your identity," claiming "they [authorities] won't question it." The user also called on people to attack food establishments by stealing their toilet paper and soap and by "put[ting] cyanide in [mountain] dew" and "cough[ing] into the potato salad at whole foods" (SITE Intelligence Group 2020).

30 March 2020

A thread on the 8chan successor site 8kun created on 30 March 2020 urged users to "exploit" the Sinophobic current that had emerged in the midst of the coronavirus pandemic. "Anyone who survives these dark and hard times has to have heart of fury and rage going after the gooks and chinese commies," said the thread's original poster. With regard to tactics, the poster suggested desecrating Chinese flags and reinforced the "Chinese virus" nomenclature. In a series of posts, one user shared videos of factory accidents to demonstrate "Chinese subhumanity" as evidence for justifying anti-Chinese sentiments within the thread. Many, however, rejected the poster's call to action. The propaganda campaign was dismissed by some as a "Jewish conspiracy" meant to distract from the pandemic's supposed effect of "showcasing the full weakness and inadequacy of liberal democracy" and of conducting a "blatant attempt at molding our minds to accept a war with China." Some responses were more nihilistic in their rejection of the poster's campaign, simply welcoming the strain the pandemic had put on the existing social order as the far right did on many occasions. "We should be celebrating [the Chinese] and supporting them," said one user. (SITE Intelligence Group 2020).

1 April 2020

According to a 1 April 2020 article published on the website of Nordic Resistance Movement (NRM), the neo-Nazi organization's leader Simon Lindberg announced at an NRM People's Conference that a demonstration scheduled for 1 May 2020 in Uppsala, Sweden, would be postponed. The postponement came with a promise to reschedule the event to "a later date this year, if conditions allow." According to Lindberg, the Swedish government's temporary ban on gatherings of fifty or more people had no bearing on NRM's decision. Had the safety of the "hundreds of nationalist-minded people" who would have attended the demonstration not been at risk, he said, the event would have been held "[i]f for no other reason than to defy the system" (SITE Intelligence Group 2020).

1 April 2020

In the neo-Nazi Whatsapp group "NSRD," members posted images claiming COVID-19 was a virus developed by "elites" to control populations and subsequently suggested the United States government was using the coronavirus as a biological weapon against its international opponents. Another user called upon followers to send unsolicited COVID-19 "stool samples" directly to Angela Merkel in a targeted harassment campaign. On 1 April 2020, member "Herr Stark" of the neo-Nazi Whatsapp group "NSRegime DE" (NSRD, "National Socialist Regime Germany") posted five consecutive images; each containing the header "Coronavirus: an invention of the elites to . . ." "Tag their property (people) with RF-ID chips like animals in order to control them better"; "Increase the profits of the chemical industry; "Pass the most restrictive laws of all time against the population"; "Reduce the freedom of demonstration and speech"; and "Increase the profit of the pharmaceutical industry with compulsory vaccination" (SITE Intelligence Group 2020).

1 April 2020

Also on 1 April 2020, the neo-Nazi group "NS" shared a video to its Telegram channel depicting members undergoing combat training. The video was captioned with a message that encouraged preparing for the "time of change" in the near future: "Though we are in quarantine, we are not wasting our time. We continue to spend our time productively, to obtain useful skills and develop existing ones. We call on everyone to not waste the opportunity for self-development. The time of change is approaching, and the future depends on each one of us!" In the video, individuals wearing "NS" shirts are shown practicing hand-to-hand combat, shooting firearms, and training with bladed weapons. All training in the video appeared to take place in an outdoor environment (SITE Intelligence Group 2020).

3 April 2020

On 3 April 2020, the neo-Nazi Telegram channel "NAR" forwarded a statement from another neo-Nazi channel known as "SMS" that has since been deleted. It indirectly asserted a "hypothetical 28 year old lone wolf domestic terrorist" could ship COVID-19-infected products to countries "like China" as a biological weapon to "expedite worldwide economic collapse." The original SMS statement: "It would be really unfortunate if a hypothetical '28 year old lone wolf domestic terrorist' were to use exports to a hypothetical country with high population density and a large but unstable economy like China as a vessel for some sort of virus to expedite worldwide economic collapse or something crazy like that *cough cough*" (SITE Intelligence Group 2020).

6 April 2020

An image depicting toxic combinations of household chemicals was shared by a neo-Nazi Telegram channel with a message suggesting toxic gases be released in busy grocery stores. The channel claimed symptoms resulting from the attack would mimic COVID-19 and send hundreds of people into an already overburdened healthcare system (SITE Intelligence Group 2020).

7 April 2020

The Russian white nationalist group Imperial Legion, a militant subsidiary of the Russian Imperial Movement (RIM), posted a statement on its official VK page framing the COVID-19 global crisis as the foretold Biblical apocalypse. The group encouraged avoiding panic and instead "[praying, training, and preparing]" for the crisis (SITE Intelligence Group 2020).

7 April 2020

Popular German neo-Nazi personality Frank Kraemer, known for his blog "The Third Perspective," uploaded a podcast in which he and his guest host Peter Steinborn (a contributor for the far right publication "Metapol") claimed the current economic crisis has not been caused by the pandemic but is rather a result of the longstanding failures of capitalism and free market systems. Kraemer asserted the virus was just being used by the "globalist elite" to distract populations from the imminent global financial collapse; thereby championing national socialism as the "bulwark that can protect the peoples of the world from the looting bankers of Wall Street and the IMF" (SITE Intelligence Group 2020).

15 April 2020

Online recruitment efforts by organized white nationalist groups were intensifying because of the increased internet traffic stemming from stay-at-home orders around the world (SITE Intelligence Group 2020).

29 April 2020

White nationalists and Neo-Nazis had been eyeing the protests as precursors "for revolution" and encouraging violence from participants. Far right groups and channels were amassing larger audiences amid the coronavirus pandemic, prompting many among them to propose coronavirus-tailored growth strategies. Some advocated for a more "approachable" image and proposed ways to reach out to non-radicalized friends and family, while accelerationists urged people to deliberately agitate the critical situation (SITE Intelligence Group 2020).

5 May 2020

Breaking stride with the far right community's otherwise persistent efforts to publicize, attend, and organize lockdown protests, prominent neo-Nazi Telegram channels advised followers to avoid the "cringe rallies." Moreover, one of the channels encouraged exploiting the "tension" building between right-wing protestors and politicians as an opportunity to distract "the System" from more accelerationist plots and implored followers not to "let a perfectly good crisis go to waste" (SITE Intelligence Group 2020).

6 May 2020

Far right extremists were continuing to seize on recent anti-lockdown protests to recruit and amplify their presence amid the COVID-19 crisis. Exacerbating societal tensions surrounding these protests, extremist actors threatened "riots" and sowed misinformation about protestors being arrested, resulting in multiple incitements to attack law enforcement. Meanwhile, conspiracy theories were continuing to fuel threats against individuals and institutions at the forefront of the coronavirus fight. Such conspiracy theories were likewise prompting attacks on 5G towers (SITE Intelligence Group 2020).

8 May 2020

"Pugilato," a Spanish-language neo-Nazi heavy metal band, released an antisemitic and antigovernment music video. The song declared that "assault troops" are ready to fight against the "new world order" of the government, Marxists, and Zionists. Although the song did not directly reference COVID-19, it appeared to be a response to lockdown measures in Spain given the timing of its release and its antigovernment sentiments (SITE Intelligence Group 2020).

8 May 2020

A clip from a yet-to-be-released film, Plandemic, promoting conspiracy theories regarding the coronavirus pandemic and highly disputing claims about the etiology of COVID-19, was banned from several major online platforms, prompting outrage and copies of the video to appear in far right online spaces. Multiple threads on 4chan decried YouTube's efforts, with some users suggesting that they removed the video because of its efficacy as a "gateway" into far right ideologies that "may actually get through to normies." Perhaps most notably, the video was shared to a chat group associated with coronavirus Central, a popular podcast hosted by white nationalist Tom Kawcyznski (SITE Intelligence Group 2020).

8 May 2020

A far right Italian Telegram channel, "ID," posted a statement tying the coronavirus crisis to a broader criticism of the existing socio-political system and offering Identitarianism as a cure-all solution. It targeted the present European liberal polity as the source of Italy's economic, political, and social difficulties. Among the criticisms "ID" made, many appealed to anti-immigration politics (SITE Intelligence Group 2020).

11 May 2020

In an article posted on 11 May 2020, Blanche Europe (BE) accused officials of taking advantage of the COVID-19 crisis to instate "repressive" measures against the public. The article was a response to a statement made by Jérôme Salomon, a top public health official in France. In the statement, Salomon likened the ongoing health crisis to the Black Plague and the Spanish flu. BE interpreted this comparison as a fear-mongering tactic used by authorities to justify the imposition of strict social measures (SITE Intelligence Group 2020).

12 May 2020

Spanish Neo-Nazi Group "Aqui la Voz de Europa" had been creating audio and video content perpetuating conspiracy theories regarding the COVID-19 pandemic since March 2020. Its productions were disseminated across Twitter, Facebook, Instagram, YouTube, and iVoox. The group promoted the pandemic as a "false world flag" and a biological weapon to bring about the "new world order." A video had been issued on 7 May 2020 titled "The Political Globalists Are the Authentic Government" in response to the fact that the "estado de alarma" (state of alarm) had not been lifted despite the drop in cases because of the country's determination to maintain restrictions at the expense of liberty, which was causing unemployment and economic collapse (SITE Intelligence Group 2020).

12 May 2020

On 12 May 2020, Democracia Nacional (DN) shared an excerpt from an article published by El Economista, a Spanish daily newspaper, discussing legal experts condemning the Sánchez government's "estado de alarma" (state of alarm) for COVID-19 and warning the country is moving toward a dictatorship. DN agreed with the sentiments but claimed most jurists in key positions "actively collaborate" in the supposed bypassing of the constitution and that these "puppets of globalism" must be driven out of their positions in politics, media, and the judiciary. A DN poster accompanying the article accused the government of being the real virus. The graphic contained images of a CCTV surveillance sign, people wearing protective masks, and the Eye of Providence, a popular symbol used by conspiracy theorists (SITE Intelligence Group 2020).

13 May 2020

As the COVID-19 crisis continued, far right communities around the world sought to capitalize on fears, disillusionment, and social tensions to advance recruitment efforts. Harnessing tensions surrounding anti-lockdown protests, numerous voices on the European far right escalated criticisms suggesting that the measures aim to impose "authoritarian" control over populations. Some rallied around those posed in the yet-to-released Plandemic movie, saying the production is a "gateway" into far right ideologies (SITE Intelligence Group 2020).

13 May 2020

Mundo Viperino, a Spanish white nationalist figure prominent among fringe far right groups in Spain, released a video in coordination with Miguel Blasco, director of the neo-Nazi media group "Aqui la Voz de Europa," claiming the COVID-19 pandemic was "accelerating" the UN's Agenda 21 conspiracy for a "global government takeover of every nation across the planet." Alba Lobera, who has made appearances on the white nationalist La Tribuna de España and manages her own media group "Mundo Viperino" (Venemous World), which has propagated conspiracy theories surrounding the COVID-19 pandemic, introduces Blasco as a "tireless warrior for the truth" before an interview where the two discuss the "2030 agenda." The video features a short promotional video from the UN outlining plans to combat climate change, followed by a declaration from Lobera that there is no climate change but rather "climate manipulation." Lobera then launches into a stream of conspiracy theories, including her uncertainty over vaccines, 5G technology, and "lies" taught in school by the "victors," with a screenshot of a January 2019 article claiming the diary of Holocaust victim Anne Frank is a fraud from a Mexican news site "La Silla Rota" (SITE Intelligence Group 2020).

15 May 2020

On 15 May 2020, the Russian far right organization "Nation and Freedom" Committee (KNS) released a video in which a masked individual, who went by the name Miroslav, discussed the potential for protest actions in Novosibirsk, Russia. He pointed out that despite quarantine measures many people in Novosibirsk had been forced to continue commuting to work in order to earn enough income to survive. Miroslav accused local authorities of lacking rigor in enforcing social distancing measures and argued public support for the government and for Putin as a leader was dwindling. Miroslav explained that the latter trend was due to the country's issues allegedly originating from "migrant populations." Migrants had supposedly disregarded the rules and regulations and consequently jeopardized the stability and prosperity of the country as a whole. The conclusion of the video posited that if the current trends are not addressed, dissenting sentiments would grow and provide a base for widespread protests (SITE Intelligence Group 2020).

18 May 2020

In a call for acts of bioterrorism, a recruitment poster released by the neo-Nazi "Waldkrieg Division" urged followers to intentionally infect "non-whites" with COVID-19. "Be part of Operation Covid-88*, join the division." The propaganda also depicted a biohazard symbol imposed over a Black Sun, which appeared to represent a movement of white nationalist-inspired bioterrorism (SITE Intelligence Group 2020).

19 May 2020

On 19 May 2020, Jeune Nation shared an article from the far right publication Militant, in which the author attacked the government response to the COVID-19 crisis, adding that the pandemic was being used as a tool to control the public. The article argued that French government officials responding to the public health crisis were dealing with the outbreak incompetently and ineffectually. Moreover, the author suggested that official information channels were deliberately overplaying the effects of the disease in order to justify restrictive social measures (SITE Intelligence Group 2020).

22 May 2020

On 22 May 2020, Jeune Nation shared information about a rally being organized by Les Nationalistes, a French far right group, in Paris on 30 May 2020. Their central demands involved reopening religious spaces and lifting the restrictive measures put in place during the quarantine (SITE Intelligence Group 2020).

27 May 2020

Far right communities remained focused on harnessing societal discontent and antiestablishment energy surrounding the coronavirus pandemic. Lockdown protests were a central pillar of this overall strategy, offering the far right entry points for outreach to the general public. Other corners of the far right continued to opt for destabilization tactics, which included calls for targeted attacks on various groups and infrastructure. However, far right proponents of both approaches continued to embrace conspiracy theories, which were used to bolster terrorist incitements and mainstream outreach alike (SITE Intelligence Group 2020).

4 June 2020

Aqui la Voz de Europa released a 7 minute, 29 second video with Spanish audio titled "The Real Virus that Is Destroying the West," on 4 June 2020. The antisemitic and racist audio rant blamed Jews and globalists for an alleged agenda to destroy European culture with a "virus" worse than COVID-19. They claimed whites in Europe and elsewhere have allegedly been "mentally conditioned to hate themselves, to hate their history, their culture, and their traditions." The "virus" apparently manifests itself in multiculturalism, anti-racism, gender ideology, anti-nationalism, and feminism, among others, which are allegedly used to make whites complicit in their own destruction. Images of destroyed cities were shown in the video, as well as landmarks in Paris, such as the Eiffel Tower and Notre Dame, which were depicted in flames (SITE Intelligence Group 2020).

9 June 2020

On 9 June user "TS" in the Telegram group chat affiliated with the neo-Nazi group "VR" posted messages claiming to have attended recent protests in Serbia's capital, Belgrade and engaged in violent confrontation with law enforcement. TS first explained why the events were taking place, claiming that citizens were protesting the "authoritarian" government's "corrupt" decisions to lift COVID-19 mitigation measures to hold an election—despite rises in cases and deaths—only to reinstate quarantine and shutdown businesses directly after the voting process concluded. When asked by other members of the group about the protests, TS claimed they were "well organized" and "had some weapons with us too . . . Some very strong firecrackers which can basically stun you . . . And some flares." TS continued by purporting they were hit with tear gas while attending the protest in Belgrade, and that they were "chasing police" while police were trying to contain the unrest (SITE Intelligence Group 2020).

19 June 2020

On 19 June 2020, the almost 4,300 subscriber accelerationist neo-Nazi Telegram channel "SSS" posted a statement discussing the devastation of the Black Plague, thereby implying COVID-19 would also be capable of committing such societal ravages. “Biological warfare is not a new concept,” the statement began, asserting that in the constant struggle over resources, mankind has used the “weaponization of disease” to “destroy their enemy with utmost efficiency.” SSS appeared to champion the potential of plagues to be used against one’s enemy, noting that the “deadliest pandemic in known history” was caused by the “Mongols catapult[ing] plague victims into a besieged city.” SSS underscored that the novel coronavirus would be more deadly than poisons and could be most effectively used “in countries with lower hygiene standards, less developed healthcare facilities and a higher population density” (SITE Intelligence Group 2020).

29 June 2020

An anonymous statement was distributed by Anarchists Worldwide on 29 June 2020 claiming an arson attack on a WISAG vehicle. WISAG was accused of benefiting from “surveillance, evictions and control” and Berliner Verkehrsbetriebe (BVG), Berlin’s main public transport company. The company was further accused of assisting in deportations, as its personnel work at airports, and participating in evictions of homeless in Berlin. The English translation from Anarchists Worldwide of the German statement Berlin, Germany: “STOP THE VIRUS OF CONTROL! – WISAG Security Vehicle Torched In solidarity with prisoners. With homeless people and with fugitives. With those who are driven out of the city and those who are being monitored by a capitalist system that meets open spaces with repression and locks away those who are too poor or too rebellious. So in solidarity with all those who are locked up or repressed, we torched a WISAG van on the night of June, 25th, 2020” (SITE Intelligence Group 2020).

Far Right Post Concerning Asia Pacific

12 May 2020

A video of a man being restrained by police and consequently separated from his child during an anti-lockdown protest in Sydney, Australia, prompted some on the far right to share a map of Sydney police stations and incite arson attacks against them. In the video, which was shared by the accelerationist Telegram channel “CA,” a man is seen in an altercation with three police officers before being restrained. The same channel then shared an additional diagram with tips for constructing a Molotov cocktail that is safe for its user (SITE Intelligence Group 2020).

Far Right Posts Concerning America

17 March 2020

On 17 March 2020, a 4chan user created a thread on the site's politics board "/pol/" in which they sensationalized conditions in New York City on account of the city and state governments increasing restrictions on activity to help contain the spread of the virus. "Businesses closing . . . Train service cut down, will be closed soon . . . Gangs of niggers and spics roaming the cities like wild dogs . . . NYPD abandoning posts. This city is fucked!" The same user then encouraged residents of the Queens neighborhoods Ridgewood and Astoria—where "most /pol/ anons in queens live—to build a militia to patrol the neighborhood. They were then advised to carry a jack of diamonds playing card to signify to others that they were allies, and to meet at Donovan's Pub in Woodside, Queens "when shit gets bad." "Use this thread to meet anons in your towns so you can form militias," the user then advised. On that call to action, groups of users began identifying their general locations to network. Others in Southern California, Kansas City, North Carolina, and Georgia also announced their locations, with some including photos of what they alleged to be their weapons stockpiles (SITE Intelligence Group 2020).

25 March 2020

As the US declared a national emergency and began mobilizing the national guard as a coronavirus relief force, the neo-Nazi Telegram channel "EFC" posted several statements inciting violence against members of the military force, calling the national guard an "unseasoned" and poorly trained military body and suggesting that anyone with basic training could "cut through [the national guard] like a hot knife" (SITE Intelligence Group 2020).

26 March 2020

Timothy R. Wilson, the Missouri neo-Nazi killed during an attempted arrest by the FBI after plotting to attack a hospital, had sought to capitalize on the coronavirus beyond his bomb plot, going as far as discussing using the virus as a bioweapon. Wilson, who was formerly enlisted in the United States military, had had connections to multiple neo-Nazi organizations, citing the leader of The Order as an inspiration and stating that white supremacists "need community . . . if [they] ever hope to win" their war against nonwhites (SITE Intelligence Group 2020).

1 April 2020

The coronavirus pandemic had led to renewed interest in a decades-old conspiracy theory among far right Telegram users that FEMA exists to establish population-wide prison camps in a time of crisis. Consequently, some users responded with a new pattern of violent incitements against FEMA and its agents (SITE Intelligence Group 2020).

3 April 2020

Far right users on platforms including Twitter and Telegram treated news a Jewish man selling a stockpile of medical supplies to doctors at a 700% markup as evidence of a broader "anti-white" sentiment within the Jewish community. Responses to the arrest of Brooklyn resident Baruch Feldheim ranged from describing him as a "parasite" to claiming his actions were part of a broader effort to "keep [non-Jewish whites] from protecting themselves while his coethnics spread [the illness]" (SITE Intelligence Group 2020).

7 April 2020

On 7 April 2020, a post from the neo-Nazi Telegram channel "SN" cited previous race riots in the United States as evidence that a wave of "civil unrest" among the black population would result from interruptions to daily life caused by the pandemic. "SN" further encouraged its audience to ready themselves for black Americans to "kill, rape, and cannibalize" en masse, thereby further exacerbating racial tensions and potentially endangering members of black communities (SITE Intelligence Group 2020).

17 April 2020

A member of an infamous and tightly-knit neo-Nazi group based in the US posted in the group's Telegram chat encouraging the spread of coronavirus conspiracy theories and misinformation, as well as far right propaganda and symbols. The goal of these initiatives was to "amplify the fear" of the public and capitalize on "5G hysteria." The user included an infographic listing five suggested methods of ensuring "Operations Security" seemingly in the event of systemic collapse: concealing weapon and ammo supplies, dressing and behaving inconspicuously in public, and prepping one's home to defend against "looters and other assorted scumbags" (SITE Intelligence Group 2020).

20 April 2020

A user known as "SPF" posted in the accelerationist neo-Nazi Telegram group "TD" claiming that the novel coronavirus "seems contrived," also adding the assertion that CNN journalist Chris Cuomo was "faking his illness." SPF further stated that the elite can "afford" to allow the markets to crash, citing the conspiracy theory that elites used the coronavirus to intentionally induce the current economic crisis in an effort to "wipe out [their] competition" and to "purge and consolidate" power (SITE Intelligence Group 2020).

20 April 2020

"Operation: Reopen Florida," read a rally event flyer posted on 20 April 2020 to the official Telegram channel of Enrique Tarrio, a leader of the influential American neo-fascist hate group the "Proud Boys" (PB). The poster provided information for upcoming rallies organized by the Proud Boys in three major Florida cities: Tallahassee, Miami, and Orlando, all supposedly scheduled to take place on 25 April at 12 PM. "Stand for freedom & against the Democrat driven unconstitutional lockdown," the poster proclaimed, urging "we must reopen Florida & rebuild our economy!" (SITE Intelligence Group 2020).

21 April 2020

A Telegram user with ties to the decades-old, United States-based neo-Nazi group National Socialist Movement (NSM) was identified at an Ohio protest of government-led efforts to mitigate the spread of COVID-19. "CTV" stated his intention to harass Jews, including on 8 April 2020, when he posted a photo of himself holding a blade and alleged he would target Jewish families during video conference Passover celebrations (SITE Intelligence Group 2020).

21 April 2020

Lists containing thousands of email addresses and login credentials allegedly belonging to employees of the World Health Organization (WHO), Gates Foundation, Wuhan Virology Lab, Center for Disease Control and Prevention (CDC), World Bank, and National Institute of Health (NIH) were widely spread among prominent far right venues. The far right's motives behind this doxxing initiative were not only to harass the staff but also to hack into the accounts and retrieve information they believed could be used as "evidence" to substantiate their conspiracy theories surrounding the origin of the novel coronavirus (SITE Intelligence Group 2020).

29 April 2020

A 29 April 2020 post by a Telegram channel claiming to represent the Yellow Vest movement shared a website promoting a series of "Massive Anti Lockdown protests being planned across the US on May 1st." The link was then shared to a number of alt-right and far right channels, which included multiple neo-Nazi groups. Far right groups had been using events like the Rally For Freedom as opportunities to network with, if not recruit, attendees. Recruitment efforts more broadly doubled as groups sought out ways to leverage the social and economic anxieties brought on by the pandemic (SITE Intelligence Group 2020).

1 May 2020

Andrew Anglin, a prominent white nationalist, praised armed anti-lockdown protesters in Michigan's state capitol and warned Governor Gretchen Whitmer and state politicians that "all kinds of riots are coming." Using a range of profane and misogynistic language, Anglin chided the governor for confining people to their houses via a stay-at-home order and wrote suggestively that she should be "run out of town . . . by an angry mob" (SITE Intelligence Group 2020).

1 May 2020

Proud Boys announced that its members will not be attending a recent protest in the capital of Michigan, in order to distance itself from purported violent threats made by a previous Proud Boys recruit toward the state's governor (SITE Intelligence Group 2020).

1 May 2020

"The Fellow Nationalist," a Neo-Nazi Telegram channel that frequently posts anti-immigrant and antisemitic content, posted a movie poster showing an edited image of "Kill Bill" actress Uma Thurman with a far right-styled facemask and illuminated eyes. Beside her, the text read, "KILL BILL GATES," followed up with, "IN MINECRAFT." The "in minecraft" addition was a reference to a popular videogame, which far right extremists commonly tagged on to incitements in a thinly veiled attempt to avoid legal culpability (SITE Intelligence Group 2020).

4 May 2020

The Philadelphia chapter of the Proud Boys promoted an upcoming quarantine protest in the city and urged others to spread word of the event as well: "OPEN PHILLY! Join this group! Rally Friday! Please share!" (SITE Intelligence Group 2020).

5 May 2020

Following the arrest and raid of a Colorado man for allegedly organizing an armed presence at an anti-lockdown protest, misinformation circulating that the FBI was "raiding" the homes of other protestors spurred far right message board users and neo-Nazi Telegram venues to target law enforcement. Discussions on 4chan and Telegram channels encouraged armed resistance in the face of the government crackdown. Furthermore, the FBI raid appeared to spur the beginning of the so-called "Boogaloo" and was seen by some far right users as justification for an accelerationist response (SITE Intelligence Group 2020).

6 May 2020

Discussing a recent lockdown protest in Michigan during which protestors openly carried weapons inside the Statehouse, users on the popular far right message board 8kun showed disappointment the protesters didn't "kill [the Governor] to make their point" (SITE Intelligence Group 2020).

6 May 2020

The Telegram channel "BMW" encouraged its followers to "raid" an online seminar hosted by the conservative political organization known as Turning Point USA. "RAID TONIGHT," the Telegram post urged. "Literal gay shabbos nigger cuckservative is holding a webinar. Crash it." The seminar was conducted by Rob Smith, a gay, black conservative writer. Additionally, a post from a user in the far right chat group "MWG" announced that "/pol/" and other similar forums "plan to raid the zoom conference with rob smith . . . Let's spread this shit like wildfire" (SITE Intelligence Group 2020).

11 May 2020

A Telegram channel run by the Proud Boys' chapter in Portland, Oregon posted a series of photos documenting a small protest held by the group in Oregon City demanding parks be reopened for recreational use. In addition to protesting the lockdown, the Proud Boys and other attendees of the rally campaigned for one of the group's members, Daniel Tooze, who was running for House Representation in Oregon's 40th district (SITE Intelligence Group 2020).

14 May 2020

The Philadelphia branch of the Proud Boys used their Telegram channel to advertise a "Reopen Pennsylvania" protest scheduled to be held the following day in the state capital, Harrisburg. This protest fit within the mold of previously observed behavior of the Proud Boys in opportunistically using a large, widely publicized event as a means of gaining recognition for their own organization (SITE Intelligence Group 2020).

20 May 2020

On 20 May 2020, Anarchists Worldwide released a Portuguese statement from the anarchist group Nucleus of Opposition to the System (NOS) that disseminated the purported personal information of a member of the Brazilian political party Republicanos 10, Antonio Fontinele, a regional coordinator for the party in the "southern region 2" of São Paulo. It included his place of birth, residential and business addresses, and his cell phone number. The anarchist group selected to release Fontinele's personal information as the first "retaliation" for the failure of the Brazilian National Congress and the government to comply with NOS' "four requirements" during the COVID-19 Pandemic: the resignation of Bolsonaro and Vice President Hamilton Mourão, the repeal of Constitutional Amendment 95 because it "prevents emergency funds to fight the pandemic," the repeal of Provisional Measure #905 for hurting labor rights, and monthly quarantine payments until the end of the pandemic. The statement encouraged further doxing attacks so the group can visit the "fascist scum" in person. NOS further claimed it is "not peaceful" and will act in the "only language" that "fascists" understand – that is "force, violence and intimidation" (SITE Intelligence Group 2020).

22 May 2020

A post by the prominent neo-Nazi Telegram channel "SSS" urged followers to accelerate and "wage war against the System on your own terms," specifying "this includes attacks on infrastructure, targeted killings, that sort of thing" (SITE Intelligence Group 2020).

1 June 2020

Anarchists Worldwide issued a second "doxxing action" from Nucleus of Opposition to the System (NOS) on 1 June 2020, in Spanish and Portuguese, releasing the personal information of Roberto Jefferson Monteiro Francisco, a Brazilian Labor Party (PTB) politician. Jefferson, who was expelled from Brazil's Congress in 2005 and banned from being elected to public office for ten years, has a strong social media presence and is vocal in his support of President Jair Bolsonaro. The latest statement from the group repeated the same threats it issued in the first doxxing action, claiming it would escalate in a violent manner to "guarantee the survival of the Brazilian people" (SITE Intelligence Group 2020).

11 June 2020

On 11 June 2020, Anarchists Worldwide distributed a Spanish and Portuguese message from Nucleus of Opposition to the System (NOS) doxxing Almino Monteiro Álvares Affonso, a member of the Brazilian Socialist Party (PSB). The statement released Affonso's personal information, calling him "corrupt" and accusing him of acquiring "enormous personal wealth stolen from the Brazilian people." NOS also alleged Affonso's inaction helped pave the way for Jair Bolsonaro's presidency (SITE Intelligence Group 2020).

19 June 2020

A 19 June 2020 message from a neo-Nazi messenger channel posted a classified ad calling for "Covid positive people" to participate in a "large scale test on transmission of the virus." A screenshot of the Craigslist ad, which was placed on Craigslist before being taken down, was posted to the Telegram channel "ST" along with a claim that "Biowarfare [is being] planned for Trump rally events." The ad called for four COVID positive individuals to "assemble" outside Tulsa's BOK Convention Center on "Saturday." The post was subsequently shared to another neo-Nazi channel, "BH," with approximately 2,600 members (SITE Intelligence Group 2020).

26 June 2020

The alleged personal information of Nílton de Albuquerque Cerqueira was released to an anarchist blog by the Nucleus of Opposition to the

System (NOS) on 26 June 2020. The statement accused Cerqueira of decades of human rights crimes including twelve murders and listed the names of the deceased. It claimed the last three alleged murders were carried out in collusion with Brazil's President Jair Bolsonaro. The General was doxxed to warn members of the military and police to withdraw their support for Bolsonaro or they will be targeted: "Our action is a warning to the pigs of the army, navy, air force and police of Brazil to back down in their support for the fascist Bolsonaro. Just like Nilton Cerqueira, any of them can be our target" (SITE Intelligence Group 2020).

29 June 2020

On 29 June 2020, Contra Media issued a statement allegedly from the "Fanni Kaplan Antagonistic Cell" (FAI) appealing for anarchists and others in Argentina to take action against the government for COVID-19 measures. They claimed the government under President Alberto Fernández was taking advantage of the pandemic to expand and implement "new control mechanisms." The FAI stated the pandemic was exposing the "harmfulness of the class society and neoliberal capitalism" of the Argentinian state. The statement also called for an end to prisons, citing the deaths of inmates (SITE Intelligence Group 2020).

8 July 2020

A far right "Boogaloo" channel, "BID," called on supporters in the US to create networks and prepare to "restore natural order," claiming the military will forcibly inject citizens with the COVID-19 vaccine. "BID" claimed the military would soon be "majority brown" and "indoctrinated to kill" those who are against multiculturalism and so could not be relied on to save white Americans. The message encouraged supporters to prepare and network as the "last generation of Europeans on the American continent that can restore natural order." The post stoked racial and political hatred by claiming "rampaging blacks and leftist cucks" will rape and pillage to get their way (SITE Intelligence Group 2020).

Far Right Posts Concerning Jewish Minorities

2 April 2020

A series of fliers created by the New Jersey European Heritage Association (NJEHA) invoked the pandemic to stoke anti-immigrant and antisemitic sentiments in states along the east coast, including New York, New Jersey, Pennsylvania, and Florida. "Stop coronavirus, deport all illegal aliens," read one NJEHA flier, a photo of which was posted to the organization's Gab account and Telegram channel. Additionally, a collection of stickers posted in the same states equated four common far right targets with "the virus," namely globalism, open borders, multiculturalism, and media. In the case of "media," the term was stylized with three sets of parentheses also known as an "echo," used online to indicate when an individual or institution is Jewish or sympathetic to Jews (SITE Intelligence Group 2020).

2 April 2020

A user on the far right message board 8kun targeted a harassment campaign against Jewish educators, providing a Hebrew academy's online class schedule as well as invitation links to the classes' virtual Zoom meetings. It encouraged far right followers to hijack the lesson and "freak them out" (SITE Intelligence Group 2020).

15 April 2020

The far right continued to urge attacks on essential businesses, services, and infrastructure to exacerbate social instability. Jews and immigrants remained the primary targets of bioterrorism-inspired attacks, with new initiatives that included chemical and explosive attacks (SITE Intelligence Group 2020).

29 April 2020

A message posted to the neo-Nazi Telegram channel "ML88" urged that "the time is now" for the far right to organize and seize power. The message was presented as a caption attached to an antisemitic cartoon, which was shared by "ML88" from the neo-Nazi Telegram channel "F" (SITE Intelligence Group 2020).

Far Right Posts Concerning 5G Infrastructure

16 April 2020

A prominent neo-Nazi Telegram channel posted a statement targeting Amazon and 5G cell towers for explosive attacks, urging people to "shoot down Amazon delivery drones" and "strap ridiculous amounts of explosives to their own drones [and fly] them toward 5G towers and detonate them." The incitement continued by encouraging people to "educate themselves on matters regarding the power grid in order to be able to sabotage it better" (SITE Intelligence Group 2020).

30 April 2020

Prominent far right Telegram channels celebrated recent attacks on 5G infrastructure as a means of pressuring "foreign occupation governments" to unveil their oppressive pandemic agendas, calling on followers to "cut down a couple 5G towers in order to force the System to make the first move" (SITE Intelligence Group 2020).

20 May 2020

An accelerationist neo-Nazi channel shared a video documenting alleged arson attacks on 5G infrastructure, celebrating the act and encouraging those who might plan on taking similar direct action in the future not to film it (SITE Intelligence Group 2020).

Far Right Post Concerning Hoax Conspiracy Theories

1 May 2020

"The Reality Report," a far right media service that promotes misinformation and conspiracy theories, compiled and shared knowledge resources meant to expose the pandemic as a hoax. Published in seven parts, the posts included a mix of mainstream and fringe sources, including the New York Times, YouTube videos, and uncited statistics (SITE Intelligence Group 2020).

References

"Anarchists Call for Action against Argentinian Government for COVID-19 Measures." 2020. Retrieved May 2022 from SITE Intelligence Group.

"Brazilian Anarchist Group Doxxes Third Politician Over COVID-19 Government Failures." 2020. Retrieved May 2022 from SITE Intelligence Group.

"Brazilian Anarchists Dox Army General Over Government COVID-19 Failures." 2020. Retrieved May 2022 from SITE Intelligence Group.

"Claiming Military Will Force COVID-19 Vaccinations, 'Boogaloo' Channel Urges Networking and Preparations." 2020. Retrieved May 2022 from SITE Intelligence Group.
"German Company Targeted in Anarchist Arson Attack for COVID-19 'Repression'." 2020. Retrieved May 2022 from SITE Intelligence Group.
"Member of Neo-Nazi Group Discusses Participation in Serbia's Protests Against COVID-19 Lockdown and Government." 2020. Retrieved May 2022 from SITE Intelligence Group.
"Neo-Nazi Channel Promotes Use of COVID-19 as Biological Weapon against Vulnerable Nations." 2020. Retrieved May 2022 from SITE Intelligence Group.
"Neo-Nazis Circulate Advertisement Calling for COVID Patients to Attend Trump Rally." 2020. Retrieved May 2022 from SITE Intelligence Group.
"Recent Far Right Updates on the COVID-19 Pandemic March 25–April 1, 2020." 2020. Retrieved May 2022 from SITE Intelligence Group.
"Recent Far Right Updates on the COVID-19 Pandemic April 2–7, 2020." 2020. Retrieved May 2022 from SITE Intelligence Group.
"Recent Far Right Updates on the COVID-19 Pandemic April 8–15 2020." 2020. Retrieved May 2022 from SITE Intelligence Group.
"Recent Far Right Updates on the COVID-19 Pandemic April 22–28, 2020." 2020. Retrieved May 2022 from SITE Intelligence Group.
"Recent Far Right Updates on the COVID-19 Pandemic April 29–May 5, 2020." 2020. Retrieved May 2022 from SITE Intelligence Group.
"Recent Far Right Updates on the COVID-19 Pandemic May 6–12, 2020." 2020. Retrieved May 2022 from SITE Intelligence Group.
"Recent Far Right Updates on the COVID-19 Pandemic May 13–26, 2020." 2020. Retrieved May 2022 from SITE Intelligence Group.
"Second Brazilian Politician Doxxed by Anarchist Group for Government Failure to Respond to COVID-19 Demands." 2020. Retrieved May 2022 from SITE Intelligence Group.
"Spanish Neo-Nazi Video Declares US and European Protests a Symptom of 'Virus' Worse than COVID-19." 2020. Retrieved May 2022 from SITE Intelligence Group.
"Weekly Report on al-Qaeda Branches and Linked Groups July 16–22, 2020." 2020. Retrieved May 2022 from SITE Intelligence Group.
"Weekly Report on al-Qaeda Branches and Linked Groups, July 23–29, 2020." 2020. Retrieved May 2022 from SITE Intelligence Group.
"Weekly Report on the Islamic State, April 22–28, 2020." 2020. Retrieved May 2022 from SITE Intelligence Group.
"Weekly Report on the Islamic State, April 29–May 5, 2020." 2020. Retrieved May 2022 from SITE Intelligence Group.
"Weekly Report on the Islamic State, May 6–12, 2020." 2020. Retrieved May 2022 from SITE Intelligence Group.
"Weekly Report on the Islamic State, May 20–26, 2020." 2020. Retrieved May 2022 from SITE Intelligence Group.
"Weekly Report on the Islamic State, May 27–June 2, 2020." 2020. Retrieved May 2022 from SITE Intelligence Group.

"Weekly Report on the Islamic State, June 3–9, 2020." 2020. Retrieved May 2022 from SITE Intelligence Group.
"Weekly Report on the Islamic State, June 17–23, 2020." 2020. Retrieved May 2022 from SITE Intelligence Group.
"Weekly Report on the Islamic State, July 1–7, 2020." 2020. Retrieved May 2022 from SITE Intelligence Group.
"Weekly Report on the Islamic State, July 30–August 4, 2020." 2020. Retrieved May 2022 from SITE Intelligence Group.

Annex B

Statistics on Extremists' COVID-19-Related Activities

How Has the Radical Islamist Threat Evolved in Syria?

IS-claimed terrorist incidents in Syria A comparison – 2018 and 2020 March 11–July 31	
Year	Number of terrorist attacks
2018	18
2020	166

IS targets in Syria A comparison – 2018 and 2020 March 11–July 31		
Target type	2018	2020
Business	2	0
Journalists/Media	1	0
Military	9	165
Private citizens/property	6	0
Government	0	1

IS modus operandi in Syria A comparison – 2018 and 2020 March 11–July 31		
Modus operandi	2018	2020
Armed assault	1	128
Assassination	1	0
Bombing/Explosion	14	35
Hostage taking	2	3

How Has the Radical Islamist Threat Evolved in Iraq?

IS-claimed terrorist incidents in Iraq A comparison – 2018 and 2020 March 11–July 31	
Year	Number of terrorist attacks
2018	194
2020	337

IS targets in Iraq A comparison – 2018 and 2020 March 11–July 31		
Target type	2018	2020
Business	3	0
Government	12	2
Journalists/Media	1	0
Military	53	295
Police	32	34
Private citizens/property	81	5
Religious figures/institutions	3	1
Transportation	1	0
Utilities	7	0

IS modus operandi in Iraq A comparison – 2018 and 2020 March 11–July 31		
Modus operandi	2018	2020
Armed assault	38	207
Assassination	14	0
Bombing/Explosion	112	130
Facility/Infrastructure attack	4	0
Hostage taking	23	0

How Has the Radical Islamist Threat Evolved in Afghanistan?

IS-claimed terrorist incidents in Afghanistan
A comparison – 2018 and 2020 March 11–July 31

Year	Number of terrorist attacks
2018	54
2020	20

IS targets in Afghanistan
A comparison – 2018 and 2020 March 11–July 31

Target type	2018	2020
Business	3	0
Educational institution	2	0
Government	19	1
Military	3	10
NGO	1	0
Police	10	5
Private citizens/property	14	2
Religious figures/institutions	2	2

IS modus operandi in Afghanistan
A comparison – 2018 and 2020 March 11–July 31

Modus operandi	2018	2020
Armed assault	8	3
Assassination	7	0
Bombing/Explosion	32	16
Hostage taking	10	1

How Has the Radical Islamist Threat Evolved in Africa?

IS-related terrorist incidents in Africa
A comparison – 2018 and 2020 March 11–July 31

Year	Number of terrorist attacks
2018	264
2020	239

IS targets in Africa
A comparison – 2018 and 2020 March 11–July 31

Target type	2018	2020
Military	120	213
Private citizens/property	65	7
Government	49	0
Police	19	17
Religious figures/institutions	12	2
Business	6	0
NGO	3	1
Transportation	2	0
Utilities	2	0
Educational institution	1	0
Telecommunication	1	0
Journalists/Media	1	0

IS modus operandi in Africa
A comparison – 2018 and 2020 March 11–July 31

Modus operandi	2018	2020
Bombing/Explosion	116	57
Armed assault	107	181
Assassination	29	0
Hostage taking	23	0
Facility/Infrastructure attack	6	0
Arson	0	1

How Has the Radical Islamist Threat Evolved in Europe?

Jihadist-related terrorist incidents in Europe
A comparison – 2018 and 2020 March 11–July 31

Year	Number of terrorist attacks
2018	4
2020	3

Jihadist targets in Europe
A comparison – 2018 and 2020 March 11–July 31

Target type	2018	2020
Private citizens/property	4	2
Police	0	1

Jihadist modus operandi in Europe
A comparison – 2018 and 2020 March 11–July 31

Modus operandi	2018	2020
Armed assault	4	2
Non-armed assault	0	1

Active jihadist groups in Europe
A comparison – 2018 and 2020 March 11–July 31

Terrorist groups	2018	2020
Jihadi-inspired extremists	4	2

How Has the Radical Islamist Threat Evolved in Southeast Asia?

Jihadist-related terrorist incidents in Southeast Asia
A comparison – 2018 and 2020 March 11–July 31

Year	Number of terrorist attacks
2018	49
2020	38

Jihadist targets in Southeast Asia
A comparison – 2018 and 2020 March 11–July 31

Target type	2018	2020
Military	14	31
Private citizens/property	11	2
Police	9	5
Business	4	0
Government	3	0
Educational institution	3	0
Religious figures/institutions	3	0
Transportation	1	0
Journalists/Media	1	0

Jihadist modus operandi in Southeast Asia
A comparison – 2018 and 2020 March 11–July 31

Modus operandi	2018	2020
Bombing/Explosion	23	3
Armed assault	17	33
Hostage taking	9	2

Active jihadist groups in Southeast Asia
A comparison – 2018 and 2020 March 11–July 31

Terrorist groups	2018	2020
Bangsamoro Islamic Freedom Movement	29	7
Abu Sayyaf Group	9	9
Jamaah Ansharut Daulah	7	0
IS	2	22
Negara Islam Indonesia	1	0
Muslim extremists	1	0

How Has the Radical Islamist Threat Evolved in the United States?

Jihadist-related terrorist incidents in the US
A comparison – 2018 and 2020 March 11–July 31

Year	Number of terrorist attacks
2018	1
2020	0

Jihadist targets in the US
A comparison – 2018 and 2020 March 11–July 31

Target type	2018	2020
Private citizens/property	1	0

Jihadist modus operandi in the US
A comparison – 2018 and 2020 March 11–July 31

Modus operandi	2018	2020
Armed assault	1	0

Active jihadist groups in the US
A comparison – 2018 and 2020 March 11–July 31

Terrorist groups	2018	2020
Jihadi-inspired extremists	1	0

COVID-19-Related Far Right Activities

COVID-19-related far right operations
2020 March 11–July 31

on the European continent	1
on the American continent	1

COVID-19-related far right incitements 2020 March 11–July 31						
	March 11–31	April	May	June	July	Total
On the European continent	4	4	2	0	2	12
On the American continent	3	5	8	2	0	18

COVID-19-related far right incitements 2020 March 11–July 31	
Incitements for armed assault	11
Preparation for armed assault	3
Incitements for depriving medical care	1
Misinformation campaign	2
Incitements for deliberate infection	2
Incitements for the release of toxic gases	1
Incitements for anti-lockdown protests	6
Incitements for alternative ways to stoke tensions	1

COVID-19-related far right incitements 2020 March 11–July 31	
Against private property	1
Against public spaces/general public	11
Against immigrants	1
Against military and law enforcement forces	3
Against critical infrastructure	2
Against countries with high population density and unstable economy	1
Against FEMA camps and agents	1
Against grocery stores	1
Against Black Americans	1
Against political figures/governments	4

COVID-19-related far right propaganda activities 2020 March 11–July 31		
	On the Europen continent	On the American continent
Outlets elaborating conspiracy theories	12	20
Outlets with recruiting purpose	1	3
Outlets advocating antigovernment narratives	5	3

COVID-19-related far right propaganda activities 2020 March 11–July 31			
Country	Operation	Incitement	Propaganda activity
Germany	1	1	2
France	0	1	2
United States	1	18	20
Ukraine	0	1	0
Russia	0	2	0
Serbia	0	1	0
Italy	0	0	1
Spain	0	0	4
Argentina	0	1	0
Brazil	0	0	4

References

"Call for Violence to Reopen Philippine Mosque Closed by COVID-19 Restrictions." 2020. Retrieved May 2022 from SITE Intelligence Group.

"Contending with ISIS in the Time of Coronavirus." 2020. International Crisis Group website. Retrieved May 2022 from https://www.crisisgroup.org/global/contending-isis-time-coronavirus.

"Corona: It Is the Prayer of the People of al-Baghouz, Whom You Burned Alive, It Has Killed You So Reap the Results of Your Actions." 2020. TRAC Terrorism Research and Analysis Consortium website. Retrieved May 2022 from https://www.trackingterrorism.org/chatter/cgi-green-b1rds-unofficial-islamic-state-corona-it-prayer-people-al-baghouz-whom-you-burned-/.

"European Union Terrorism Situation and Trend Report 2020." 2019. Europol website. Retrieved May 2022 from https://www.europol.europa.eu/activities-services/main-reports/european-union-terrorism-situation-and-trend-report-te-sat-2020.

"Global Terrorism Database." Retrieved May 2022 from University of Maryland's website https://www.start.umd.edu/gtd/.
"Imam in Hamas TV Friday Sermon a Day before Coronavirus Cases Confirmed in Gaza: 'This Virus Is a Soldier of Allah.'" 2020. Memri website. Retrieved May 2022 from https://www.memri.org/tv/gaza-friday-sermon-palestinian-sheikh-jamil-mutawa-coronavirus-allah-soldier-praise-victims.
"Indonesia." 2020. International Crisis Group website. Retrieved May 2022 from https://www.crisisgroup.org/crISwatch/database?location percent5B percent 5D = 44&date_range = last_6_months&from_month = 01&from_year = 2020&to_month = 01&to_year = 2020.
"Indonesian IS-Aligned Account Urges Supporters Carry Out Attacks during COVID-19 Pandemic." 2020. Retrieved May 2022 from SITE Intelligence Group.
"Interactive Data Table: World Muslim Population by Country." 2019. Pew Research Center website. Retrieved May 2022 from https://www.pewforum.org/chart/interactive-data-table-world-muslim-population-by-country/.
"IS-aligned Group Mocks 'Disbelieving' Countries over Inability of Scientific Progress to Stop COVID-19." 2020. Retrieved May 2022 from SITE Intelligence Group.
"IS-Aligned Maldivian Channel Urges for Attacks during COVID-19 Crisis." 2020. Retrieved May 2022 from SITE Intelligence Group.
"Islamic World." Nations Online website. Retrieved May 2022 from https://www.nationsonline.org/oneworld/muslim-countries.htm.
"Jihadist Threat Alert IS-aligned Group Portrays COVID-19 Pandemic as Revenge for Muslims of Baghuz." 2020. Retrieved May 2022 from SITE Intelligence Group.
"Murder and Extremism in the United States in 2019." 2020. ADL Center on Extremism website. Retrieved May 2022 from https://www.adl.org/media/14107/download.
"Philippines." 2019. International Crisis Group website. Retrieved May 2022 from https://www.crisisgroup.org/asia/south-east-asia/philippines
"Recent Global Jihadist Updates on the COVID-19 Pandemic April 1–7, 2020." 2020. Retrieved May 2022 from SITE Intelligence Group.
"Recent Jihadist Updates on the COVID-19 Pandemic April 28–May 6, 2020." 2020. Retrieved May 2022 from SITE Intelligence Group.
"Security Council Press Statement on Terrorist Attack in Afghanistan." 2020. United Nations Security Council.
"Security Situation in Somalia." 2019. ECOI.NET website. Retrieved May 2022 from https://www.ecoi.net/en/countries/somalia/featured-topics/security-situation/.
"Situation in West Africa, Sahel 'Extremely Volatile' as Terrorists Exploit Ethnic Animosities, Special Representative Warns Security Council." 2020. United Nations Security Council website. Retrieved May 2022 from https://www.un.org/press/en/2020/sc14245.doc.htm.
"Spotlight on Global Jihad April 23–30, 2020." 2020. Retrieved May 2022 from The Meir Amit Intelligence and Terrorism Information Center.
"Spotlight on Global Jihad April 2–6, 2020." 2020. Retrieved May 2022 from The Meir Amit Intelligence and Terrorism Information Center.

"Spotlight on Global Jihad April 7–22, 2020." 2020. Retrieved May 2022 from The Meir Amit Intelligence and Terrorism Information Center.

"Spotlight on Global Jihad July 16–22, 2020." 2020. Retrieved May 2022 from The Meir Amit Intelligence and Terrorism Information Center.

"Spotlight on Global Jihad July 23–29, 2020." 2020. Retrieved May 2022 from The Meir Amit Intelligence and Terrorism Information Center.

"Spotlight on Global Jihad July 2–8, 2020." 2020. Retrieved May 2022 from The Meir Amit Intelligence and Terrorism Information Center.

"Spotlight on Global Jihad July 30–August 5, 2020." 2020. Retrieved May 2022 from The Meir Amit Intelligence and Terrorism Information Center.

"Spotlight on Global Jihad July 9–15, 2020." 2020. Retrieved May 2022 from The Meir Amit Intelligence and Terrorism Information Center.

"Spotlight on Global Jihad June 11–17, 2020." 2020. Retrieved May 2022 from The Meir Amit Intelligence and Terrorism Information Center.

"Spotlight on Global Jihad June 18–24, 2020." 2020. Retrieved May from The Meir Amit Intelligence and Terrorism Information Center.

"Spotlight on Global Jihad June 25–July 1, 2020." 2020. Retrieved May 2022 from The Meir Amit Intelligence and Terrorism Information Center.

"Spotlight on Global Jihad June 4–10, 2020." 2020. Retrieved May 2022 from The Meir Amit Intelligence and Terrorism Information Center.

"Spotlight on Global Jihad March 12–18, 2020." 2020. Retrieved May 2022 from The Meir Amit Intelligence and Terrorism Information Center.

"Spotlight on Global Jihad March 19–25, 2020." 2020. Retrieved May 2022 from The Meir Amit Intelligence and Terrorism Information Center.

"Spotlight on Global Jihad March 26–April 1, 2020." 2020. Retrieved May 2022 from The Meir Amit Intelligence and Terrorism Information Center.

"Spotlight on Global Jihad May 14–20, 2020." 2020. Retrieved May 2022 from The Meir Amit Intelligence and Terrorism Information Center.

"Spotlight on Global Jihad May 1–6, 2020." 2020. Retrieved May 2022 from The Meir Amit Intelligence and Terrorism Information Center.

"Spotlight on Global Jihad May 21–26, 2020." 2020. Retrieved May 2022 from The Meir Amit Intelligence and Terrorism Information Center.

"Spotlight on Global Jihad May 27–June 3, 2020." 2020. Retrieved May 2022 from The Meir Amit Intelligence and Terrorism Information Center.

"Spotlight on Global Jihad May 7–13, 2020." 2020. Retrieved May 2022 from The Meir Amit Intelligence and Terrorism Information Center.

"Syria Security Situation." 2020. European Asylum Support Office website. Retrieved May 2022 from https://coi.easo.europa.eu/administration/easo/PLib/05_2020_EASO_COI_Report_Syria_Security_situation.pdf.

"The Voice of Hind." 2020. Issue 3.

"Virus Fears Spread at Camps for ISIS Families in Syria's North East." International Crisis Group website. Retrieved May 2022 from https://www.crisisgroup.org/middle-east-north-africa/eastern-mediterranean/syria/virus-fears-spread-camps-isis-families-syrias-north-east.

"Weekly Report on al-Qaeda Branches and Linked Groups July 16–22, 2020." 2020. Retrieved May 2022 from SITE Intelligence Group.

"Weekly Report on al-Qaeda Branches and Linked Groups, July 23–29, 2020." 2020. Retrieved May 2022 from SITE Intelligence Group.

"Weekly Report on the Islamic State, April 22–28, 2020." 2020. Retrieved May 2022 from SITE Intelligence Group.

"Weekly Report on the Islamic State, April 29–May 5, 2020." 2020. Retrieved May 2022 from SITE Intelligence Group.

"Weekly Report on the Islamic State, July 1–7, 2020." 2020. Retrieved May 2022 from SITE Intelligence Group.

"Weekly Report on the Islamic State, July 30–August 4, 2020." 2020. Retrieved May 2022 from SITE Intelligence Group.

"Weekly Report on the Islamic State, June 17–23, 2020." 2020. Retrieved May 2022 from SITE Intelligence Group.

"Weekly Report on the Islamic State, June 3–9, 2020." 2020. Retrieved May 2022 from SITE Intelligence Group.

"Weekly Report on the Islamic State, May 20–26, 2020." 2020. Retrieved May 2022 from SITE Intelligence Group.

"Weekly Report on the Islamic State, May 27–June 2, 2020." 2020. Retrieved May 2022 from SITE Intelligence Group.

"Weekly Report on the Islamic State, May 6–12, 2020." 2020. Retrieved May 2022 from SITE Intelligence Group.

Abdul-Zahira, Qassim. 2020. "Iraq Officials Say IS Targets Intelligence Bureau; 3 Wounded." AP News, 28 April.

Al-Lami, Mina. 2020. "Africa's Sahel Becomes Latest al-Qaeda-IS Battleground." BBC, 11 May.

Broches, Emma. 2020. "Southeast Asia's Overlooked Foreign Fighter Problem." Lawfare 5 June.

Campbell, John. 2020. "Niger Attack Demonstrates Islamic State in West Africa's Growing Reach." Council on Foreign Relations. Retrieved May 2022 from https://www.cfr.org/blog/niger-attack-demonstrates-islamic-state-west-africas-growing-reach.

Cordesman, Anthony H. 2020. "The Real World Capabilities of ISIS: The Threat Continues." CSIS website. https://www.csis.org/analysis/real-world-capabilities-isis-threat-continues.

Damora, Brittany. 2020. "COVID-19: Impact on Kidnap for Ransom Activity." Security Magazine, 13 April.

Gartenstein-Ross, Daveed, Emelie Chace-Donahue, and Colin P. Clarke. 2020. "The Threat of Jihadist Terrorism in Germany." International Centre for Counter-Terrorism website. Retrieved May 2022 from https://icct.nl/publication/the-threat-of-jihadist-terrorism-in-germany/.

Grierson, Jamie, Dan Sabbagh, Matthew Weaver, Simon Murphy, and Molly Blackall. 2020. "Libyan Held over Reading Multiple Stabbing 'Known to Security Services.'" The Guardian, 21 June.

Hoffman, Bruce, and Jacob Ware. 2020. "The Terrorist Threat from the Fractured Far Right." Lawfare, 1 November.

Johnson, Bridget. 2020. "ISIS Lauds 'Death and Terror' of Coronavirus Outbreak." Homeland Security Today, 27 January.

Jones, Seth G., Catrina Doxsee, and Nicholas Harrington. 2020. "The Escalating Terrorism Problem in the United States." CSIS Briefs. Retrieved May 2022 from https://csis-website-prod.s3.amazonaws.com/s3fs-public/publication/200612_Jones_DomesticTerrorism_v6.pdf.

Levenia, Ultra, and Alban Sciascia. 2020. "How COVID-19 Is Reshaping Terror Threats in Indonesia." The Diplomat, May.

Lurie, Devin. 2020. "ISIS in the Philippines: A Cause for Concern." American Security Project website. Retrieved May 2022 from https://www.americansecurityproject.org/isis-in-the-philippines-a-cause-for-concern/.

Mashal, Mujib, and Najim Rahim. 2020. "Taliban Stage a Major Attack, as Violence Intensifies in Northern Afghanistan." The New York Times, 13 July.

Perkins, Brian M. 2020. "IS-CAP Attack Claims in DRC Increase, but Capabilities Largely Remain the Same." Terrorism Monitor 18(14).

Pikulicka-Wilczewska, Agnieszka. 2020. "The Islamic State Remains Alive in Afghanistan." The Diplomat, April.

Rahmah, Unaesah. 2021. "Southeast Asia, Indonesia, Philippines, Malaysia, Myanmar, Thailand, Singapore." Counter Terrorist Trends and Analyses 13(1).

Rolbieczki, Tomasz, Pieter van Ostaeyen, and Charlie Winter. 2020. "The Islamic State's Strategic Trajectory in Africa: Key Takeaways from Its Attack Claims." CTC Sentinel 13(8).

Ross, Rachel. 2018. "What Is Ramadan?" Live Science website. Retrieved May 2022 from https://www.livescience.com/61815-what-is-ramadan.html.

Rubio, Pablo. 2020. "Egypt a Recurrent Target of Jihadist Terrorism." Atalayar website. Retrieved May 2022 from https://atalayar.com/en/content/egypt-recurrent-target-jihadist-terrorism.

Seldin, Jeff. 2020. "Pushed to the Brink Again, Islamic State's Afghan Affiliate Claims Deadly Attacks." VOA News, 12 May.

Umar, Haruna, and Sam Olukoya. 2020. "In Nigeria, an Islamic State-Linked Group Steps Up Attacks." AP News, 26 June.

Von Hein, Matthias. 2020. "'Islamic State' Exploiting Coronavirus and Conflict to Rise Again." DW, 22 May.

Wang, Amy B. 2018. "A Teen with Former Neo-Nazi Ties Claims His 'Muslim Faith' Led Him to Stab Three, Police Say." The Washington Post, 22 March.

Weiss, Caleb. 2020. "Islamic State in Somalia Suffers Setbacks Despite Uptick in Claimed Activity." Long War Journal, 1 June.

Zenn, Jacob. 2020. "ISIS in Africa: The Caliphate's Next Frontier." Newlines Institute for Strategy and Policy website. Retrieved May 2022 from https://newlinesinstitute.org/isis/isis-in-africa-the-caliphates-next-frontier/

Index

www.ingramcontent.com/pod-product-compliance
Lightning Source LLC
Chambersburg PA
CBHW051543020426
42333CB00016B/2080
* 9 7 8 1 8 0 5 3 9 7 4 7 2 *

Terrorism and the Pandemic